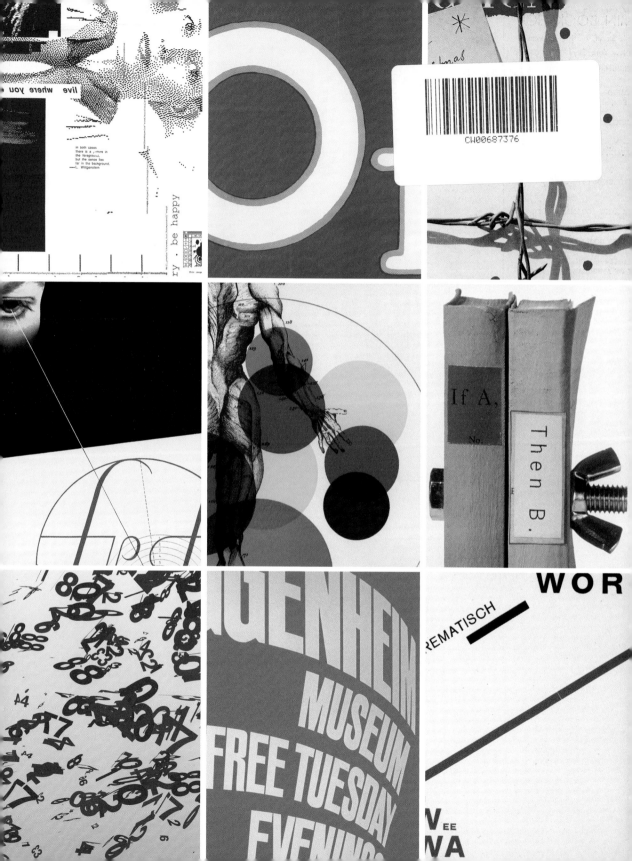

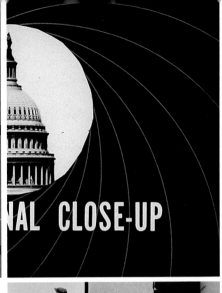

NAL CLOSE-UP

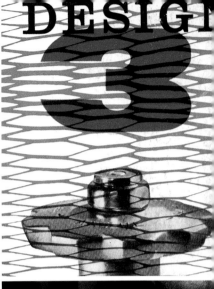

DESIGN 3

neu ulph

ility

een nodelijtheld voor de

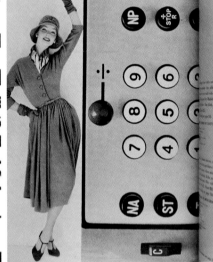

VOOR DE BEELDEND
CTIE THEO VAN DOES
E X. HARMS TIEPEN

NHONDERDACHTTIEN

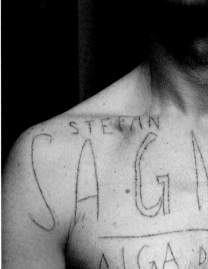

STEFAN SAGM ALGA

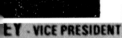

EY - VICE PRESIDENT

(DEMOCRATIC)

RESIDENT

VICE PRESIDENT

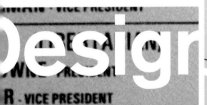

Design

VICE PRESIDENT

R - VICE PRESIDENT

(GREEN)

VICE PRESIDENT

DUKE - VICE PRESIDENT

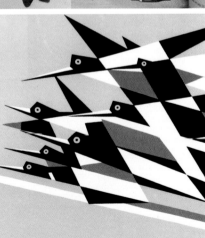

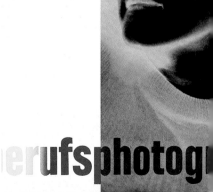

erufsphotog

GRAPHIC ICONS

VISIONARIES WHO SHAPED
MODERN GRAPHIC DESIGN

JOHN CLIFFORD

Graphic Icons: Visionaries Who Shaped Modern Graphic Design

John Clifford

Peachpit Press

Find us on the Web at: www.peachpit.com
To report errors, please send a note to errata@peachpit.com

Peachpit Press is a division of Pearson Education.

Copyright © 2014 by John Clifford

Acquisitions Editor: Nikki Echler McDonald
Production Editor: Tracey Croom
Development Editor: Bryn Mooth
Copy Editor: Elaine Merrill
Proofer: Liz Welch
Indexer: FireCrystal Communications
Cover and Interior Design: Think Studio

ISBN 13: 978-0-321-88720-7
ISBN 10: 0-321-88720-4

9 8 7 6 5 4 3 2 1

Printed and bound in the United States of America

To my family, Tim and Will

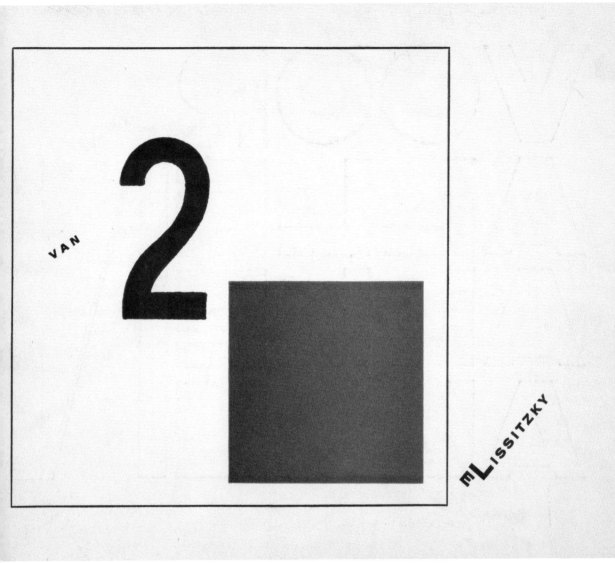

El Lissitzky, 1922

PREFACE

This is a book about names. Many people know the names of architects, artists, and fashion designers, but not many know the names of graphic designers. It's strange to me, since graphic designers create so much of our everyday world: books, magazines, web sites, logos, posters, packaging, infographics, wayfinding signs, mobile apps, and film and television graphics.

This list of influential 20th century graphic designers is not, and cannot be, definitive. There are designers I wanted to include, but couldn't get permission to publish. For example, two designers in this book name Tibor Kalman as an influence, yet his work isn't featured. Not because I don't think he's worthy, but because I couldn't get permission, much as I tried. There were others who were simply too expensive to feature. (Believe it or not, design books don't have unlimited budgets.)

This book is about people, not about themes or movements. I've loosely grouped the designers chronologically, within four broad time periods. So while a particular work may not technically be considered early modern, for example, I've opted to include it in Chapter 1, more as a reference to its era than to a particular artistic movement. Many of these designers had (and have) lengthy bodies of work that grew and evolved over long careers, so I didn't want to label them under any one movement or style.

I was a design student at California College of Arts and Crafts (now California College of the Arts) in the 1990s. Graphic design, or at least the design I noticed, was pretty complex then, with layers upon layers of texture, distorted images, and blurred or distressed type. It was chaotic. Messy. Sometimes illegible. I liked it in a way, I guess, but didn't think I could ever design anything like that. I've always preferred being neat and clear and direct. In my uneducated mind, since all designers seemed to be doing grunge (or, *the* grunge, as my friends and I called it), you had to do grunge if you wanted to be a designer. That, and the fact that I struggled through my first studio classes, made me unsure about this whole design thing.

Then I took a graphic design history class with Steve Reoutt. I used to think of history classes as stuffy and dull. Not this one. I was floored: the simplicity and starkness of El Lissitzky; the bright colors of Edward McKnight Kauffer; the bold type of Herbert Bayer; the asymmetry and white space of Jan Tschichold; the abstraction and restraint of Herbert Matter. Each of these designers gave me hope: If they could accomplish a lot with a little, maybe I could, too.

This is the book I have always wanted for myself. Although I'm not an academic, I teach, and I want a simple primer on history for my students. I'm a practicing designer, not a historian, and I'd love an easy reference on modern designers for inspiration.

Of course, there are excellent design history books already out there, like the classic textbook *Meggs' History of Graphic Design*, by Philip B. Meggs and Alston W. Purvis. This book doesn't attempt to replace them. Instead, I hope it will lead readers to them. Suggestions for further reading and exploring pop up throughout this book.

Ultimately, *Graphic Icons* is a very personal list. These are the people who have influenced me and my work. In addition to the pioneers I learned about in school, the dean of my design school is here, along with my old boss. Some of those messy designers from the '90s are here, too. While this list is personal, I think a strong case can be made for all the designers in this book: They changed the field of graphic design. I hope you'll learn something from reading it, as I've learned from writing it.

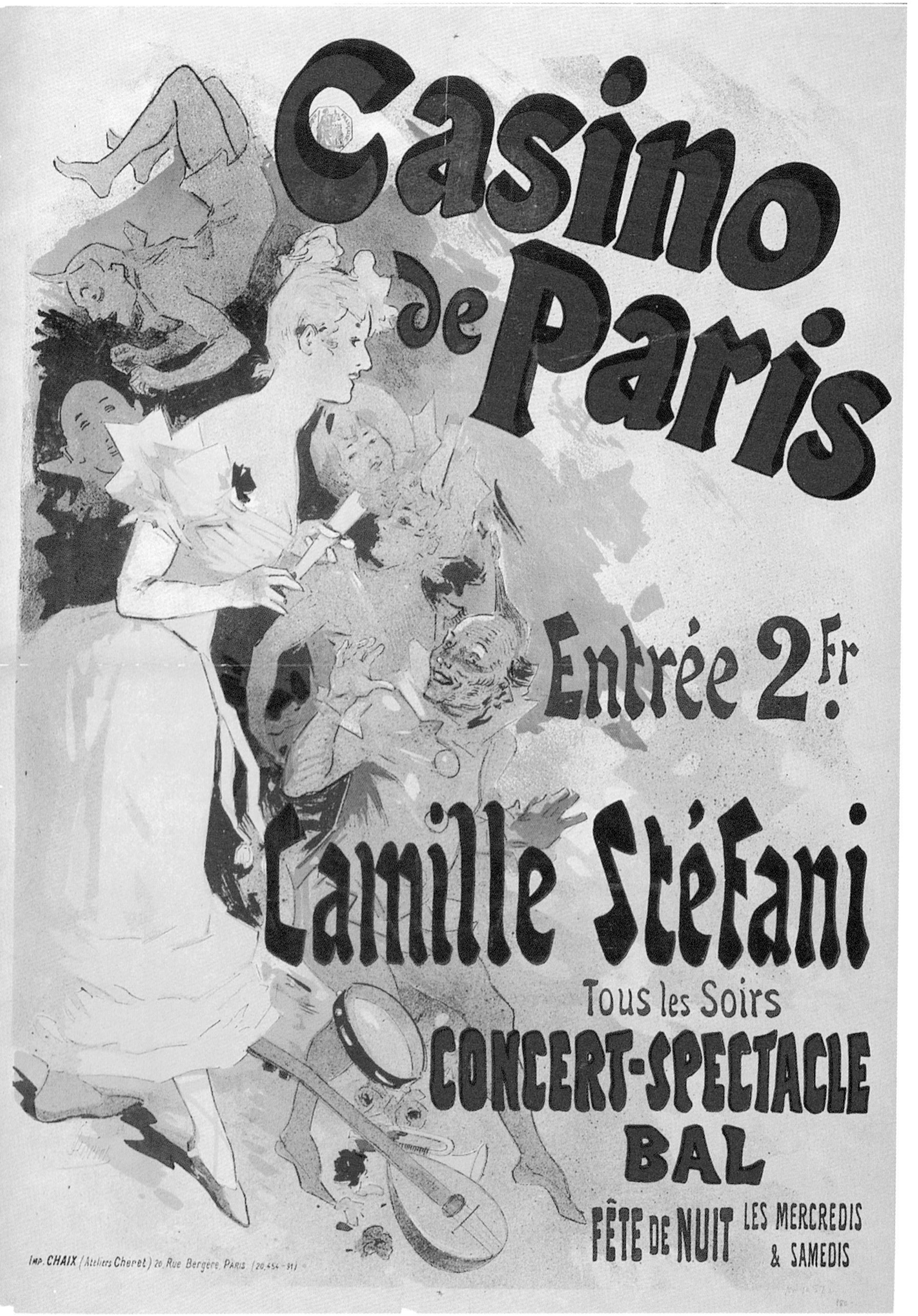
Casino de Paris
Entrée 2 Fr.
Camille Stéfani
Tous les Soirs
CONCERT-SPECTACLE
BAL
FÊTE DE NUIT LES MERCREDIS & SAMEDIS
IMP. CHAIX (Ateliers Cheret) 20, Rue Bergère, PARIS (20.454-91)

INTRODUCTION—ARTS AND CRAFTS, ART NOUVEAU: INDUSTRIALIZATION SHAPES VISUAL CULTURE

As the 20th century approached, the world had already experienced huge changes. The Industrial Revolution, which began in the mid-1700s in England and continued through the 1800s in Europe and the United States, created new ways of doing almost everything—manufacturing, traveling, and communicating. The rise of the machine enabled mass production, making goods more accessible and inexpensive. It also created jobs in growing, centralized urban areas. People left farms in the country for work in the city.

Population shifts, industrialization, mass communication: All of these forces would shape visual culture—and the artists and designers who created it—across the world for decades to come.

As cities grew, street posters became the most efficient way to reach consumers. Steam-powered printing presses could produce posters, books, newspapers, and magazines faster and in greater quantity than manual processes. Printed materials were no longer precious, handmade items available only to the wealthy; they were accessible to working classes, as well. As education became more widely available, literacy rates rose—which furthered the development of printed communication.

Not everyone embraced mass production and efficiency, however. William Morris rejected the machine aesthetic and founded the Arts and Crafts movement in England around 1880. Its goal? To unite aesthetic excellence and traditional craftsmanship. Morris wasn't against just the machine; he was against the mediocre: Most mass-produced goods were low-quality and clichéd. Morris founded the Kelmscott

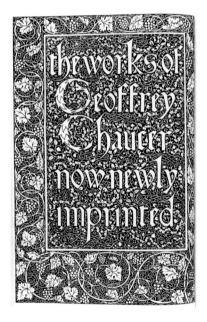

ABOVE: William Morris, title page, *The Works of Geoffrey Chaucer*, 1896

OPPOSITE: Jules Cheret, *Casino de Paris* poster, 1891

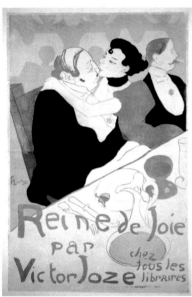

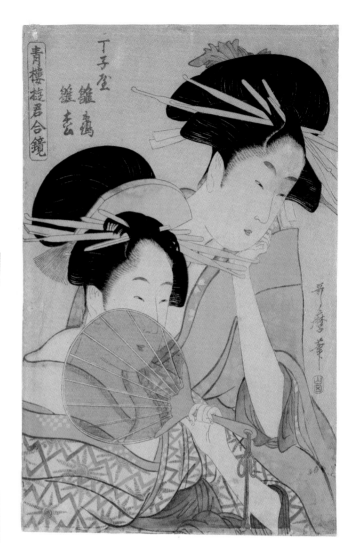

ABOVE, LEFT: Henri de Toulouse-Lautrec,
Reine de Joie par Victor Joze poster, 1892

ABOVE: Kitagawa Utamaro, Chojiya
hinazuru hinamatsu, woodblock print,
between 1798 and 1801

OPPOSITE: Alphonse Mucha, Sarah
Bernhardt American tour poster, 1896

Press and published his own books, using detailed woodcut borders and decorations, and typefaces inspired by type from the 15th century. However, running a publishing house at that time without mechanization was unsustainable: Kelmscott's labor-intensive books were very expensive, putting them out of reach for the general population. The movement's influence carried on, though, as decorative forms based on nature and plants continued, becoming a big part of Art Nouveau.

In Paris, poster art thrived—not just for advertisers, but also for collectors. Artists found opportunities creating work that promoted products and entertainment. Jules Cheret, often called the father of the modern poster, married art and utility: He didn't just paint the posters, he also developed a method for reproducing them. Cheret's overprinting technique lent texture, splashes, and scratches to his brightly colored designs. Cheret and other European artists were influenced by the asymmetrical simplicity and flat color of Japanese woodblock prints, an art form that reached the continent after Japan began trading with western countries in the mid-1800s. Cheret developed a distinct style with his use of female figures and hand lettering. The women in his posters were usually animated and enjoying life—dancing, drinking, and smoking—an unusual depiction at the time. Artists, such as his fellow Frenchman Henri de Toulouse-Lautrec and Italy's Leonetto Cappiello, followed suit.

Czech-born Alphonse Mucha worked in Paris and exemplified the decorative Art Nouveau ("New Art") movement: flat color, creative lettering, and stylized organic forms. He added detailed mosaic backgrounds, and often gave his female subjects long, flowing curves of hair. The actress Sarah Bernhardt, convinced that Mucha captured her as no other artist had, signed him to an exclusive contract under which he designed her posters, theater sets, and costumes.

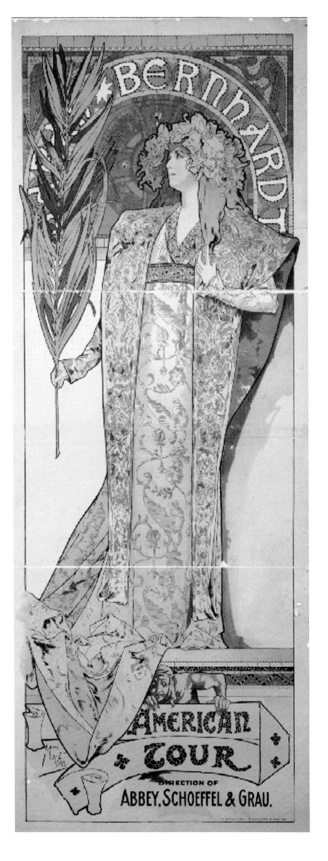

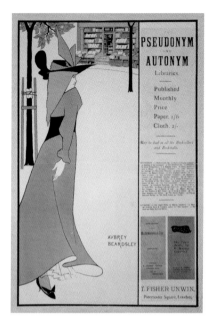

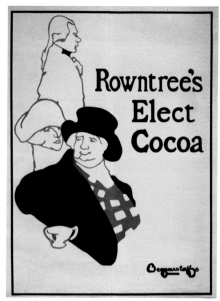

In England, illustrator Aubrey Beardsley simplified forms from nature and became well-known for his black-and-white images, heavy outlines, and distorted bodies. While Beardsley separated image and lettering (usually in different boxes), painters James Pryde and William Nicholson, brothers-in-law who were known as the Beggarstaffs, integrated lettering into their compositions. Their illustrations, made of flat shapes of colored paper, were often incomplete, inviting viewers to mentally finish the picture. The Beggarstaffs' partnership was short-lived: although their work was admired in art circles, they didn't make any money.

Will Bradley introduced Art Nouveau to the United States, reflecting the influence of Aubrey Beardsley and William Morris in the design of his posters, books, and journals, many of which he published through his Wayside Press in Springfield, Massachusetts. The look he developed, though, was his own, as he worked at unifying the visuals with the text.

In Germany, Art Nouveau was known as *Jugendstil* ("Young Style"); German artists and designers experimented with the style before moving on to something new. Peter Behrens was initially inspired by French Art Nouveau, but started stripping his work of ornament around the turn of the century. Behrens and other designers became more objective, moving away from floral motifs toward a more geometric logic and order. The shift to more geometric designs was also taking place with the members of the Vienna Secession in Austria, like Gustav Klimt and Koloman Moser.

Printed materials—posters, books, periodicals—became increasingly simple and structured in their design as modernism spread throughout Europe after the turn of the century. Soon, the artists and craftsmen who created them would have new titles: graphic designers.

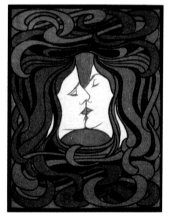

ABOVE, TOP: Aubrey Beardsley, poster, 1894

ABOVE, RIGHT: Beggarstaffs, Rowntree's elect cocoa poster, 1895

ABOVE: Peter Behrens, *The Kiss*, 1898

OPPOSITE: Will Bradley, Springfield Bicycle Club Tournament poster, 1895

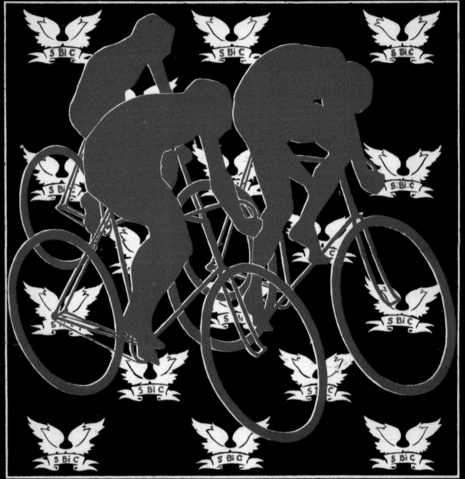

SPRINGFIELD BICYCLE CLUB TOURNAMENT

WILL H. BRADLEY '95

SPRINGFIELD MASS
SEPT. 11 AND 12, 1895

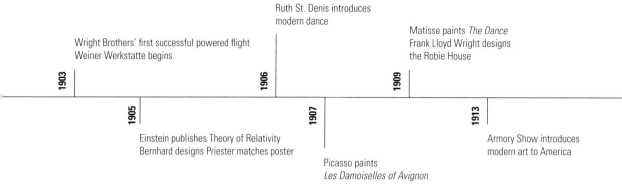

Ruth St. Denis introduces
modern dance

Matisse paints *The Dance*
Frank Lloyd Wright designs
the Robie House

Wright Brothers' first successful powered flight
Weiner Werkstatte begins

1903

1906

1909

1905

1907

1913

Einstein publishes Theory of Relativity
Bernhard designs Priester matches poster

Picasso paints
Les Damoiselles of Avignon

Armory Show introduces
modern art to America

EARLY MODERN: SIMPLICITY MEETS THE AVANT-GARDE

The 20th century brought experimentation, innovation, and change, which echoed throughout society, culture, and everyday life. Artists, writers, architects, and designers rejected historical styles and ideas that they felt had no place in the Industrial Age, developing new concepts in response to the era's needs and possibilities.

These emerging aesthetic approaches were reactions to what came before. For example, artists and designers adopted abstract, geometric forms, casting aside the decorative, organic flourishes of Art Nouveau. Graphic design—even though nobody would call it that for years to come—was heavily influenced by movements in modern art at the time. These movements—Cubism, Futurism, Constructivism, De Stijl, and Dada—encouraged simplicity and new ways of expression. In design, a more functional approach was emerging. The goal? Clear communication. Posters with this new design sensibility became a popular form of advertising in Europe, fueling the commercial and economic activity that dominated the Industrial Age.

The era's political unrest, like the Russian Revolution of 1917, inspired artists to believe that radical shifts in design could change the world, and that the development of a visual

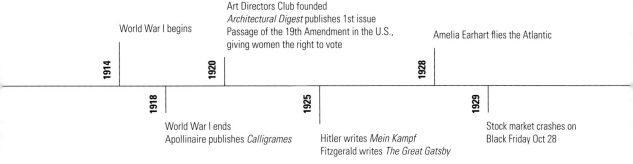

World War I begins

Art Directors Club founded
Architectural Digest publishes 1st issue
Passage of the 19th Amendment in the U.S.,
giving women the right to vote

Amelia Earhart flies the Atlantic

1914

1920

1928

1918

1925

1929

World War I ends
Apollinaire publishes *Calligrames*

Hitler writes *Mein Kampf*
Fitzgerald writes *The Great Gatsby*

Stock market crashes on
Black Friday Oct 28

language made of geometric shapes, photography, and simple typography could unite people from different cultures and classes. Like-minded designers and thinkers formed groups to discuss and promote these new ideas.

At the same time, technological developments made it possible for designers and artists to reach a broader audience and exert more influence. Advancements in photography, like film replacing plates and the availability of mass-market cameras, allowed more creative control. The Industrial Age's emphasis on mass production meant that ordinary people could adorn their homes with items that were beautiful as well as functional, and this created new opportunities for designers. Even the machines that produced all these goods were themselves considered beautiful. And printing shifted from a decorative craft to a powerful means of communicating new ideas and information.

New ideas met new technology in this Early Modern era, transforming the way people, companies, and governments used visual media to communicate.

LUCIAN BERNHARD

1883–1972 | BORN: Stuttgart, Germany | EDUCATION: Munich Art Academy

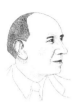

Invented the "object poster," focusing on the product being sold

Rejected Art Nouveau's decorative complexity

Designed several typefaces

Lucian Bernhard's submission to the Priester matches advertising competition was not immediately embraced— the judging panel initially tossed his poster in the trash. But another judge, Ernst Growald, arrived late. Spying Bernhard's work in the bin, he took it out, studied it, and declared, "Here is a genius." Growald persuaded the other jurors, and Bernhard's poster won first prize.

Lucian Bernhard was in his early 20s when he entered his design in an advertising poster contest sponsored by Priester matches. (Consider this an early form of crowdsourcing.) Although Art Nouveau was popular at the time, with its complex ornaments and floral embellishments, Bernhard took a different creative direction, painting a simple scene showing a smoking cigar in an ashtray with matches. A friend saw the artwork and thought it advertised cigars. So Bernhard reduced all unnecessary detail until all that remained was a pair of red matches. He then painted the brand name. There was no slogan, nothing to distract from the visual of the product and its name.

Bernhard's design was influenced by the reduced silhouettes and minimalism of England's Beggarstaff Brothers (brothers-in-law, actually, who ran an advertising design studio under a pseudonym). Like the Beggarstaffs, Bernhard used flat planes of solid color, but unlike them, he didn't outline individual shapes in his artwork.

Not only did Bernhard's design win Priester's poster contest, it also launched a new, straightforward style of advertising. German companies in particular embraced this new flat minimalism, which they called *Sachplakat* (object poster, which led to the broader *Plakatstil*, or poster style)—advertisers felt that Art Nouveau's intricate decoration could obscure or compete with their product. Posters need to make a quick impression—people passing by are not likely to stop and spend time deciphering the message. Bernhard's focus on the product and its name addressed this issue.

Bernhard opened his own firm in 1906, employing more than 20 designers. Later, he moved to New York, where he expanded into interior design and helped start the collective Contempora, which sold products like textiles and home goods. He also designed typefaces that are still used today, like Bernhard Modern and Bernhard Gothic.

OPPOSITE: Priester matches poster, c. 1905

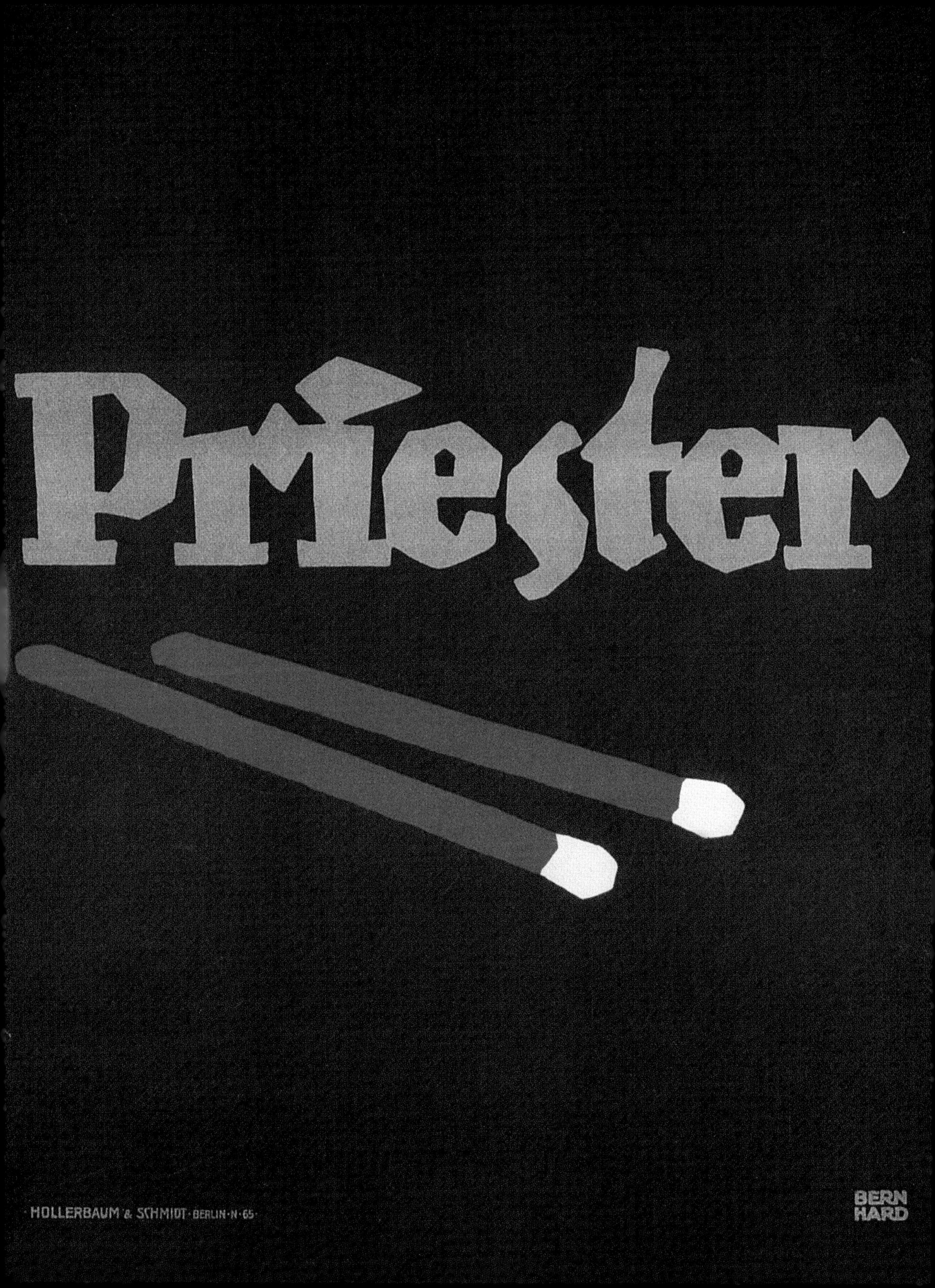

Priester

HOLLERBAUM & SCHMIDT · BERLIN · N · 65 ·

BERN
HARD

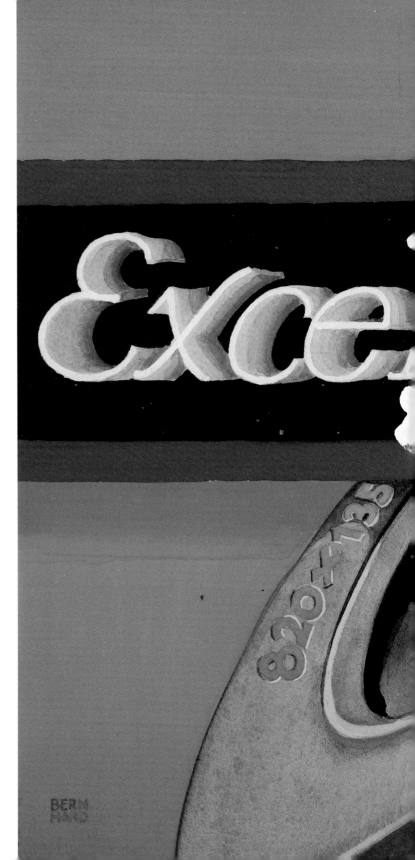

READ: *History of the Poster*, by Josef Müller-Brockmann, for a smart overview of poster design from the late 1800s to the 1970s.

DO: Bernhard's poster style stripped the imagery down to the essentials in order to clearly communicate a message. Consider a recent design project you've completed: What elements can you remove from the design? How much can you edit and still retain the work's meaning and message?

Excelsior poster (gouache maquette), c. 1914

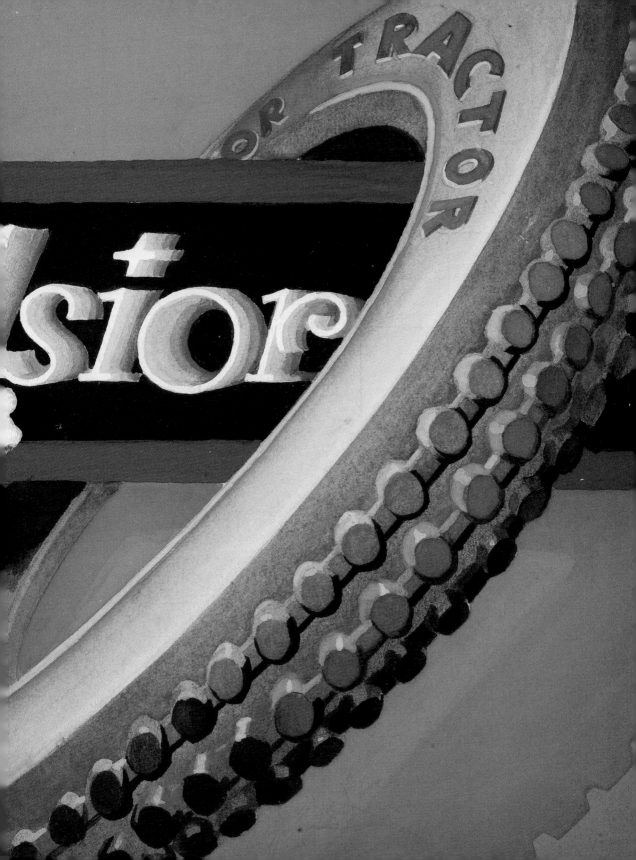

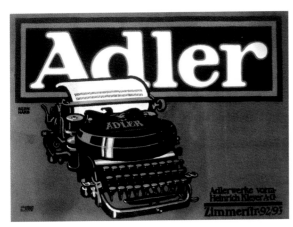

ABOVE: Adler Typewriters poster, c. 1909

OPPOSITE: Bosch poster, 1914

"Lucidity, clarity, fitness is the aim. New rules must complement the old. As the automobile has found its own specific beauty, so will commercial typography find its own expression—quite different from the art of the book, though many mistakes may still be necessary before the goal is reached."[1]

—Lucian Bernhard

The quote is set in a digital version of Bernhard Modern, a typeface he designed

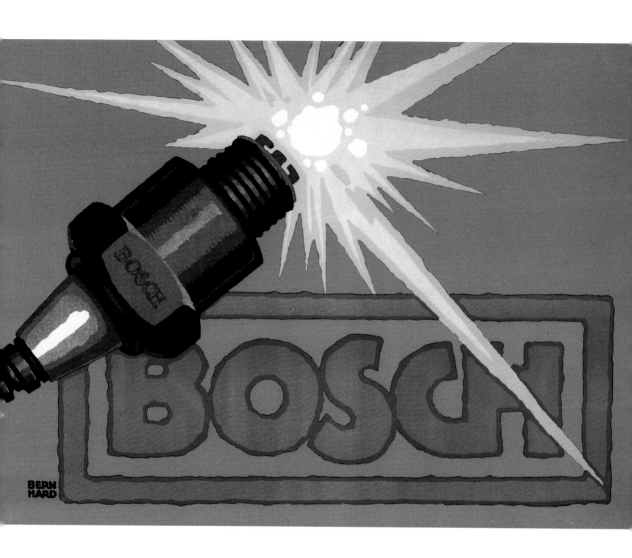

HANS RUDI ERDT

1883–1918 | BORN: Benediktbeuern, Germany | EDUCATION: Munich School of Applied Arts

Further developed *Plakatstil* (poster style) movement in Germany

Used visual tricks to suggest the product, rather than show it

Designed classic war posters

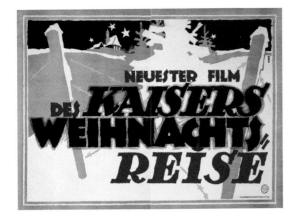

ABOVE: Poster for film *Des Kaisers Weihnachtsreise*, 1917

OPPOSITE: Poster for Opel automobiles, 1911

Like Lucian Bernhard, Berlin-based Hans Rudi Erdt used a lean approach to design: flat colors, simple shapes, and bold typography. While Bernhard focused on the product being sold, Erdt took a less literal approach in his designs. His poster for Opel automobiles, for example, doesn't show the car. The face of a man with driving goggles and a cap on his head is placed above and behind the brand name. Nothing more. People tend to connect with people better than with objects, so featuring a person in a design can lead to a more emotional connection.

Erdt was skilled at integrating type into his layouts. Although he doesn't show the car, he suggests its presence: The letter "O" is at a larger scale than the other letters. And it's a perfect circle, like a steering wheel. It looks like the man is driving the car that we cannot see. A visual device that associates the brand name with a steering wheel helps people remember that Opel is a car company.

Printer Hollerbaum and Schmidt signed Erdt to an exclusive contract, along with other progressive designers like Bernhard, Julius Klinger, and Julius Gipkens. Erdt designed for clients like Manoli and Problem cigarettes, and Nivea skin care. During World War I, he designed several projects for Germany, including posters for war movies for the government's film committee. He died at the young age of 35 from tuberculosis.

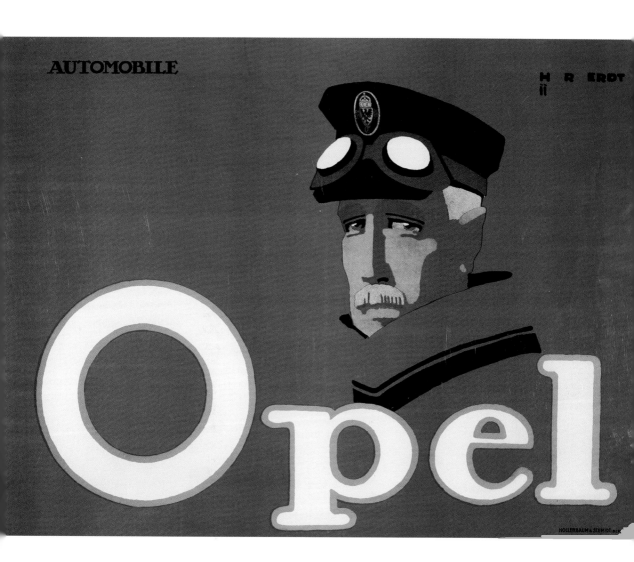

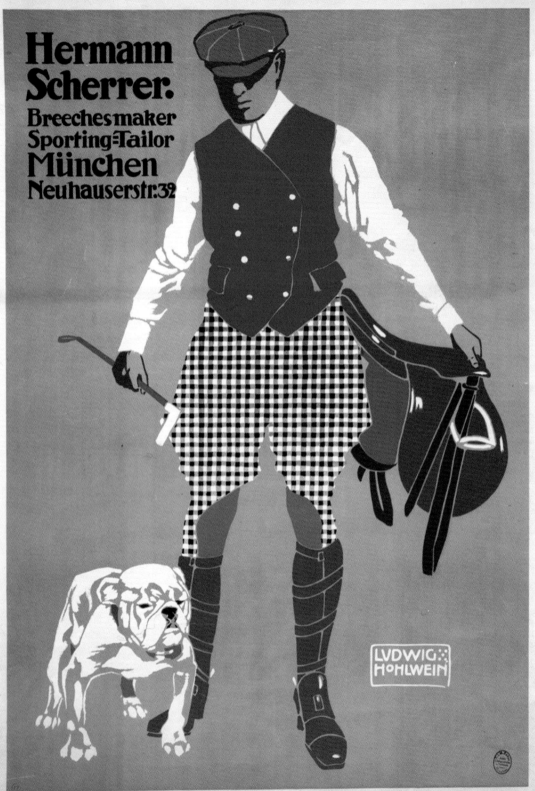

LUDWIG HOHLWEIN

1874–1949 | BORN: Wiesbaden, Germany | EDUCATION: Technical University in Munich; Dresden Academy

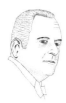

Incorporated depth and pattern in poster designs

Evolved stylistically throughout his career, from flat to painterly to severe

Another influential German designer, Ludwig Hohlwein, drew inspiration from the Beggarstaffs and their flat, simple, graphic style. Trained as an architect, Hohlwein left Munich in 1911 for Berlin, where he worked as a poster artist. While he worked in the *Plakatstil* (poster style) that Bernhard had pioneered, the two differed in some important aesthetic ways. Rather than total flatness, Hohlwein incorporated depth in his poster designs; pattern, texture, and color gave his work more volume, which was well suited for his clothing and retail clients.

Hohlwein's designs evolved as the world around him changed. His work became richer and more painterly. His posters during World War I used light and shadow to give them more of a human touch. For instance, in his poster promoting an exhibit of artwork by German prisoners of war, the balance of the graphic cross with the soldier's expressive face appeals to the viewer's emotions.

As Adolf Hitler rose to power, Hohlwein designed many posters for the Nazi party. His work grew more sharp and severe, and featured figures that exhibited muscular, Aryan ideals. Although Hohlwein was a very talented designer, his legacy has been tainted by his close ties to the Nazi party.

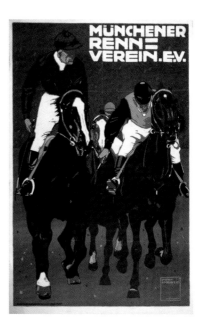

ABOVE: Poster for Munich Racing Association, 1909

OPPOSITE: Hermann Scherrer poster, 1911

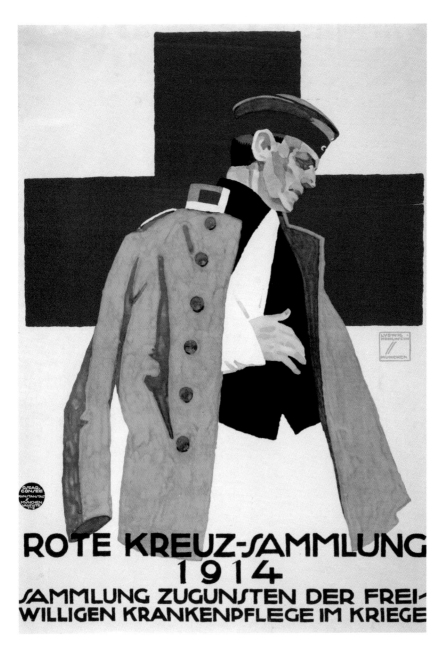

ABOVE: Red Cross Collection Drive fund-raising poster, 1914

OPPOSITE: Berliner Sport Club poster, 1914

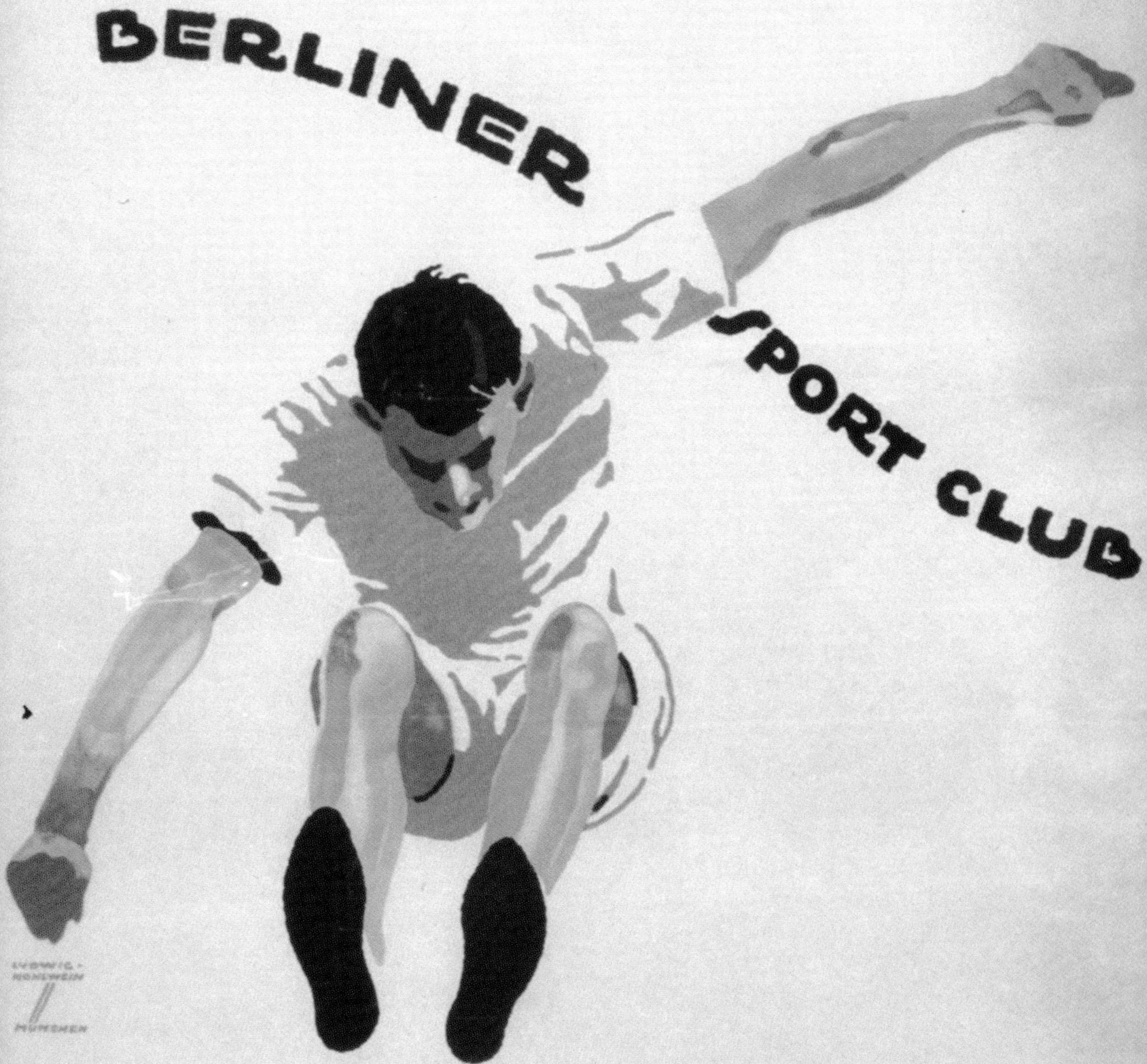
BERLINER
SPORT CLUB

FILIPPO TOMMASO MARINETTI

1876–1944 | BORN: Alexandria, Egypt | EDUCATION: the Sorbonne, University of Pavia

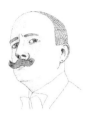

Broke typographical rules and influenced modern design

Founded Italian Futurism

Combined words with typography to create a new form of expressive poetry

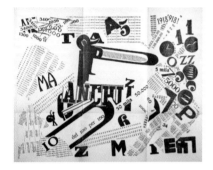

ABOVE: "Une assemblee tumultuese" (A Tumultuous Assembly) foldout, from *Les mots en liberte futurists*, 1919

OPPOSITE: Cover for *Zang Tumb Tumb* poetry book, 1914

READ: *Futurism: An Anthology*, edited by Lawrence Rainey, Christine Poggi, and Laura Wittman, collects manifestos, artwork, and poems, including the work of Fortunato Depero, the most commercially successful Futurist artist and designer.

Speed. Machines. Aggression. War. Change. These were the important elements of life in the 20th century, according to Italian Futurism founder Filippo Tommaso Marinetti. Although better known as a poet, Marinetti brought a new form of expression to this literary art by breaking all the rules of typography—and graphic design still reflects his profound influence.

In 1909, Marinetti published his "Futurist Manifesto" in a French newspaper, calling for a revolution in art, poetry, and design. He called for the demolition of traditional means of creating, and urged artists to embrace the speed, mechanical processes, and violence of the industrialized world. He saw war as a method of defeating the past and moving into the future. The married father of three daughters was also a big old sexist, as feminism was among the issues he railed against.

He published his first book, *Zang Tumb Tumb*, in 1914. Based on his experiences during the Balkan War of 1912, the title is a graphic representation of the mechanized sounds of gunfire, grenades, and other weapons. It was one of his experiments in "words in freedom," where he broke away from conventional linear writing by using only nouns—no adjectives or verbs. Defying traditional typography, he designed the cover using a mixture of typefaces at varying scales and angles and scrambled around the page. He pioneered expressive typography, giving it a pictorial quality; his words *looked* the way they *sounded*.

Marinetti furthered his Futurist theories in areas like music, dance, film, and textiles. He even published *Futurist Cookbook*, in which he proposed to ban pasta because it made the body sluggish (perhaps he foreshadowed the low-carb diet craze). He also became more political and embraced Fascism, even though his support for Italian dictator Benito Mussolini didn't last long.

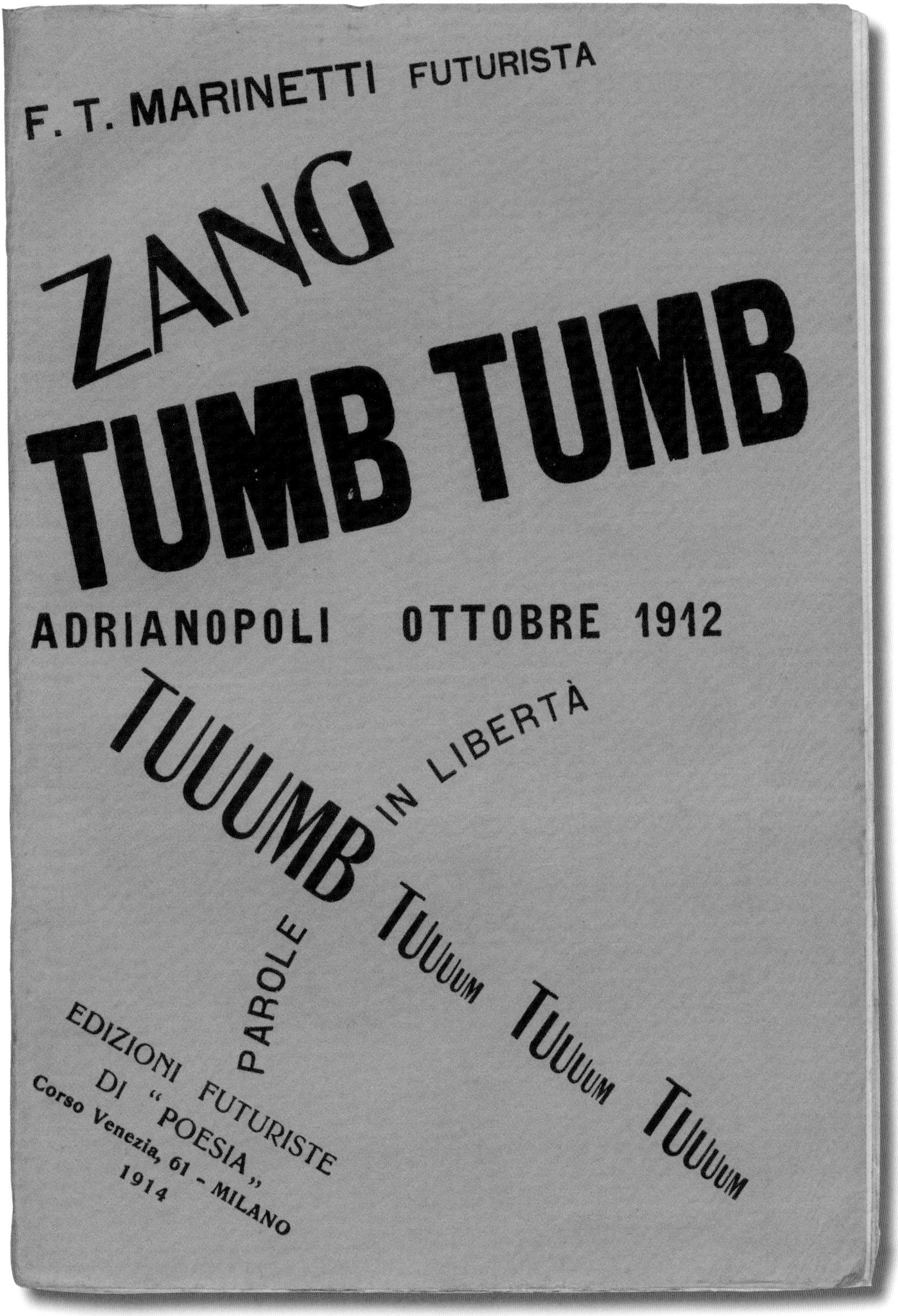

F. T. MARINETTI FUTURISTA

ZANG
TUMB TUMB

ADRIANOPOLI   OTTOBRE 1912

TUUUMB Tuuum Tuuum Tuuum

IN LIBERTÀ

PAROLE

EDIZIONI FUTURISTE
DI "POESIA"
Corso Venezia, 61 - MILANO
1914

EDWARD McKNIGHT KAUFFER

1890–1954 | BORN: Great Falls, Montana | EDUCATION: Mark Hopkins Institute; Chicago Art Institute

Adapted knowledge of modern painting to design

Designed radical poster incorporating Cubism, Futurism, and Vorticism

Helped establish the discipline of graphic design in England

Edward McKnight Kauffer was born in Montana, but it was Chicago that opened his artistic eyes, where the famous 1913 Armory Show introduced American patrons to European avant-garde art. Inspired, he traveled abroad to study. He saw the influential poster work of Ludwig Hohlwein in Germany, studied painting in Paris, and launched his career in advertising design in London.

Frank Pick, an administrator for the London Underground, became an important client for Kauffer. Pick was a strong supporter of modern design and believed in its commercial value. At a time when the Underground was known for generating pollution, Pick and Kauffer began a bold campaign to give the transit system a more positive reputation by creating a series of travel posters that focused on the system's interesting destinations. Throughout their lengthy collaboration, Kauffer designed more than 100 posters for Pick.

In 1919, Kauffer submitted work for a poster to promote London newspaper *The Daily Herald*. To illustrate the tagline, "Soaring to Success! Daily Herald—The Early Bird," he used his 1916 painting *Flight*, a dynamically radical interpretation of birds flying that looks like it was inspired by Japanese prints. In the painting, Kauffer married his own observations of birds in flight with a heavy dose of influence from the Futurists, as well as the Vorticists, a movement of British avant-garde abstract artists who idolized machines and speed. The poster went on to become an icon of Kauffer's work, and it led to commissions for book covers, interiors, store windows, theater sets, photomurals, and rugs.

Kauffer was smart and sophisticated, and he understood that he needed to build friendly relationships with clients to get the best results. Frank Pick and Shell-Mex Oil's Jack Beddington agreed with him philosophically. But most clients didn't automatically embrace Kauffer's radical views on modernism, so he gently prodded them to get to the best design solution. In addition to socializing with clients, he was a part of London's art and literary scenes, hanging out with people like T.S. Eliot and Virginia Woolf.

After building an influential advertising career in London, Kauffer moved to New York in 1940. It didn't go well. His symbolic designs with minimal text were popular among the museum set, but not yet accepted in the conservative world of American commercial advertising. He became restless and lost his confidence when faced with the competitive scene in New York, and died in 1954.

OPPOSITE: Poster for the *Daily Herald*, 1918

OVERLEAF: Aeroshell poster, 1932

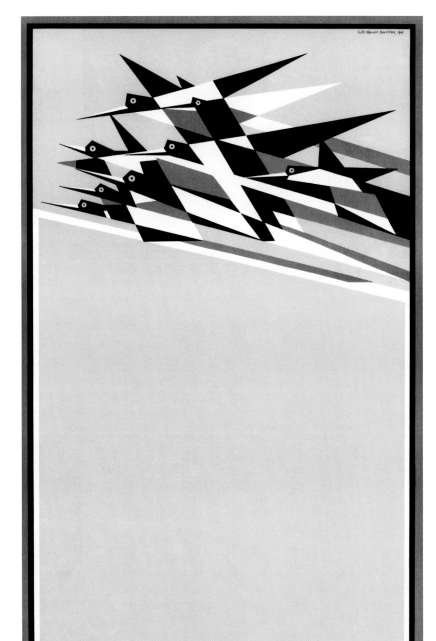

Soaring to Success !

DAILY HERALD

— the Early Bird.

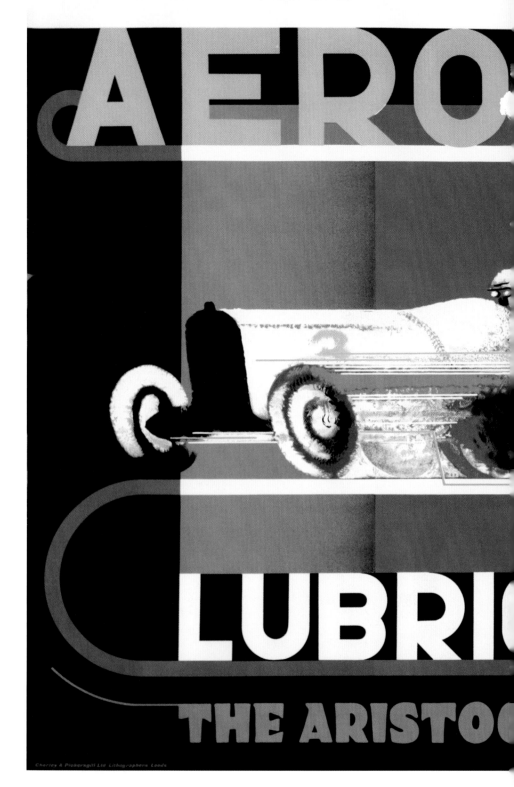

Charley & Pickersgill Ltd. Lithographers, Leeds

E MCKNIGHT
KAUFFER 1932

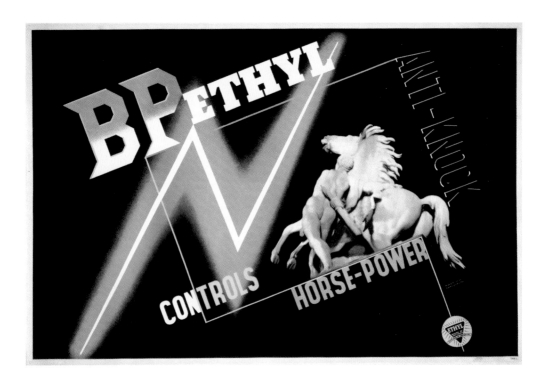

SEE: The London Transport Museum includes 127 Kauffer posters in its collection, with a number of them regularly on display.

ABOVE: BP ethyl poster, 1934

OPPOSITE: London Underground poster, 1930

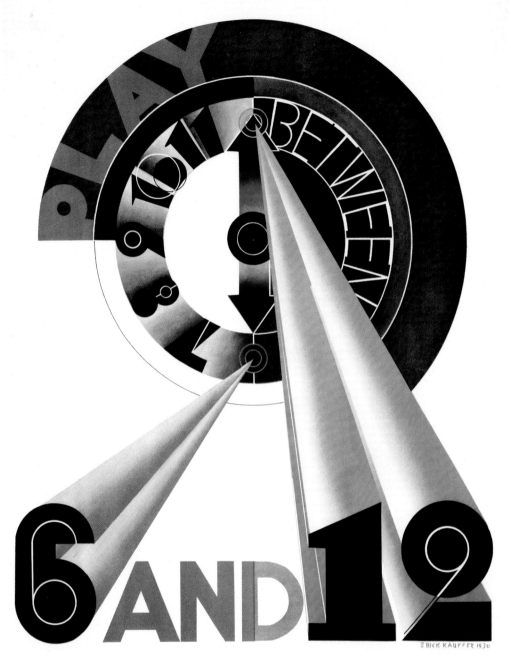

PLAY BETWEEN

6 AND 12

THE BRIGHT HOURS
GO BY
UNDERGROUND

EL LISSITZKY

1890–1941 | BORN: Pochinok, Russia | EDUCATION: Technische Hochschule, Polytechnic Institute of Riga

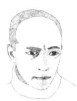

Influenced the design of books, exhibitions, and type

Pioneered the use of diagonal axes, asymmetry, white space, and bold sans serif type

Believed that visual communication could reach the uneducated masses and prompt social and political change

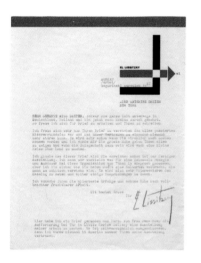

ABOVE: Letterhead, 1926

OPPOSITE: Cover for *Veshch* magazine, 1922

OVERLEAF: Pages from *For the Voice*, poetry book by Vladimir Mayakovski, 1923

It's not surprising that Russian designer El Lissitzky drew influence from the Suprematists early in his career; his work often combined elements on a strong diagonal axis, giving his designs a new, dynamic quality.

The Suprematist movement was born in Russia, the brainchild of painter Kasimir Malevich, who advocated for art built on abstract geometric shapes and flat colors. (The appropriately named *Black Circle* is one of Malevich's works.) Followers of Suprematism believed art need not serve any function beyond its intrinsic, spiritual value. In 1921, Lissitzky was among a group of artists who broke away from the Suprematists to focus on practical design to aid Russia's new communist state. These were the Constructivists.

Lissitzky believed that art and design could communicate in a nation where much of the population was illiterate. He aimed to establish a visual language using shape and color instead of letterforms; in his famous political poster *Beat the Whites with the Red Wedge*, geometric shapes tell the story of the revolutionaries shattering the establishment.

Lissitzky's design work had several distinguishing characteristics—layouts structured on a grid, limited color palettes, tense diagonals, sans serif type, and repetition of pure geometric forms. He experimented with photomontage, a method of layering and superimposing multiple images. To him, sequencing the pages of a book felt like cinema. The way he organized space gave words a new energetic power.

His diverse talents in painting, architecture, typography, and design allowed him to connect movements like Constructivism, De Stijl, Dada, and the Bauhaus. That integration produced layouts that not only engaged the eye, but also clarified and emphasized the content. Although he suffered from tuberculosis, he rarely slowed down. Teaching, writing, traveling, and working for publications like *Veshch-Objet-Gegenstand*, along with his friendly demeanor, helped spread his ideas around the world.

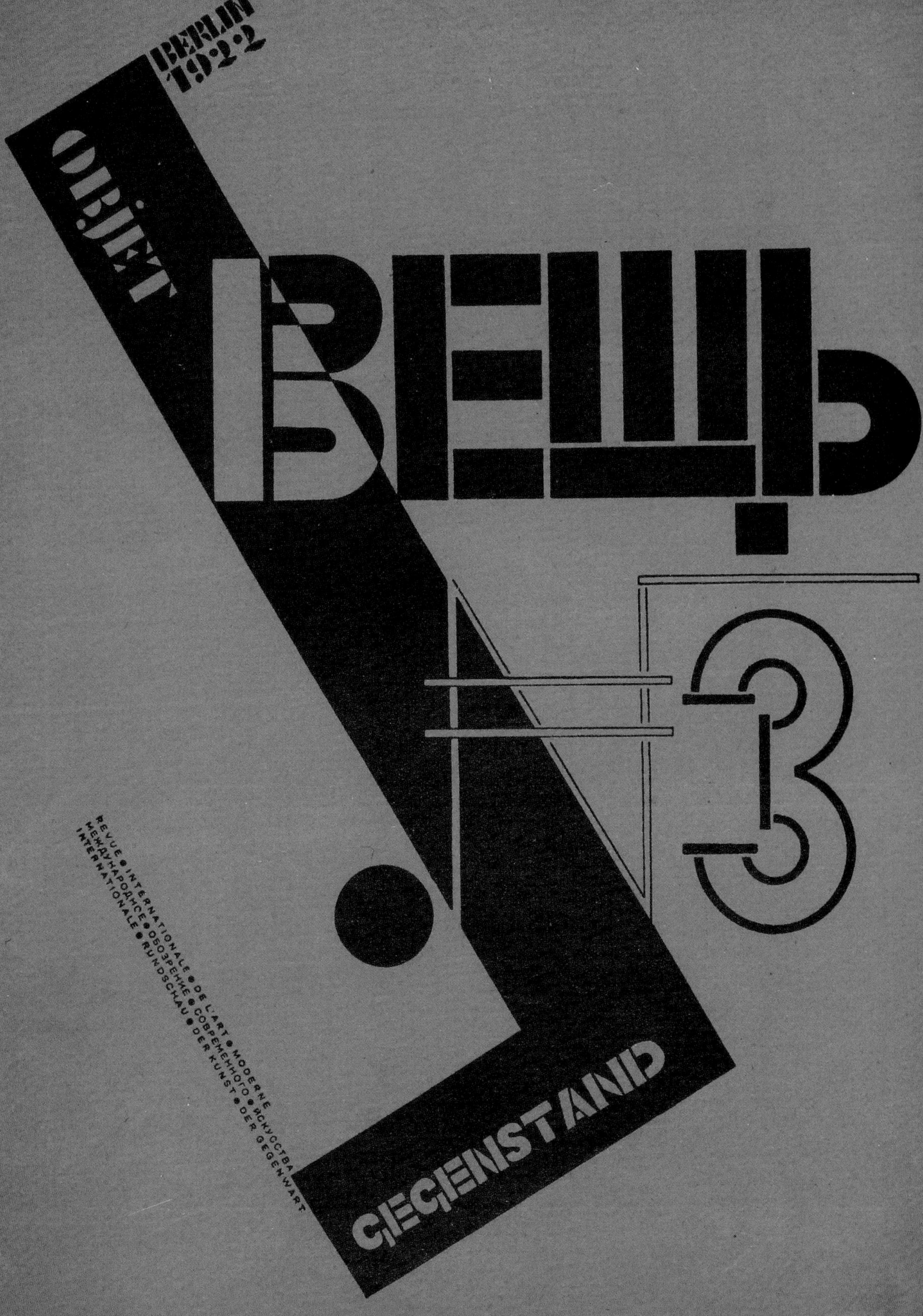

BERLIN 1922

OBJET

ВЕЩЬ

1-2

GEGENSTAND

REVUE • INTERNATIONALE • DE L'ART • MODERNE
МЕЖДУНАРОДНОЕ • ОБОЗРЕНИЕ • СОВРЕМЕННОГО • ИСКУССТВА
INTERNATIONALE • RUNDSCHAU • DER KUNST • DER GEGENWART

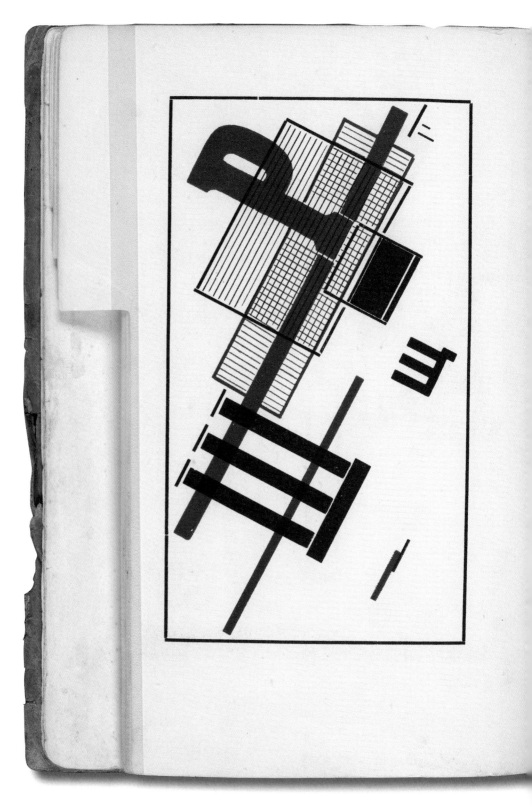

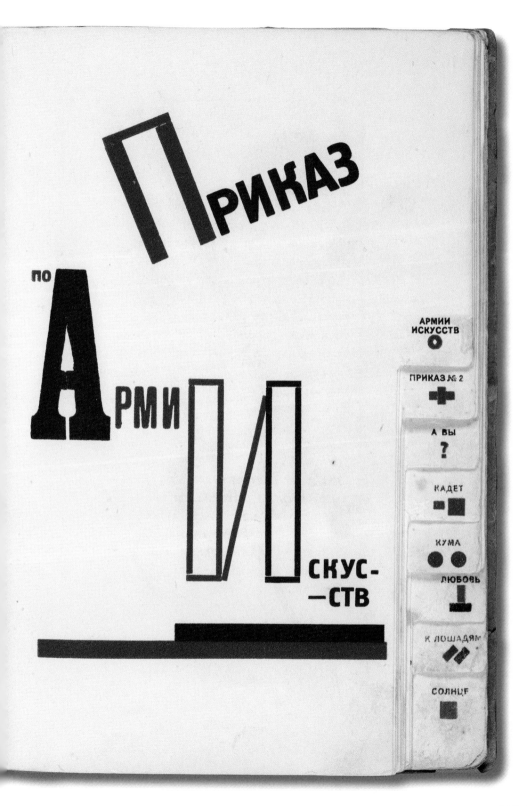

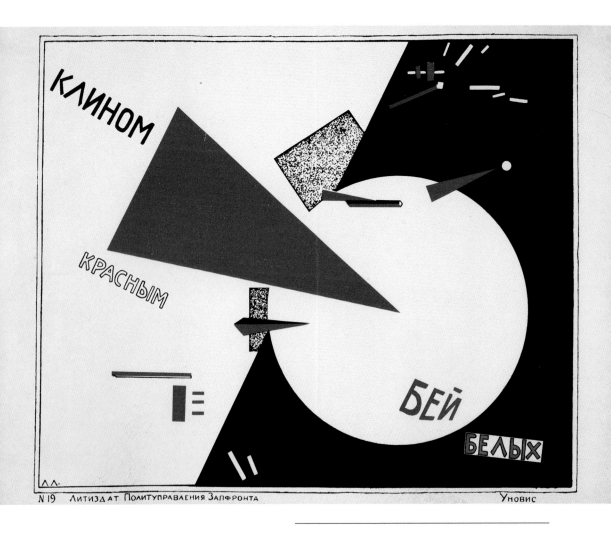

READ: Explore how contemporary designers are using their talents as Lissitzky did to prompt social change: *Designing for Social Change: Strategies for Community-Based Graphic Design*, by Andrew Shea, Ellen Lupton, and William Drenttel
The Design Activist's Handbook: How to Change the World (or Your Part of It) with Socially Conscious Design, by Noah Scalin and Michelle Taute

ABOVE: "Beat the Whites with the Red Wedge," poster, 1919

OPPOSITE: Cover of Arckhitektura (Architecture), 1927

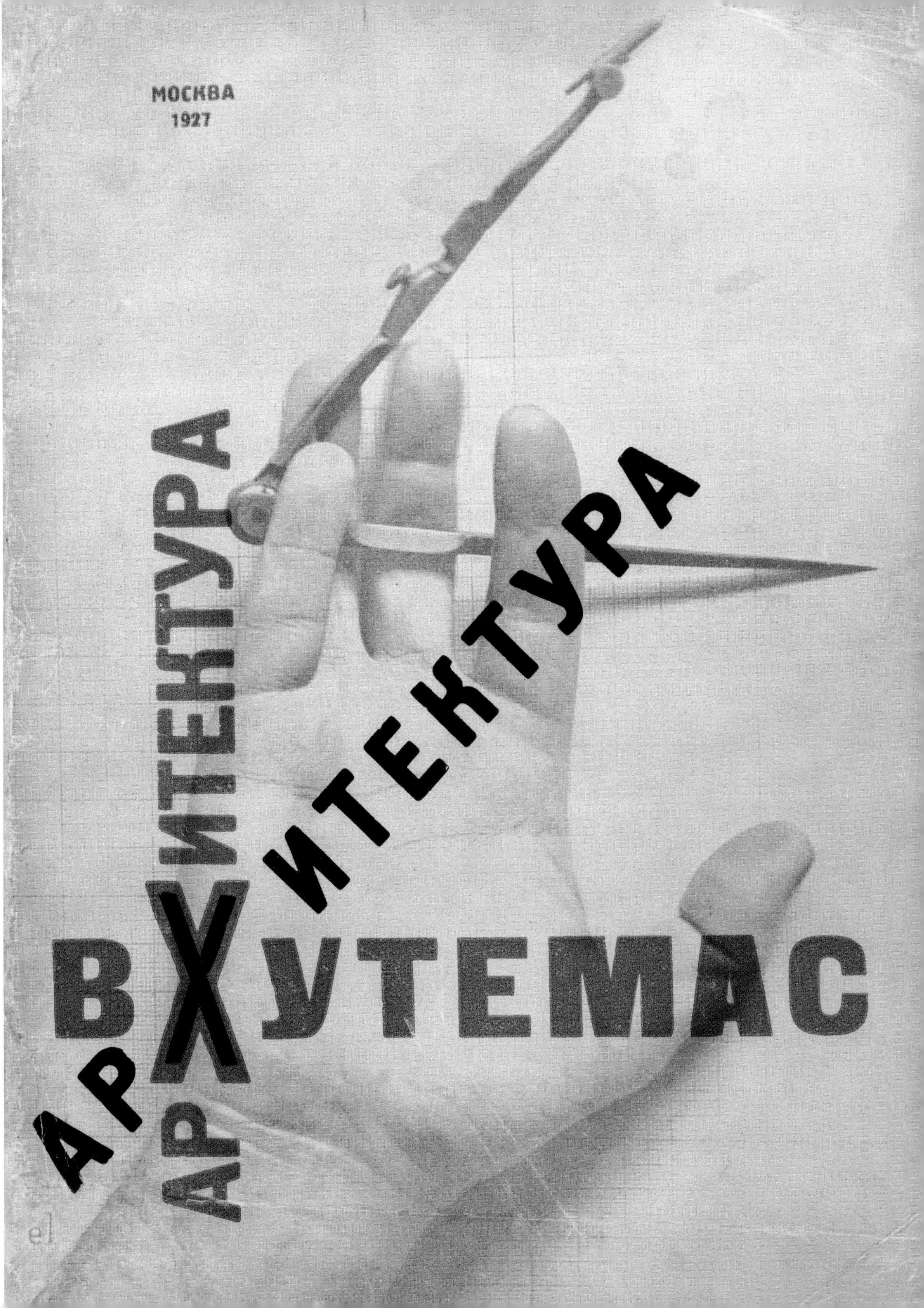

МОСКВА
1927

АРХИТЕКТУРА

АРХИТЕКТУРА

ВХУТЕМАС

el

ALEXANDER RODCHENKO

1891–1956 | BORN: St. Petersburg, Russia | EDUCATION: Kazan School of Art

Pioneered photomontage

Worked among diverse media, including design, painting, and photography

Embraced dramatic angles and bold perspectives

While in art school, Rodchenko met fellow student Varvara Stepanova (1894–1958), who became his wife and partner in art. She was also an accomplished member of the Russian avant-garde who painted, photographed, wrote, and designed. She is best known for her designs for theater sets, costumes, and textiles. Her set designs included innovative collapsible structures that served multiple functions. Like her husband, she collaborated with Vladimir Mayakovsky on poster design. Her later work included magazine design for publications like *Sovetskaya Zhenshchina (Soviet Woman)*.

Alexander Rodchenko began his career in the visual arts as a painter, but politics steered him down a commercial design path. He joined El Lissitzky and Vladimir Tatlin in founding the Constructivist movement, but then he quit painting to serve the Russian Revolution in a practical manner. Putting his avant-garde ideals to use in promoting the message of the revolution became much more important to him than what he called "easel painting."

Like other Constructivists, Rodchenko's work was characterized by strong diagonals, asymmetry, sans serif type, heavy rules, white space, and bold photography. He pioneered the use of photomontage, combining different photographs into one composition. Juxtapositions in scale, perspective, and subject matter aimed to surprise viewers, awakening them to the new medium's revolutionary power.

In 1923, Rodchenko began collaborating with poet and activist Vladimir Mayakovsky. They started an advertising agency together and worked for several state organizations. This work also promoted the ideals of the revolution and brought modern design into advertising. Around the same time, Rodchenko created the visuals to accompany Mayakovsky's poems in his book *Pro Eto (About This)*. Interpreting abstract poetry was a good fit for Rodchenko's artwork.

His work often had a cinematic quality to it, and he designed film posters for Sergei Eisenstein's *Battleship Potemkin* and Dziga Vertov's *Kino Glaz (Cinema Eye)*, as well as the latter's title sequence.

Rodchenko's sense of humor and diverse interests probably helped him survive under Josef Stalin's dictatorship. His versatility meant he was always beginning something new, which helped him stay optimistic. He found most of his success as a photographer, using radical compositions and experimenting with dramatic angles and perspectives. He later worked as a photojournalist and returned to painting.

OPPOSITE: *Kino Glanz* (Film Eye), 1924

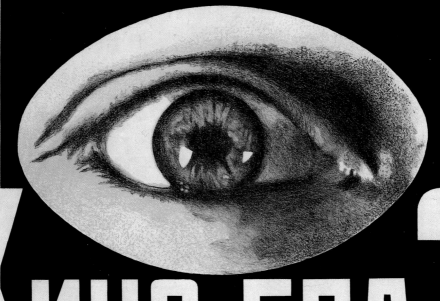

КИНО ГЛАЗ

РОДЧЕНКО

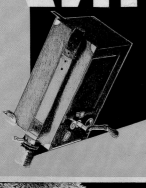

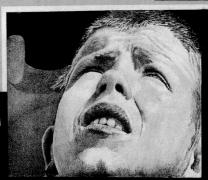

6
СЕРИЙ

**РАБОТА
ДЗИГИ ВЕРТОВА
ОПЕРАТОР
КАУФМАН**

Главлит. №253. Типо-литография Госкино ул.Коммуны 35. Телеф. 5-75-09. Тираж 8000.

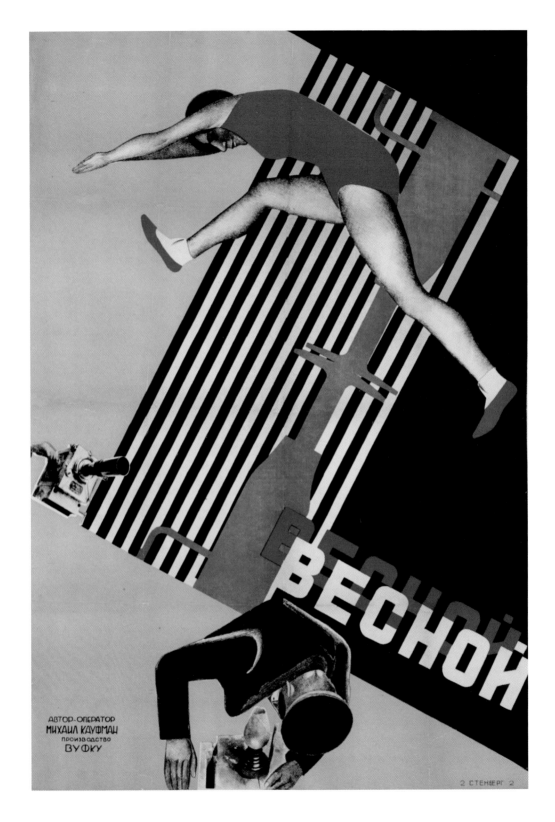

АВТОР-ОПЕРАТОР
МИХАИЛ КАУФМАН
производство
ВУФКУ

2 СТЕНБЕРГ 2

STENBERG BROTHERS

Vladimir: 1899–1982 | BORN: Moscow, Russia | EDUCATION: Stroganov School of Applied Art

Georgii: 1900–1933 | BORN: Moscow, Russia | EDUCATION: Stroganov School of Applied Art

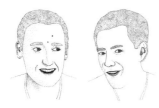

Created a groundbreaking style in movie posters

Invented a projector to enlarge still images from film

Infused dynamic movement into design

Today, it's hard to find movie posters that demonstrate graphic design excellence. They weren't much better in the 1920s Soviet Union. After the Russian Revolution, though, the Bolshevik party saw film as an important way to win over the masses, 60 percent of whom were illiterate, with propaganda. Foreign films were also popular. Brothers Vladimir and Georgii Stenberg created more than 300 posters to advertise these films.

Up to that point, movie posters often focused on the film's star during a key moment in the film, a conceptual approach we still see today. The Stenbergs took different elements and combined them, using dramatic changes in scale, extreme close-ups, and vivid color, creating a unique image reflecting the general feel of the movie. Their look was Constructivist, and their methods were similar to Alexander Rodchenko's photomontage. But while the Stenbergs' work looks photographic, it was all created by hand. Reproducing large-scale photos was very difficult at the time. The brothers invented a projector so they could enlarge images from film frames, then trace, distort, and combine them.

They incorporated movement into their work, which had not been seen before: people leaping, kicking, and falling through the air; and type and graphic elements spinning and curving. They also used bright, saturated colors, which was unusual, given that they were advertising black-and-white films. These colors were strong and jarring: a person's skin color might be green, yellow, or blue. Backgrounds were often urban and architectural.

Born a year apart, they shared a desk at school after Vladimir was left behind in the second grade. They continued to collaborate inseparably as adults, working on the same project simultaneously. Members of Russia's avant-garde, they also sculpted and designed theater sets, shoes, and train cars. In 1933, Georgii was killed when a truck collided with his motorcycle. Soviet leader Joseph Stalin was punishing Constructivist artists at the time who went against his favored socialist realism, so Vladimir always feared that it had been no accident, but rather a murder carried out by the secret police.

READ: *Art of the Modern Movie Poster: International Postwar Style and Design,* by Judith Salavetz, Spencer Drate, Sam Sarowitz, and Dave Kehr, contains some of the best movie poster designs created after World War II.

SEE: Find classic examples of vintage movie posters at Posteritati Movie Poster Gallery, in New York's Little Italy, or L'imagerie Gallery, in North Hollywood.

OPPOSITE: *In The Spring* film poster, 1929

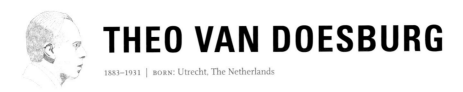

THEO VAN DOESBURG

1883–1931 | BORN: Utrecht, The Netherlands

Co-founded the De Stijl movement

Aimed to develop a universal language of order, abstraction, and geometric shapes

Experimented with typography

ABOVE: Poem written by I.K. Bonset, van Doesburg's pseudonym, from *De Stijl*, 1921

OPPOSITE: Cover of *De Stijl* art journal, woodcut by Vilmos Huszar, 1919

As they did in Russia, politics met art in The Netherlands. During World War I, Dutch painter, designer, architect, and poet Theo van Doesburg joined people like painter Piet Mondrian and furniture designer Gerrit Rietveld to try to refine the ideas behind Cubism. They called this new movement De Stijl, or The Style. The group blamed nationalist pride and self-centered individualism for the war, and they aimed to establish a universal sense of order through a visual language of abstraction and geometric forms. This new vocabulary was rigid in its use of straight lines, blocks, asymmetry, and primary colors.

Though Mondrian might be more well-known, van Doesburg was considered the main theoretical force behind the movement. He disagreed with Mondrian's thinking that De Stijl's ideals applied only to painting, and in his work for the group's magazine (also called *De Stijl*), which he designed and edited, van Doesburg experimented with typography and layout. Van Doesburg's diagonal compositions for the magazine broke with Mondrian's pure vertical and horizontal structures—and this stylistic difference actually ended their friendship.

While the gregarious van Doesburg was a part of this rational movement, he also was a part of its exact opposite: Dada, the "non-art" movement that mocked accepted art forms through inconsistency and absurdity. Under the assumed name I.K. Bonset, he edited the Dada magazine called *Mécano*, wrote Dada poetry, and experimented with typography in the same artistic vein.

Though he died at the young age of 47, during his life he wrote, lectured, attended conferences, and organized exhibitions, in addition to designing and painting. Through those activities, he heavily influenced the avant-garde of his time, which has, in turn, shaped contemporary visual culture.

ABONNEMENT
BIJ VOORUITBETA-
LING BINNENLAND
4.50 BUITENLAND
5.50 PER JAAR-
GANG. VOOR AN-
NONCES WENDE
MEN ZICH TOT
DEN UITGEVER.

DE STIJL

MAANDBLAD VOOR DE BEELDENDE
VAKKEN. REDACTIE THEO VAN DOES-
BURG. UITGAVE X. HARMS TIEPEN.

ADRES VAN RE-
DACTIE: KORT
GALGEWATER 3
LEIDEN. ADMI-
NISTRATIE: X.
HARMS TIEPEN,
HYPOLITUSBUURT
37 DELFT, INTERC.
TEL. 729 EN 690.

1e JAARGANG.   APRIL   NEGENTIENHONDERDACHTTIEN.   NUMMER 6.

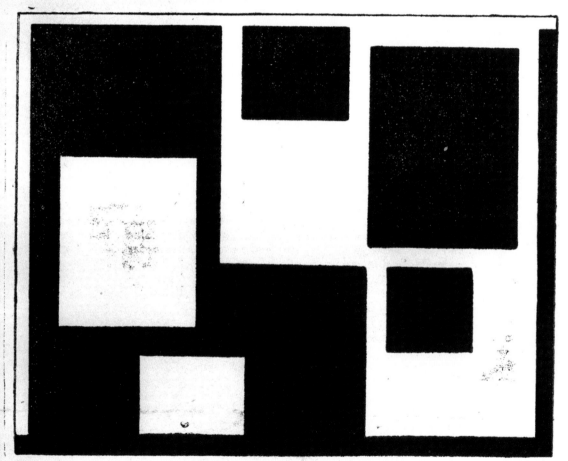

KOMPOSITIE VI.   V. HUSZAR.

VIERDE JAARGANG 1921

DE STIJL

ANTHOLOGIE-BONSET

INTERNATIONAAL MAANDBLAD VOOR NIEUWE KUNST WETENSCHAP EN KULTUUR REDACTIE THEO VAN DOESBURG

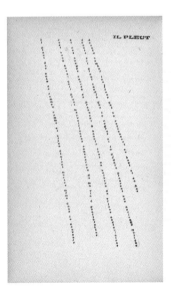

French avant-garde poet Guillaume Apollinaire created a book of poems in 1918 called *Calligrames*. Breaking with the standard horizontal lines of type reading from left to right, he arranged the text in ways to visually express the poems' meanings. "Il Pleut" ("it's raining"), is pictured at left. It was a one-time experiment for him, but it influenced the typographic experiments of the Futurists and the Dadaists.

PRIJS 25 CENTS.

théo van doesburg

WAT is DADA?

? ? ? ? ? ? ?

ABOVE: Pamphlet cover, 1923

OPPOSITE: Cover of *De Stijl*, 1921

THE BAUHAUS

The Bauhaus ("building house") was a progressive experiment in design education. Led by architect Walter Gropius, it was the model for a new design school, one where theory and practice were integrated. The school's philosophy and teaching approach have had a profound and lasting influence on modern design.

In Germany's Weimar Republic in 1919, the school began with the idea of uniting the artist and the builder. William Morris's Arts and Crafts movement was a big influence, as were Russia's Constructivism and Holland's De Stijl. Gropius put together an impressive faculty. The focus was on architecture, and there was very little graphic design instruction at this time. However, the curriculum evolved over its 14-year run, and graphic design emerged as a fundamental discipline.

Part of that evolution embraced industry and the machine, as the school moved away from traditional craftsmanship. Hungarian László Moholy-Nagy joined the faculty in 1923 and began teaching typography and photography. He also directed the Bauhaus Press and designed its visual identity: a composition of a circle, triangle, and square—the basic geometric forms. He articulated the school's philosophies in 14 books, and published an article defining the "New Typography," a movement that would be further developed by designer Jan Tschichold.

Students learned traditional design skills like lettering and composition, but were encouraged to use principles such as asymmetry, balance, and structured space while exploring technological developments in photography and printing. Herbert Bayer and Joost Schmidt were both students at the Bauhaus who later taught there.

After only 14 years, the Nazi party saw the school as a threat and forced it to close. Many of the teachers and students left Germany. Moholy-Nagy moved to Chicago to form the short-lived

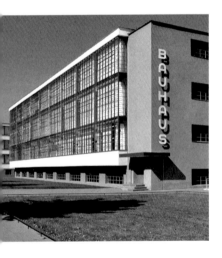

ABOVE: Bauhaus Building in Dessau, Germany

OPPOSITE: László Moholy-Nagy, brochure cover for a set of 14 Bauhaus books, 1929

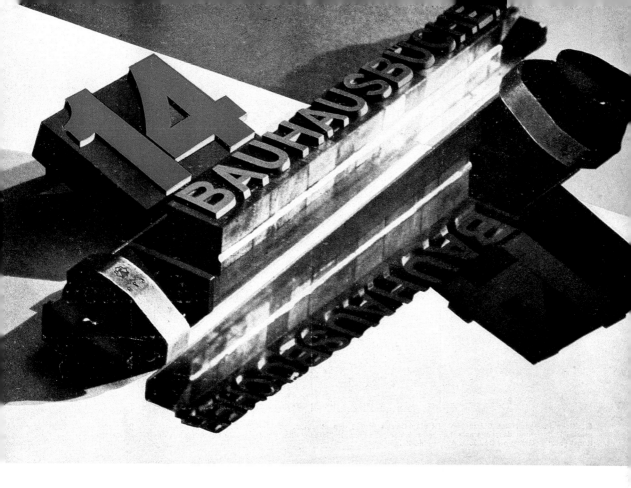

New Bauhaus. He then started the School of Design, which later became part of the Illinois Institute of Technology (IIT). The institute, then called Chicago's Armour Institute of Technology, also employed architect Ludwig Mies van der Rohe, who was the director of the Bauhaus at the end, to head its architecture school. Painter Paul Klee moved to Switzerland, while Wassily Kandinsky relocated to Paris. Graphic designer Josef Albers joined the faculty at North Carolina's Black Mountain College, while Gropius and also architect/furniture designer Marcel Breuer taught at the Harvard Graduate School of Design. Everyone took the Bauhaus ideals with them wherever they went, helping to spread the school's influence far and wide.

READ: *Bauhaus: Weimar, Dessau, Berlin, Chicago,* by Hedwig Wingler, catalogs public and private documents relating to the Bauhaus, and exhibits furniture, ceramics, posters, ads, and other works created by Bauhaus students and teachers.

SEE: The 1994 British TV documentary *Bauhaus: The Face of the 20th Century* features both new and archival footage, including interviews of noted Bauhaus students and educators, such as Walter Gropius, Wassily Kandinsky, Ludwig Mies van der Rohe, and Kurt Krantz.

HERBERT BAYER

1900–1985 | BORN: Haag, Austria | EDUCATION: the Bauhaus

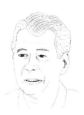

Continued to spread the influence of the Bauhaus

Built a noteworthy advertising career in the United States

Established design as a valuable corporate asset

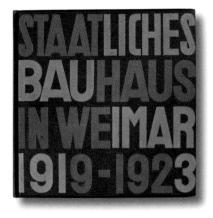

ABOVE: Exhibition catalog cover, 1923

OPPOSITE: Thuringian Banknotes, 1923

Herbert Bayer was a "young master" at the Bauhaus: a student who then became a teacher. He studied under László Moholy-Nagy and Wassily Kandinsky. With them, he helped form a functional design ideology that spanned design disciplines. He served as the school's director of the printing and advertising workshop, helping graphic design become a bigger part of the curriculum.

During Germany's Weimar Republic, the hyperinflated economy was so unstable that each region had its own emergency currency. Bayer's design of these bank notes was a major departure from the conventional national symbols, swirls, and serif type. His modern look used grids, geometry, and sans serifs. Due to the unstable economy, though, the bills quickly became useless, and people began burning them for heat.

His work covered a broad range: the signage at the Bauhaus building in Dessau, magazines like *Vogue* and *Fortune*, and a prefabricated newspaper stand. Fed up with bad typography, Bayer designed the sans serif font Universal in 1925 with no uppercase letters, since, he reasoned, we don't speak in upper and lowercase.

Moving to the United States at the age of 38, Bayer began a noteworthy career in advertising. With his background in European modernism, he brought fresh ideas to corporate America. He had a lengthy association with the Container Corporation of America, a major supporter of modern design known for innovative advertising. Compared to his earlier work, Bayer's new designs became more illustrative as he continued to explore ways to communicate effectively. During this time he also designed and organized exhibitions, such as the Bauhaus exhibit at New York's Museum of Modern Art. He later moved to Aspen, Colorado, and Montecito, California.

1000000

EINE MILLION MARK

WEIMAR, DEN 9. AUGUST 1923
DIE LANDESREGIERUNG

1000000 Mark zahlt die Kasse der Thüringischen Staatsbank dem Einlieferer dieses Notgeldscheines.— Vom 1. September 1923 ab kann dieses Notgeld aufgerufen und gegen Umtausch in Reichsbanknoten eingezogen werden.

Wer Banknoten nachmacht oder verfälscht oder nachgemachte oder verfälschte sich verschafft und in den Verkehr bringt, wird mit Zuchthaus nicht unter zwei Jahren bestraft.

1000000

EINE MILLION MARK

WEIMAR, DEN 9. AUGUST 1923
DIE LANDESREGIERUNG

1000000 Mark zahlt die Kasse der Thüringischen Staatsbank dem Einlieferer dieses Notgeldscheines.— Vom 1. September 1923 ab kann dieses Notgeld aufgerufen und gegen Umtausch in Reichsbanknoten eingezogen werden.

Wer Banknoten nachmacht oder verfälscht oder nachgemachte oder verfälschte sich verschafft und in den Verkehr bringt, wird mit Zuchthaus nicht unter zwei Jahren bestraft.

1000000

EINE MILLION MARK

WEIMAR, DEN 9. AUGUST 1923
DIE LANDESREGIERUNG

1000000 Mark zahlt die Kasse der Thüringischen Staatsbank dem Einlieferer dieses Notgeldscheines.— Vom 1. September 1923 ab kann dieses Notgeld aufgerufen und gegen Umtausch in Reichsbanknoten eingezogen werden.

Wer Banknoten nachmacht oder verfälscht oder nachgemachte oder verfälschte sich verschafft und in den Verkehr bringt, wird mit Zuchthaus nicht unter zwei Jahren bestraft.

why should we write and print in two alphabets? we do not speak a capital 'a' and a small 'a.'[2]

—Herbert Bayer,
explaining the thought behind his
all-lowercase typeface Universal. The quote
is set in a digital version of that face.

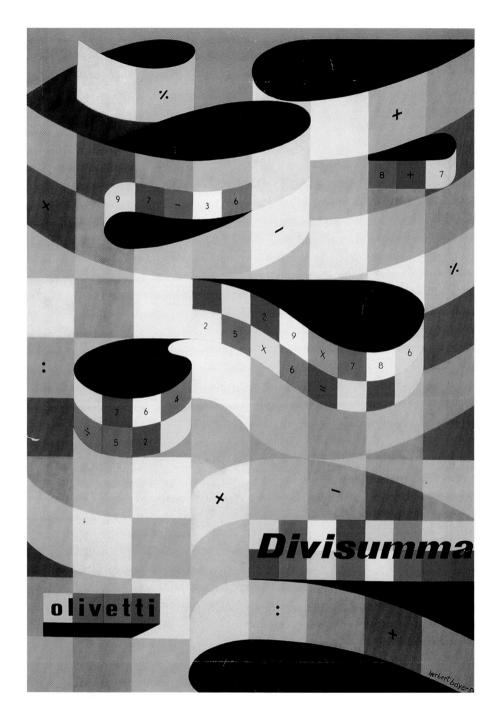

Poster for Olivetti adding machines, 1953

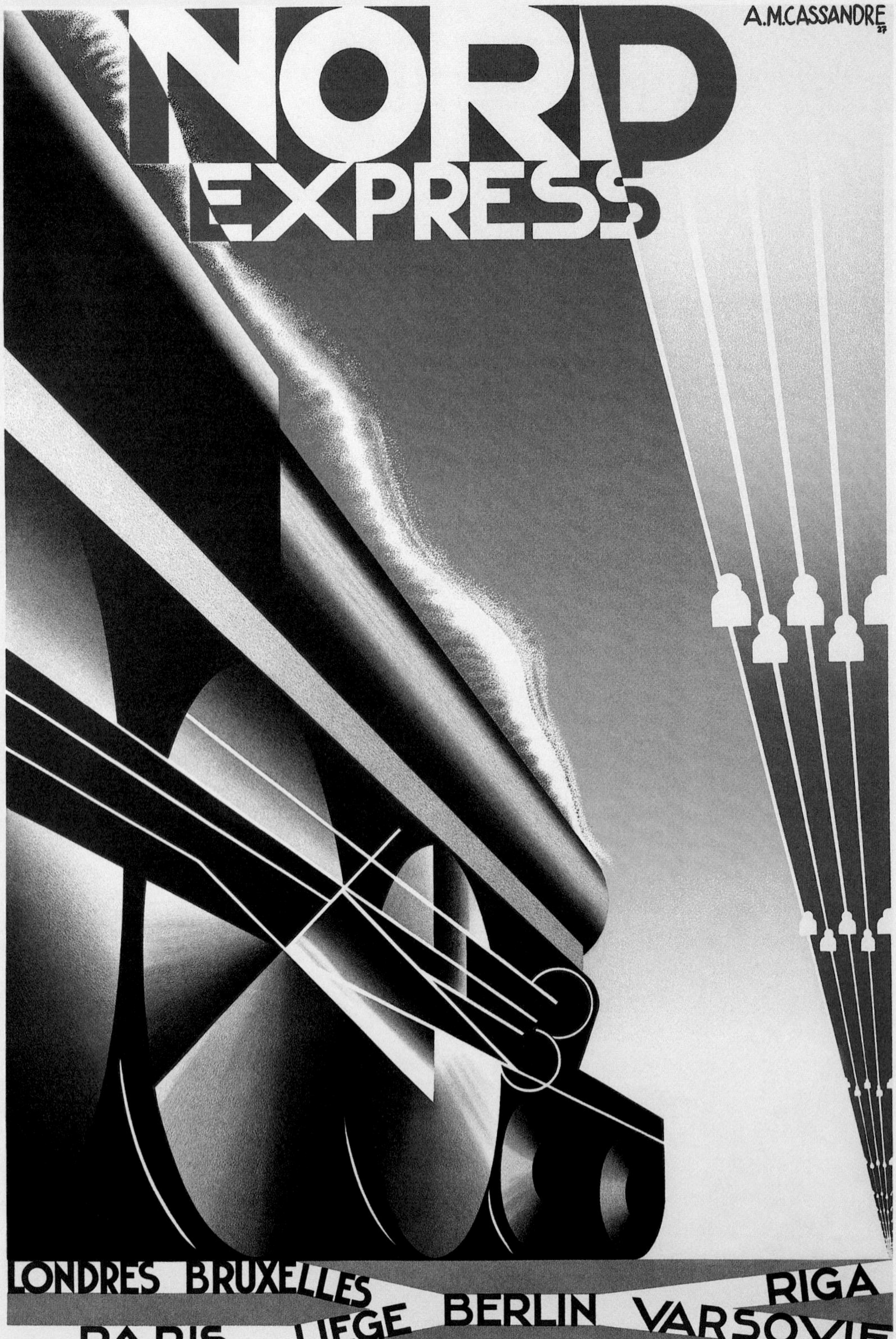
A.M.CASSANDRE 27
NORD
EXPRESS
LONDRES BRUXELLES
PARIS
LIEGE
BERLIN
VARSOVIE
RIGA

A.M. CASSANDRE

1901–1968 | BORN: Ukraine | EDUCATION: École des Beaux Arts and Académie Julian in Paris

Applied concepts of modern painting, like those of Fernand Léger and Picasso, to French poster design

Used strong perspective to imply three-dimensional space

Designed typefaces

From a time when the poster was emerging as an iconic advertising medium, one artist's work stands out, thanks to its simple forms and striking perspectives. Adolphe Mouron was a French painter who made a living designing posters under the pseudonym A.M. Cassandre. Cassandre used geometry, shadow, and silhouettes to create the illusion of space, and he pioneered airbrushing techniques to add smoothness and depth to his illustrations. A true commercial artist, he incorporated type as a vital part of his compositions, not as an afterthought.

Cassandre's work had a geometric, architectural quality; like other creatives at the time (architect Le Corbusier notably among them), Cassandre found beauty in machines. Among the more than 200 posters that Cassandre designed, some of the most famous glorify gritty mechanical subjects like railroad cars, airplanes, and ocean liners.

Like the Russian Constructivists, Cassandre believed that art should not be for the elite, but for everyone. But unlike the Constructivists, he was not committed to avant-garde philosophies. By borrowing elements from different movements and using them as more of a decorative style, his work represented the popular style later known as "Art Deco." His type designs—the fonts Bifur, Acier Noir, and Peignot—were more elegant than functional.

Cassandre cofounded Alliance Graphique, an advertising agency in Paris, before spending some time in New York to work for clients like Forbes and the Container Corporation of America. He eventually moved back to Paris to focus on painting and stage design. His personal life did not go as well as his professional one. He was divorced twice, and committed suicide at his home in 1968.

ABCDEFGHIJ
KLMNOPQRS
TUVWXYZabc
defghijklmno
pqrstuvwxyz
1234567890

OPPOSITE: Express Nord train poster, 1927

ABOVE: Specimen of Peignot, based on Cassandre's type design.

WILLIAM ADDISON DWIGGINS

1880–1956 | BORN: Martinsville, Ohio | EDUCATION: Frank Holme School of Illustration, Chicago

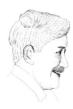

Coined the term "graphic design"

Designed books and typefaces

Wrote the influential book *Layout in Advertising*

William Dwiggins remains recognized for his book and type designs—but his most lasting influence lies in two words: graphic design.

After studying under prolific type designer Frederic W. Goudy, Dwiggins became a freelance calligrapher and illustrator in the advertising industry. He moved on to book design for clients like Alfred A. Knopf, where he worked on over 300 projects and helped develop the company's high standards for design. He loved making books, and excelled at combining type, hand lettering, and nature-inspired flourishes into cohesive designs.

But perhaps Dwiggins made the biggest contribution to the field with his writing. In 1922, he wrote an article for the *Boston Evening Transcript* titled "New Kind of Printing Calls for New Design." In it, Dwiggins coined a new phrase for commercial art: graphic design (although the term didn't come into widespread use until the 1940s). His 1928 book, *Layout in Advertising*, not only shared his design theories, but also revealed his sense of humor, as he poked fun at his fellow designers for low standards in design and production.

Dwiggins wanted to be remembered as a type designer—and he is. He'd be pleased that two of his five full typefaces, Caledonia and Electra, remain popular today.

In his spare time, Dwiggins enjoyed his very detailed miniature marionette theater, which he built himself. Described as modest and funny, he said before his death on Christmas day in 1956: "It was a grand adventure; I am content."³

OPPOSITE: Paper sample book, c. 1920

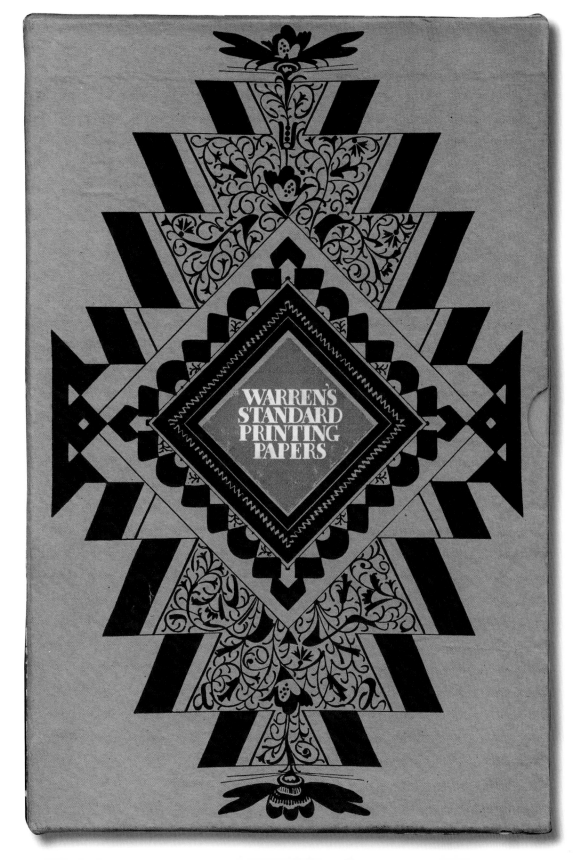

WARREN'S
STANDARD
PRINTING
PAPERS

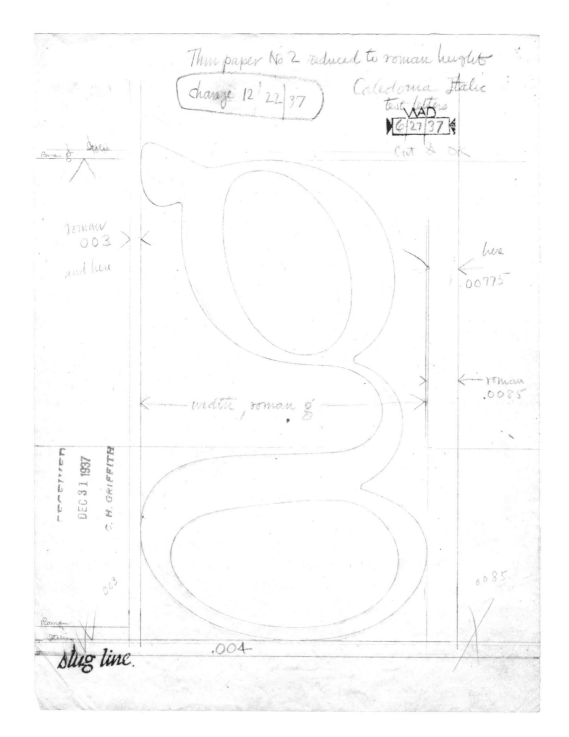

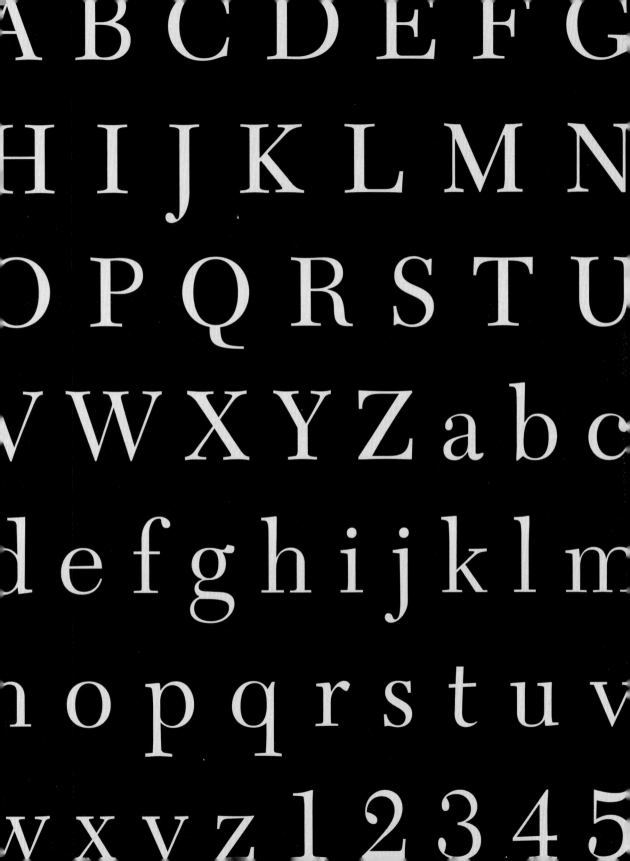

● vom 16. januar bis 14. februar 1937

kunsthalle basel

konstruktivisten

van doesburg
domela
eggeling
gabo
kandinsky
lissitzky
moholy-nagy
mondrian
pevsner
taeuber
vantongerloo
vordemberge
u. a.

JAN TSCHICHOLD

1902–1974 | BORN: Leipzig, Germany | EDUCATION: Leipzig Academy for Graphic Arts and Book Trades

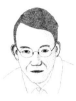

Wrote *The New Typography*, a radical type and design guide that remains influential

Raised the standards of book design

Evolved beyond strict Modernism throughout his career

Just as his design predecessors influenced Jan Tschichold, so he shaped graphic design long after his own death. After growing up in the heart of Germany's book industry, Tschichold had a formal education in classical typography and calligraphy. A Bauhaus exhibition in 1923 introduced him to Constructivism, and he soon began incorporating modern elements into his designs. His photomontage posters for Munich movie theater Phoebus Palast show the influence of László Moholy-Nagy and El Lissitzky.

In 1928, Tschichold published a manual that continues to influence people today: *Die neue Typografie (The New Typography)*, which is still in print. The strict standards in this book aimed to free designers from traditional restrictions and move them beyond centered type and ornaments. He believed design should be clear and efficient—and that the tools of clarity were sans serif type, asymmetric compositions, photography, and white space.

As the Nazi party felt Modernism was "un-German," they arrested Tschichold in 1933 and imprisoned him for four weeks. He and his family then moved to Basel, Switzerland. His work began to drift away from the rigid New Typography. Centered type, serif faces, and ornaments began to appear in his work, as he understood that different projects called for different solutions.

After a move to London in 1947, he standardized the look for the inexpensive paperbacks of Penguin Books. He color-coded the horizontal bands on the covers (orange = fiction, blue = biography), a design touch that is still in use today. In addition to design and typographic principles, he considered how the book felt in the hand, and established rules for printing, paper weight, and binding. Demanding and inflexible, he raised the level of quality and set standards that influenced the entire publishing industry.

"In addition to being more logical, asymmetry has the advantage that its complete appearance is far more optically effective than symmetry."[4]

—Jan Tschichold

OPPOSITE: Exhibition poster for
Konstructivism (Constructivism), 1937

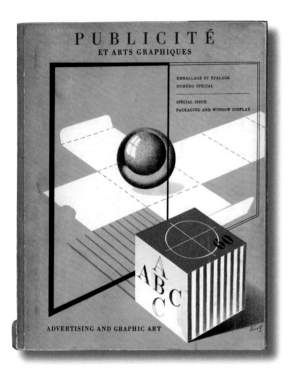

ABOVE: *Advertising and Graphic Art* cover, 1947

OPPOSITE: Exhibition poster for *Der Berufsphotograph*
(The Professional Photographer), 1938

gewerbemuseum basel   ausstellu

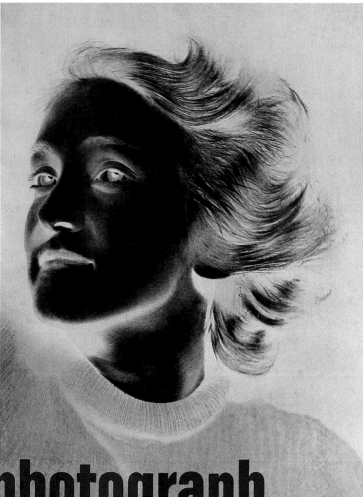

entwurf jan tschichold swb   photo spring swb   cliché schreiter ag basel   druck benno schwabe & co. basel   1938

berufsphotograph

seine arbeiten — sein werkzeug

8. mai — 6. juni

werktags	14-19	
mittwochs	14-19	19-21
sonntags	10-12	14-19

eintritt frei

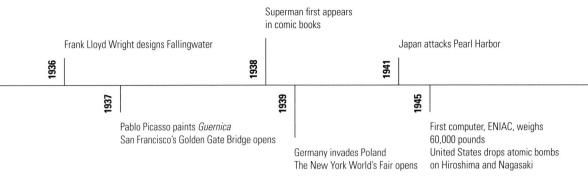

Superman first appears
in comic books

Frank Lloyd Wright designs Fallingwater

Japan attacks Pearl Harbor

1936

1938

1941

1937

1939

1945

Pablo Picasso paints *Guernica*
San Francisco's Golden Gate Bridge opens

Germany invades Poland
The New York World's Fair opens

First computer, ENIAC, weighs
60,000 pounds
United States drops atomic bombs
on Hiroshima and Nagasaki

MIDCENTURY MODERN: MODERNISM COMES TO AMERICA

The Stock Market Crash of 1929 started a chain of events that resulted in the Great Depression of the 1930s, devastating global economies and putting millions of people out of work. The effects rippled through politics, culture, and society around the world: In Germany, for example, financial support for the Weimar Republic from American loans disappeared, and the Nazi party took advantage of this economic vulnerability as it began its rise to power in Europe. Designers and artists needed to either conform to Hitler's policies or move elsewhere. Many came to the United States, bringing their European modern sensibilities with them.

Entering World War II helped the United States claw its way out of the Depression, as the war effort created jobs and pumped money back into the economy. When the conflict was over, growing consumer demand and an increase in births (the Baby Boom) fueled an economic surge. Cars and a new interstate highway system, both job creators, enabled more travel, which spawned hotels and fast-food restaurants along the way. Thanks to easily affordable mortgages for military returnees, the housing sector exploded beyond city limits and launched a new suburban way of life. In 1949, *Arts & Architecture* magazine sponsored the Case Study Home contest, challenging designers to marry good design with affordable materials and production. That same

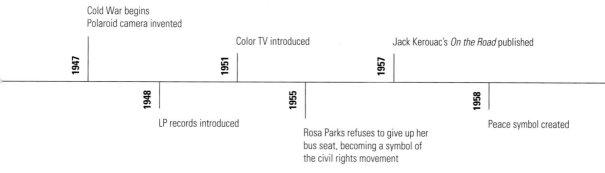

Cold War begins
Polaroid camera invented

Color TV introduced

Jack Kerouac's *On the Road* published

1947

1951

1957

1948

1955

1958

LP records introduced

Rosa Parks refuses to give up her
bus seat, becoming a symbol of
the civil rights movement

Peace symbol created

year, designers Charles and Ray Eames built their case study house, which became a functional model of accessible design.

This new American economy led to new opportunities for graphic designers—there were so many new products to promote and so many media outlets through which to do so. In addition to advertising, magazine publishing, film and television, and the music industry all attracted top design talent. Corporations began taking design more seriously, and the field of corporate identity creation began to flourish. And it wasn't just the émigré Europeans who were thriving in the design profession—several American-born designers built successful careers on modernism, as well.

In Europe during the 1950s, the international typographic style, or Swiss style, advanced the philosophies of the Bauhaus and the De Stijl movement. This rational approach, based on a mathematical grid to structure layouts, was so clean and simple it took modernism to a new minimal level. The style became more common as corporations began adopting it.

Together, the Stock Market Crash and World War II produced economic changes that united people and ideas during the middle of the century, resulting in new ways to design and communicate.

LESTER BEALL

1903–1969 | BORN: Kansas City, Missouri | EDUCATION: University of Chicago

Launched the modern graphic design movement in the United States

Designed famous posters pushing the benefits of electricity

Advanced corporate-identity design

Lester Beall studied art history in Chicago, but his true education in modernism came from French magazines and Bauhaus books. Beall became the first American graphic designer to successfully integrate the European avant-garde into corporate America, and he did it through his designs of posters, magazines, packaging, and identities.

In the mid 1930s, nine out of ten rural homes in the United States did not have electricity. As part of President Franklin Delano Roosevelt's New Deal, Beall designed posters to support the Rural Electrification Administration's efforts to bring power to rural residents. Beall's first posters, created in 1937, were simple and graphic, with flat illustrations. They were designed to appeal to an audience with little education, much like El Lissitzky's work with the Constructivists a generation before had been. After the first posters, Beall produced two more sets, each becoming more complex. The third set, designed around the time the United States entered World War II, used photomontage: silhouetted photographs, graphic patterns, and angled type. The patriotic colors and implications that electricity would benefit the war effort appealed to people's sense of national pride.

In 1935, moving from Chicago to New York brought Beall new design opportunities. Corporate identity design—an entire visual language for a company, with detailed guidelines on how to use it—is now a well-established discipline, but back then, it was not. Beall designed strong graphic identities and extensive usage guidelines for companies like Connecticut General Life Insurance and Caterpillar Tractors. His work for International Paper set forth guidelines on usage for everything—including correspondence, delivery vehicles, building signs, and packaging.

Beall eventually moved his family and studio out of the city to a farm in nearby Connecticut, where he was surrounded by natural beauty and peace and quiet. He achieved something many people search for today: a good work/life balance. "By living and working in the country I felt I could enjoy a more integrated life," he wrote. "The way a man lives is essential to the work he produces. The two cannot be separated."[5]

Also, he believed that art and design cannot be separated. He counted artists Paul Klee, Henri Matisse, Pablo Picasso, and Jean Arp; photographer Man Ray; and designers Jan Tschichold and László Moholy-Nagy among his strongest influences. Constantly seeking visual inspiration, Beall always traveled with a camera and drew regularly. A big music fan, he frequently listened to jazz, as well as the works of composers Sergei Prokofiev and Igor Stravinsky.

OPPOSITE: Rural electrification administration poster, 1937

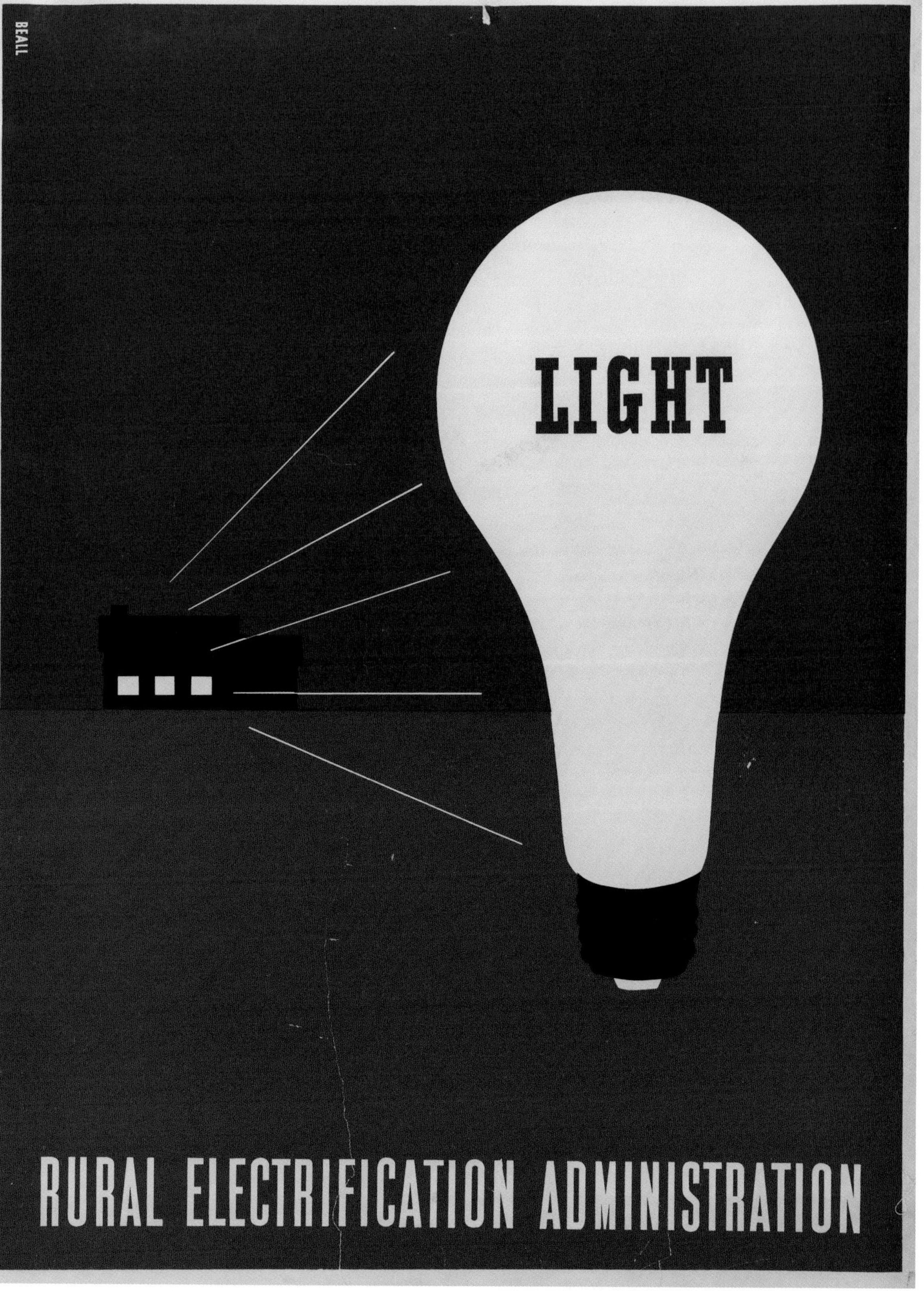
BEALL
LIGHT
RURAL ELECTRIFICATION ADMINISTRATION

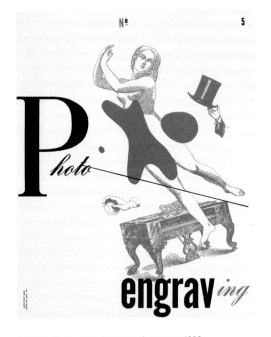

ABOVE: *Photoengraving* magazine cover, 1938

OPPOSITE: International Paper Company logo, designed with Richard Rogers, 1960

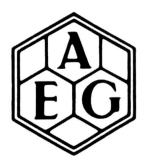

Peter Behrens designed the first major corporate identity program in 1908, for German electrical manufacturer AEG. He unified all communication for the company by establishing clear guidelines for consistent use of the logo, type, and layouts, which were reflected in AEG's products, buildings, and advertising.

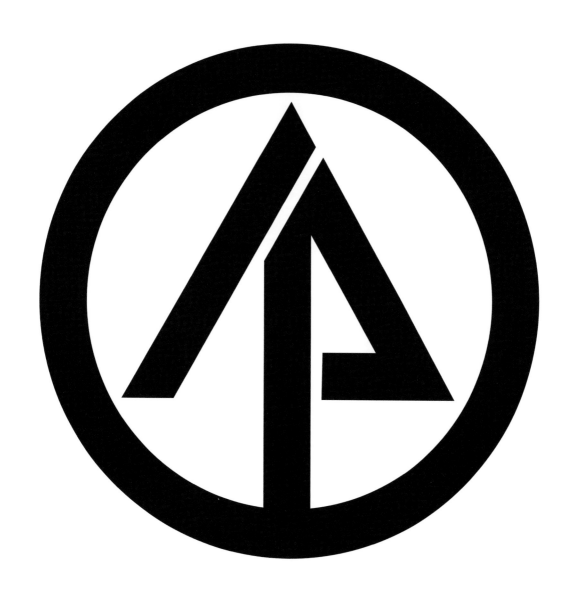

ALEXEY BRODOVITCH

1898–1971 | BORN: Ogolitchi, Russia

Incorporated white space and the double-page spread into American magazine design

Designed and edited *Portfolio*, an important graphic design magazine

Collaborated with photographers like Richard Avedon, Irving Penn, and Man Ray

"Astonish me!"[6] was Alexey Brodovitch's persistent challenge to the designers, photographers, and students he directed. A Russian émigré who moved from Paris to New York in 1930, he loved change, and looked at each issue of the magazines under his creative leadership as a chance to do something new.

Before Brodovitch became art director at *Harper's Bazaar*, most American magazines were crowded and fussy. Text and images were usually kept separate, and models were often posed like stiff mannequins. Brodovitch changed all that. He added white space to give the images and text some breathing room. He combined type and pictures seamlessly. And, he ushered in a more elegant, sophisticated, and dynamic look in fashion photography; instead of asking models to stand perfectly still in a studio setting, Brodovitch encouraged his photographers to express themselves more and shoot on location, setting the models free to move.

The photos in *Harper's Bazaar* didn't just show a piece of clothing or illustrate the text; they were crucial to Brodovitch's vision. He nurtured the careers of Richard Avedon and Irving Penn. Photographers are known for not liking anyone cropping their images, but Brodovitch was so good at it that even legends like Henri Cartier-Bresson and Man Ray didn't object.

It's common now for magazine articles to open with a double-page spread. That's because of Alexey Brodovitch. He allowed feature stories to make a grand entrance—with a single large cropped photo bleeding off the page, a headline, a small block of text, and plenty of white space. Brodovitch took a fairly restrained approach to typography, although he sometimes experimented with setting type in shapes that echoed an accompanying photo.

Brodovitch was also art editor of the influential design magazine *Portfolio*, where he helped develop the content. *Portfolio*'s creative team aspired to produce an entirely new kind of publication, with elaborate die-cuts, fold-outs, and special papers. But since *Portfolio* accepted no advertising, its business model was doomed, and it closed after just three issues. Today, original copies sell for hundreds of dollars.

Throughout his career, Brodovitch taught the "Design Laboratory," first at the Philadelphia Museum of Art's newly established art and design school, and later at the New School in New York. This workshop, open to designers, photographers, and illustrators, launched many a creative career; Design Lab students included Diane Arbus and Richard Avedon. Brodovitch's critiques were harsh but inspiring, as he, of course, expected to be astonished all the time.

His personal life was not as successful as his professional. He was an alcoholic in an unhappy marriage, and his son had serious physical and emotional problems. Brodovitch's legendary tenure at *Harper's Bazaar* ended unceremoniously in 1958 when he was fired, likely because of his drinking. His health slowly deteriorated until his death ten years later.

OPPOSITE: *Harper's Bazaar* cover, photograph by Richard Avedon, 1953

OVERLEAF: Front and back cover for *Portfolio* magazine #1, 1950

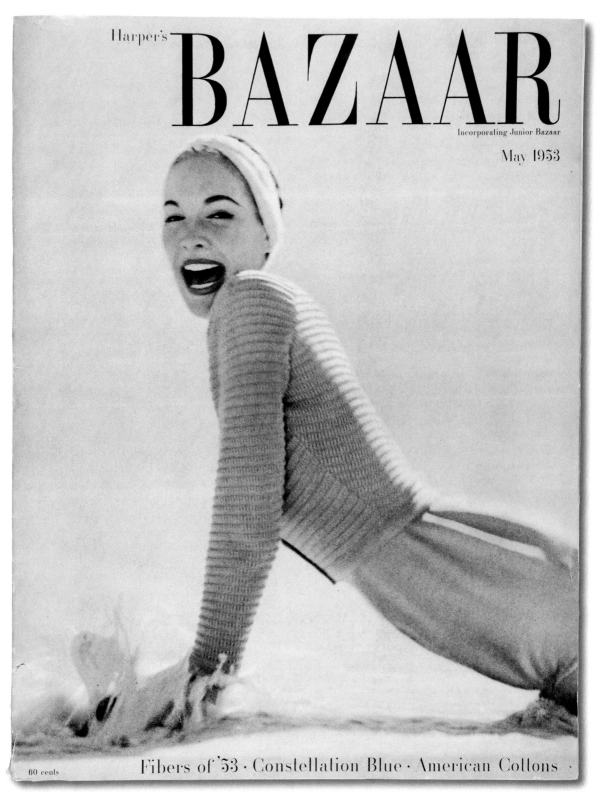

Harper's **BAZAAR**

Incorporating Junior Bazaar

May 1953

60 cents

Fibers of '53 · Constellation Blue · American Cottons ·

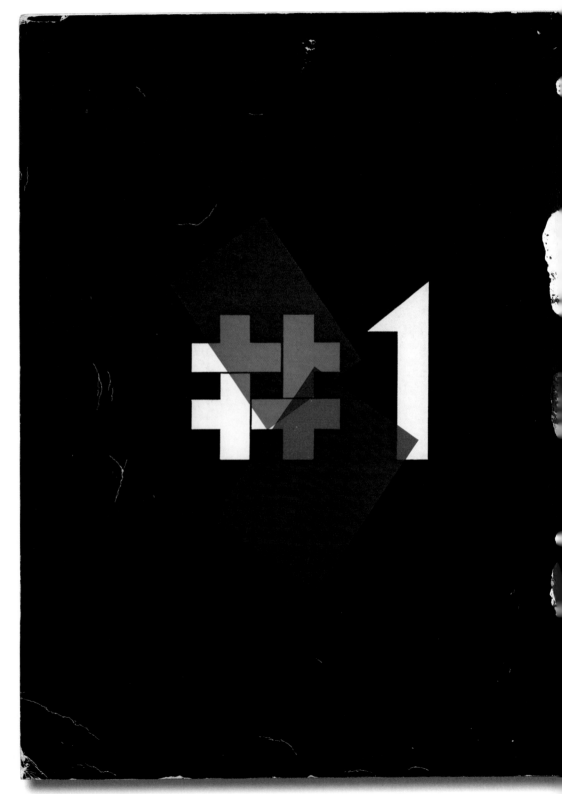

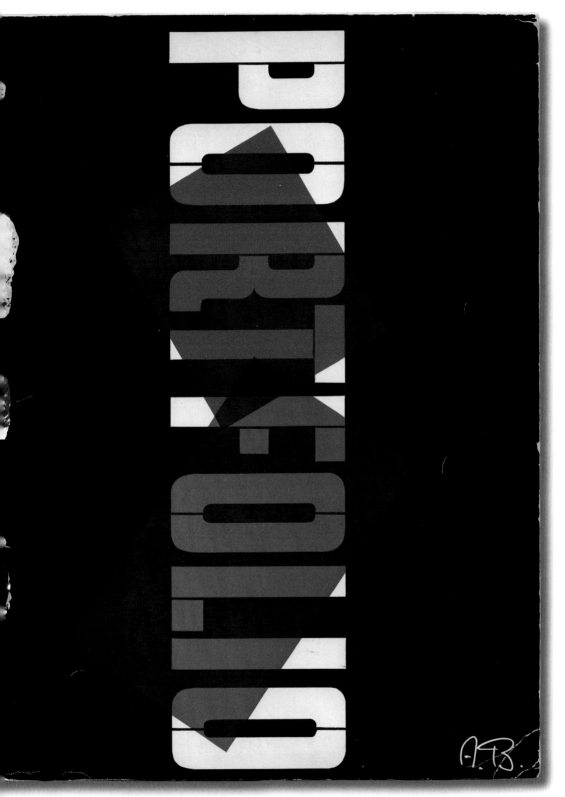

PORTFOLIO

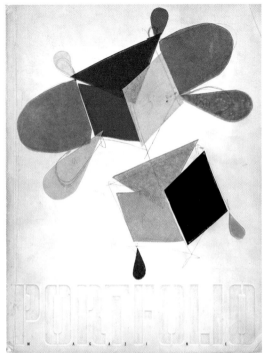

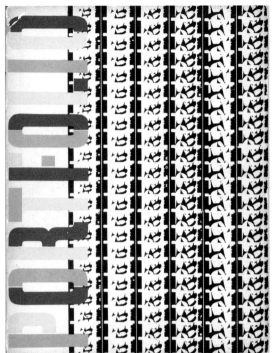

READ: *Alexey Brodovitch,* by Kerry William Purcell

WATCH: The 1957 musical *Funny Face* stars Fred Astaire as a Richard Avedon-like fashion photographer who transforms Audrey Hepburn into a top model. Dovitch, the magazine art director, is based on Alexey Brodovitch.

GET TO KNOW: Other influential magazine designers and art directors include Mehemed Fehmy Agha, Henry Wolf, Walter Bernard, Roger Black, Neville Brody, Fred Woodward, Luke Hayman, and Janet Froelich. (See also Cipe Pineles on page 100.)

ABOVE: Covers for *Portfolio* magazine #2 1950; #3, 1951

OPPOSITE: Dylan Thomas book cover, 1964

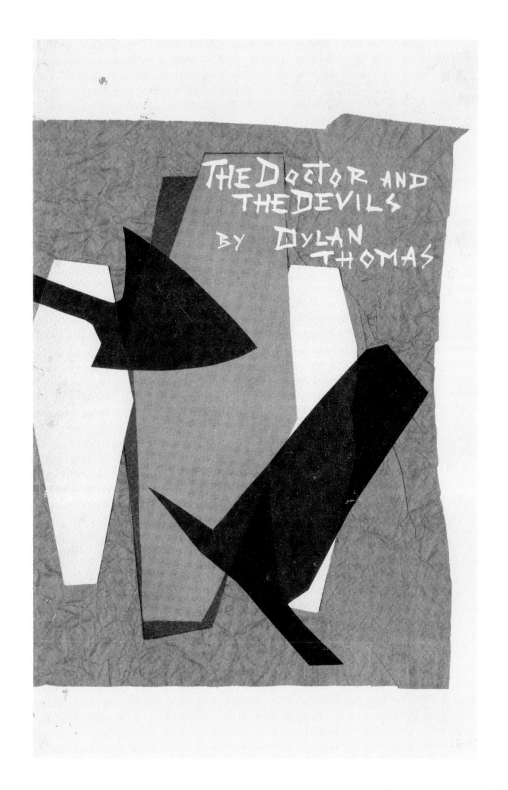

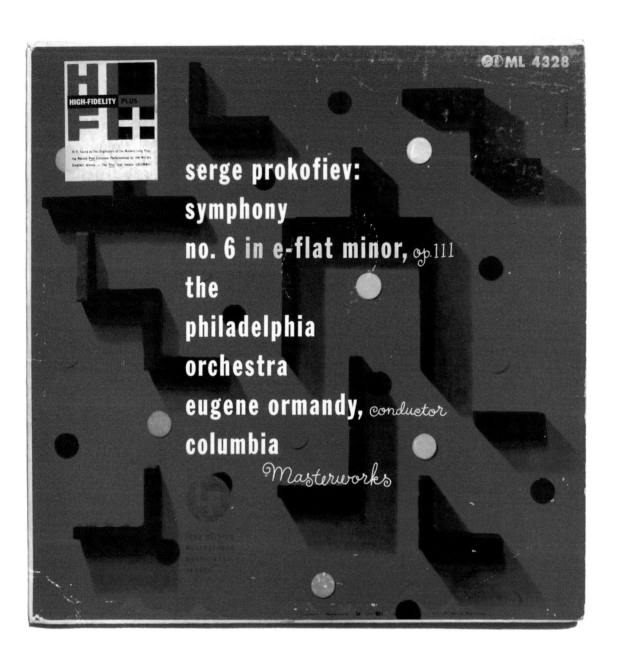

ABOVE: Serge Prokofiev
album cover, 1950

OPPOSITE: Rudolf Serkin
10-inch package

ALEX STEINWEISS

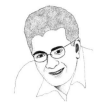

1917–2011 | BORN: Brooklyn, New York | EDUCATION: Parsons School of Design

Designed inventive record covers

Developed the cardboard LP sleeve

In an era of digital distribution, it's hard to imagine that packaging ever played a significant role in marketing new music. But it certainly did, and Alex Steinweiss paved the way for a golden age of album design.

In 1939, Columbia Records hired Steinweiss to design posters and in-store displays to market their records. Retailers needed these promotions, because the records themselves—78-RPM discs wrapped in plain paper and packaged in boxed sets—did nothing to sell themselves. Other labels, like Decca, featured some artwork on their covers, usually a stock decoration or a photo of the recording artist or composer. In a brilliant innovation, Steinweiss applied his beautiful poster designs to the actual record sleeves.

Steinweiss pioneered a conceptual approach to album design; he didn't think a buyer would be attracted to a stuffy portrait of a classical composer. Always a big music fan, he'd listen to the album before beginning the design, letting the music guide his work. For a recording of composer Bela Bartok's *Concerto No. 3*, Steinweiss created an abstract illustration of a piano, rendered in a contemporary color palette. He mixed stylized illustrations, simple geometric shapes, and musical symbols, incorporating type as part of the overall design. Although he was influenced by A.M. Cassandre and Lucian Bernhard, he had his own approach: playful, lively, and fresh.

Necessity dictated some of Steinweiss's creative decisions and helped shape his distinctive style. The Columbia office was in Bridgeport, Connecticut, where there were no typesetters. So he often drew type by hand, and he later developed his curly script into a font called Steinweiss Scrawl. Process printing, which enabled colors to mix, was very expensive then, so Steinweiss usually worked with three or four flat colors.

In 1948, Columbia introduced the LP—long-playing record. Because the old 78-sized packaging scratched the new records, Steinweiss developed the folded cardboard sleeve, which is still used to package vinyl today.

He also designed magazines, film titles, and product packaging, but most of his work was music. When he was in his 50s, Steinweiss felt out of place in the record industry, as photography became more popular for cover designs. In 1974, he and his wife moved to Florida, where he focused on ceramics and painting. Fortunately, he was able to see a revived interest in his design work before he died, in 2011.

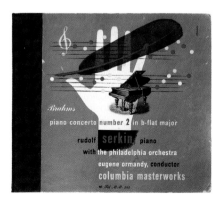

READ: *Alex Steinweiss: The Inventor of the Modern Album Cover,* by Kevin Reagan and Steven Heller

GET TO KNOW: Other influential designers for the music world include Charles Murphy, Reid Miles, Hipgnosis, Jamie Reid, Barney Bubbles, Vaughan Oliver, Art Chantry, and Jason Munn.

HERBERT MATTER

1907–1984 | BORN: Engelberg, Switzerland | EDUCATION: École des Beaux Arts in Geneva, Academie Moderne in Paris

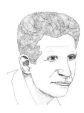

Excelled at design, photography, and teaching

Broadened the use of photography in design

Experimented throughout his career

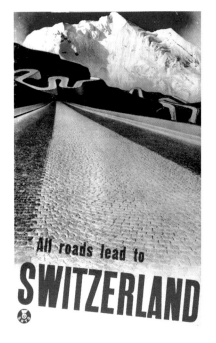

ABOVE AND OPPOSITE: Swiss tourism posters, 1935 and 1934

Herbert Matter learned typography from A.M. Cassandre, geometry from Le Corbusier, and abstraction from Fernand Leger. He put these design sensibilities fully to use in his native Switzerland and later in the United States in the course of a career marked by constant experimentation.

After studying in Paris, Matter was forced to leave France and return to his homeland when immigration authorities discovered he didn't have the proper documentation. After settling in Zurich, Matter designed a series of posters for the Swiss Tourist Office that were radically different from the era's typical travel posters of pretty landscapes and exciting city scenes. Matter collaged different photographs together, using dramatic changes in scale and striking perspectives to create imagery that was more expressive and artistic than realistic.

In 1936 he left for a photography job in New York, and there he met with *Harper's Bazaar* art director Alexey Brodovitch. Brodovitch was already a fan—two of Matter's posters hung in his office—and he commissioned several fashion shoots from the Swiss photographer. Matter's photography grew more experimental over time.

After a few years designing furniture in California for Charles and Ray Eames, Matter returned to New York. In 1944, he embarked on a collaboration with modern furniture manufacturers Hans and Florence Knoll that spanned many years and produced a body of work marked by abstract product photography and clean type. In designing an identity for the New Haven Railroad, Matter explored more than a hundred options before deciding on a logo of stacked, slab-serif letterforms in red and black. It was powerful and identifiable, and part of a comprehensive program that included trains, tickets, timetables, and marketing materials.

Matter's influence remains strong today, thanks in part to his years in the photography department at Yale, where he taught more by doing than by lecturing. Always modest, he felt his work should do the talking.

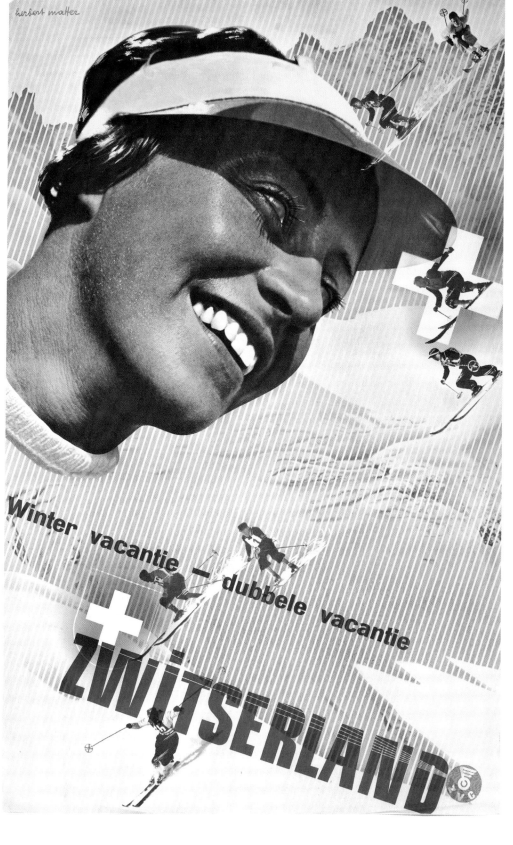

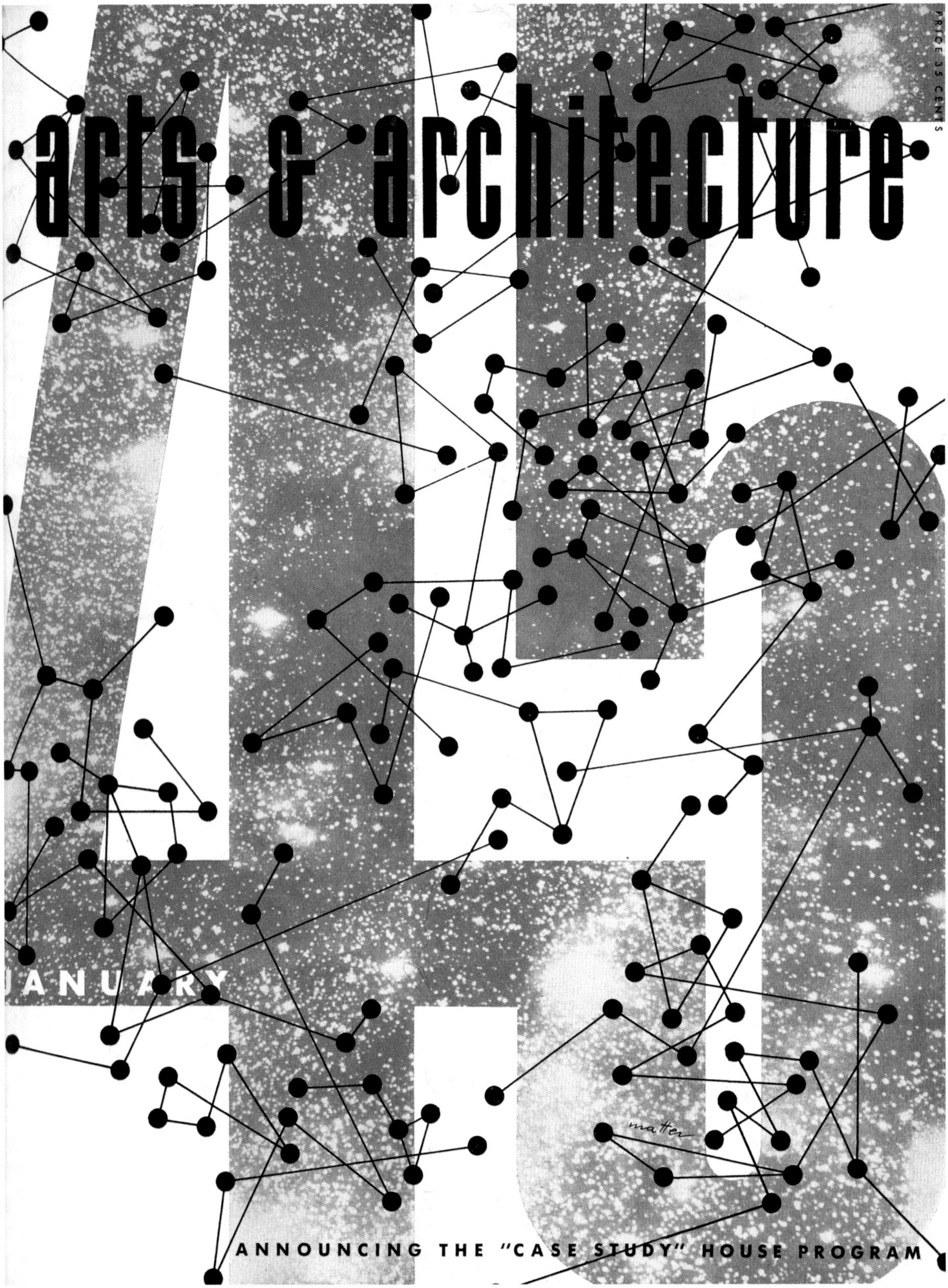

arts & architecture

PRICE 35 CENTS

JANUARY

matter

ANNOUNCING THE "CASE STUDY" HOUSE PROGRAM

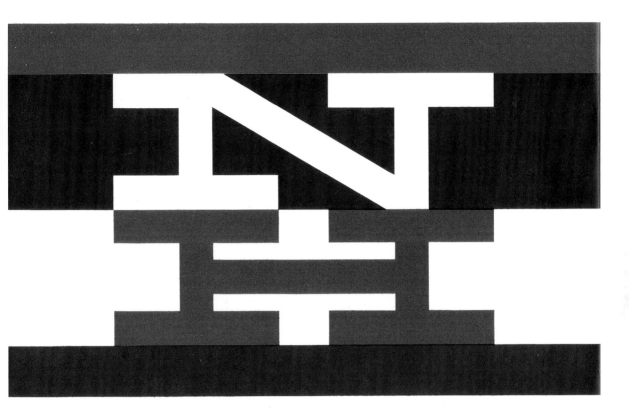

"…Industry is a tough taskmaster.

Art is tougher.

Industry plus Art, almost impossible.

Some artists have done the impossible.

Herbert Matter, for example.

His work of '32 could have been done in '72 or even '82.

It has that timeless, unerring quality one recognizes instinctively."[7]

—Paul Rand
from a poem he wrote for an exhibition catalog of Matter's work

ABOVE: New Haven Railroad
trademark, 1954

OPPOSITE: *Arts & Architecture*
magazine cover, 1945

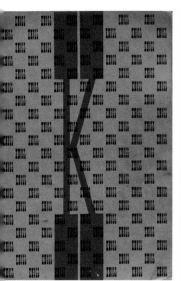

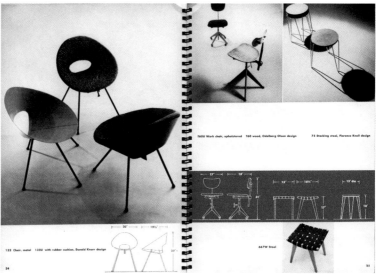

133 Chair, metal   133U with rubber cushion, Donald Knorr design

24

760U Work chair, upholstered   760 wood, Odelberg Olson design   75 Stacking stool, Florence Knoll design

667W Stool

25

Matter's commitment to modernism was reflected not only in his work, but in his personal relationships as well. Painter Jackson Pollack was a close friend. The two met through their wives, who knew each other after being jailed together for protesting cutbacks to the Workers Progress Administration. Franz Kline, Robert Frank, and Willem de Kooning were also friends. Matter directed a film for the Museum of Modern Art on the sculpture of his friend Alexander Calder, and made photographs of his neighbor Alberto Giacometti and his sculptures, which were published in a book after Matter's death. His wife and muse, Abstract Expressionist painter Mercedes Matter, founded the influential New York Studio School of Drawing, Painting, and Sculpture in New York's Greenwich Village in 1963.

ABOVE: Knoll Index of Designs catalog, cover and spread, 1950

OPPOSITE: Knoll ad

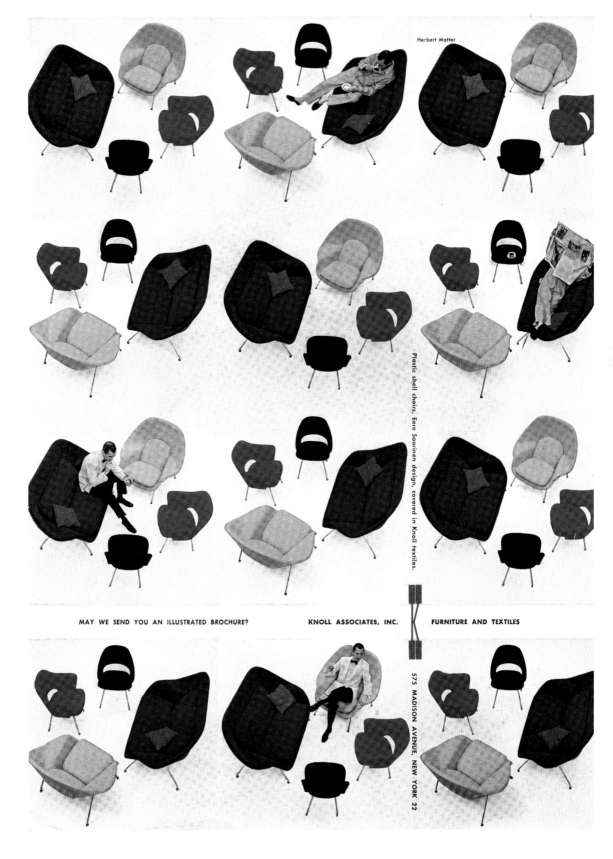

Herbert Matter

Plastic shell chairs, Eero Saarinen design, covered in Knoll textiles.

MAY WE SEND YOU AN ILLUSTRATED BROCHURE?   KNOLL ASSOCIATES, INC.   FURNITURE AND TEXTILES

575 MADISON AVENUE, NEW YORK 22

LADISLAV SUTNAR

1897–1976 | BORN: Pilsen, Czechoslovakia | EDUCATION: School of Applied Arts, Charles University, and the Czech Technical University (all in Prague)

Pioneered what we now call information design

Wrote books laying out important guidelines for design systems

Designed catalogs, books, exhibits, toys, and more

Ladislav Sutnar had intended to work in the United States temporarily. But global events kept him in New York, where he built a highly influential design career.

Sutnar's work designing book covers, theater sets, and exhibitions in Prague led the Czech government to invite him to design the country's exhibit for the 1939 World's Fair in New York. In March of that year, Hitler invaded Czechoslovakia, so Sutnar remained in New York and became friendly with other émigrés, including designers like Walter Gropius and Herbert Bayer. He also met writer Knud Lönberg-Holm, who would become his partner in developing new methods of designing information for business.

Lönberg-Holm worked at Sweet's Catalog Service, which compiled the catalogs of different manufacturers in the construction industry into one volume. These multi-source catalogs were convenient for the user, but visually they were a bit of a mess, as each manufacturer's section of the compilation looked different. Sutnar joined the company to improve the catalogs' design.

Recognizing that people look for products in different ways, Sutnar and Lönberg-Holm developed a system that cross-referenced each item by company, trade, and product name. Sutnar clarified the vast amount of information, using colors, shapes, and graphic symbols to guide the reader. He established hierarchy by emphasizing type—changing scale and weight, reversing out of color, and using italics and parentheses—which made skimming, reading, and remembering

easier. (He also established the standard protocol of putting phone number area codes in parentheses.) Like Alexey Brodovitch was doing with magazines around the same time, Sutnar was moving beyond the single page and embracing the double-page spread, creating designs that weren't just visually interesting, but also helpful to the reader.

Sutnar and Lönberg-Holm also collaborated on three books: *Catalog Design* (1944), *Designing Information* (1947), and *Catalog Design Process* (1950). These guides explained their methods, and encouraged designers to set consistent standards while still creating visual excitement.

Influenced by the functional Constructivist and De Stijl movements, Sutnar always worked at developing a visual language that communicated directly. The fact that English was his second language, causing some struggles to understand and be understood, may have motivated him. Charts, graphs, and images simplified information, helping busy people save time. The way Sutnar steered readers through complex information sounds much like what we now call information design or information architecture, which has been further developed by Edward Tufte and Richard Saul Wurman, as well as by digital and web designers everywhere.

As someone who believed that design should influence every part of daily life, Sutnar designed pretty much everything: furniture, fabrics, glassware and dishes, even toys. His colorful and geometric building block set, Build the Town, was never actually produced, in spite of Sutnar's efforts to design packaging and promotional materials for it.

OPPOSITE: Catalog cover for Cuno Engineering Corporation, 1946

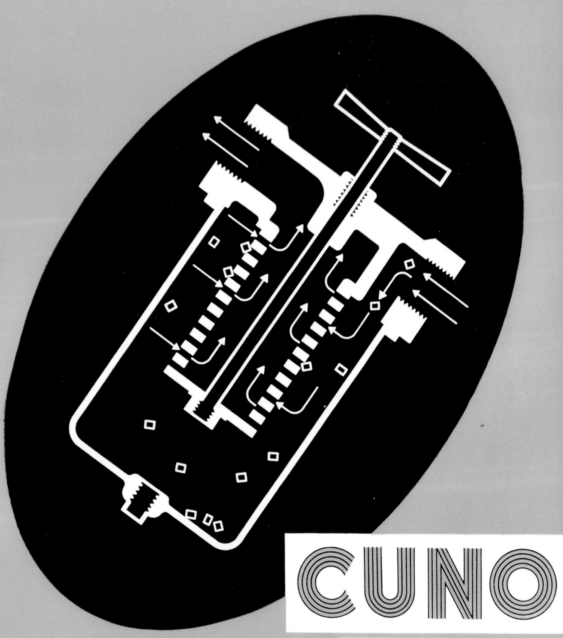

CUNO

continuously
cleanable filters

Cuno Engineering Corporation

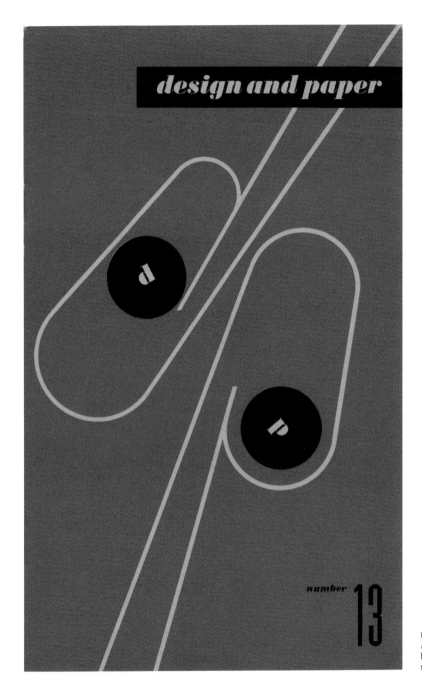

LEFT AND OPPOSITE:
Design and Paper
booklet, cover and
spreads, 1943

Words, pictures, drawings and color are the elements with which printed information is designed. These should be composed in space in such a way that they work together as smoothly as the gears of a machine.

This catalog index shows first the product, then its applications, then specifications for each application. The design coordinates these various units of information.

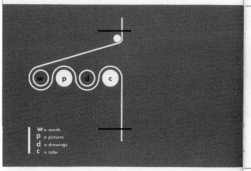

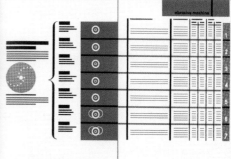

The principles of controlled visual flow can be applied not only to the double spread, but to the book as a whole. The purpose is the same: to lead the eye on the desired path for more efficient reading, and to integrate the whole work into a cohesive design. In the design below, for the cover and section heading pages of an industrial catalog, the repetition of the same pattern unifies the design, while the horizontal flow leads the reader through the catalog.

The same principles, worked out in a different way, have been used in planning this issue of "Design and Paper". Not only each unit, but the booklet itself is intended to be an example of controlled visual flow. The identifying upper right hand corners, the alternating color scheme, and the spatial relationships are designed to lead the reader smoothly through the booklet and to integrate the information it contains.

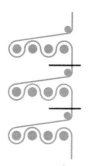

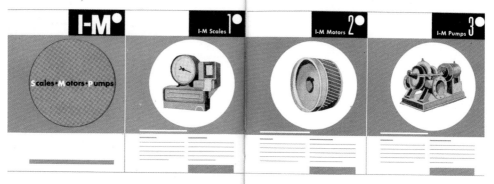

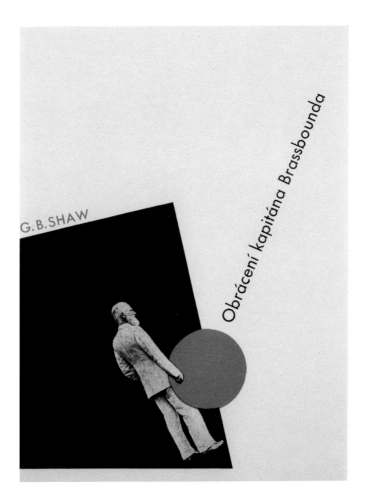

READ: *Envisioning Information,* by Edward Tufte, shows and explains some of the best examples of information design from around the world.

SEE: Visit TED.com for an extensive video library of TED (Technology, Entertainment, Design) Talks, taken from a series of conferences founded by information designer Richard Saul Wurman and featuring short, energetic presentations by some of today's most creative thinkers.

ABOVE: George Bernard Shaw book cover, 1932

OPPOSITE: Build the Town building block set, c. 1942

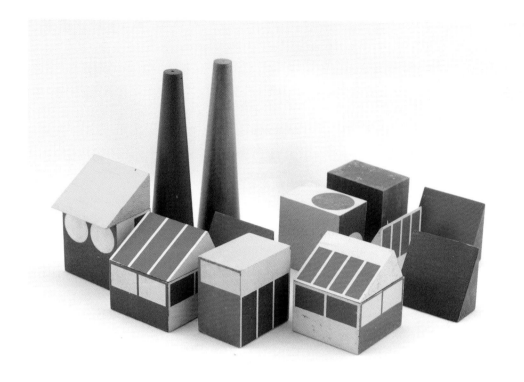

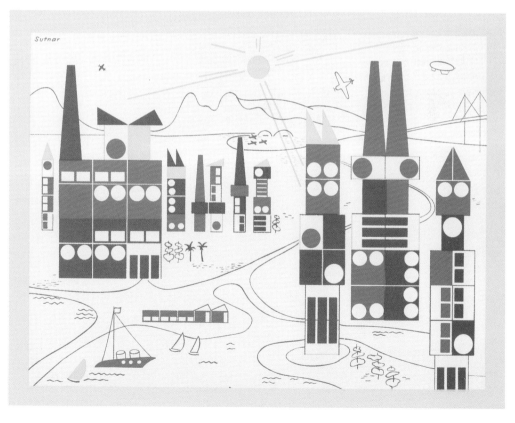

ALVIN LUSTIG

1915–1955 | BORN: Denver, Colorado | EDUCATION: Los Angeles Community College, Art Center School

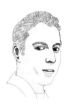

Worked in multiple design disciplines

Took an intellectual approach to solving problems

Designed groundbreaking book covers

Magazines, interiors, book jackets, packaging, fabrics, hotels, mall signage, the opening credits of the cartoon *Mr. Magoo*—even a helicopter—Alvin Lustig designed all of them. He always felt the title "graphic designer" was too limiting, and it's clear why: He designed *everything*. And he did it all before dying at the young age of 40.

Lustig started in Los Angeles, and moved between there and New York a few times. During his first stint in New York, while working for *Look* magazine Lustig started designing interiors, which he continued to do after moving to Los Angeles a few years later. Work like this inspired him to design the total package for his clients, from corporate identity to office environment.

But he is best known for his book covers. New Directions publisher James Laughlin had been packaging reprints of modern literary titles in a pretty traditional format, and they weren't selling. Lustig came on board and gave the books new life with bright colors and abstract visuals that echoed the art of Joan Miró and Paul Klee. Rather than showing an image that explicitly represented the story, Lustig read the work and created symbolic visuals that interpreted the book's overall meaning. The approach worked: stores began displaying the books prominently,

and sales tripled. While Laughlin hoped readers weren't buying the books solely for their covers, he was grateful that the design exposed more people to quality writing.

Like Herbert Matter, Lustig transformed the realistic qualities of photography and created an abstract art form. A series of conceptual black-and-white covers for the New Directions Modern Reader collection marked Lustig's shift away from illustration and toward photo collage. His 1953 cover for Federico Garcia Lorca's *Three Tragedies* is a great example: Lustig photographed the author's name written on a sandy beach, effectively integrating type and image. That design, along with inexpensive one-color printing, helped the book to stand out in a market dominated by painterly colors and traditional type.

As a teenager, Lustig was diagnosed with diabetes. His vision began failing around 1950, and by 1954 he was totally blind. But that didn't stop him from working: He could see a design in his mind, and his wife, Elaine Lustig Cohen, or another assistant would produce it under his careful direction. The disease continued taking its toll, though, and he died in 1955. Elaine took over the many works in progress at the time of Lustig's death, and she went on to become an acclaimed designer herself.

OPPOSITE: *Three Lives,* Gertrude Stein book cover, 1945

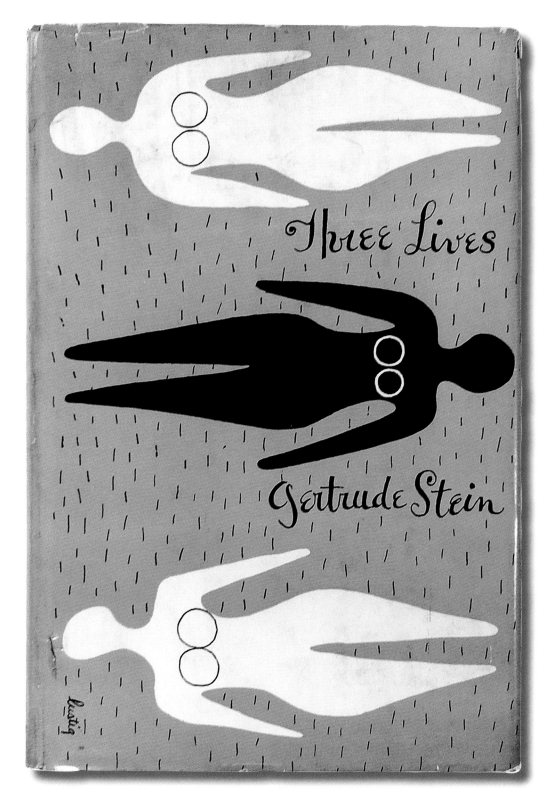

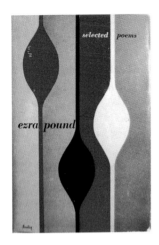
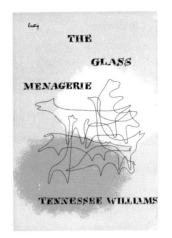
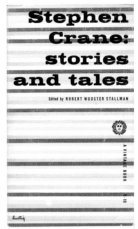

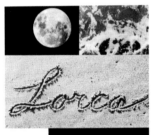
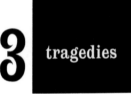
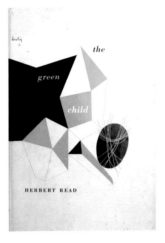
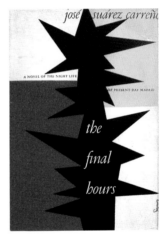

TOP ROW: *Selected Poems*, Ezra Pound, 1949

The Glass Menagerie, Tennessee Williams, 1949

Stephen Crane: Stories And Tales, 1955

BOTTOM ROW: *3 Tragedies*, Federico Garcia Lorca, paperback version, 1955

The Green Child, Herbert Read, 1948

The Final Hours, Jose Suarez Carreno, 1953

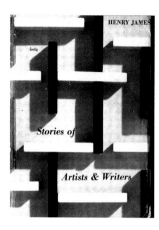

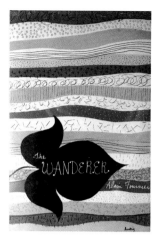

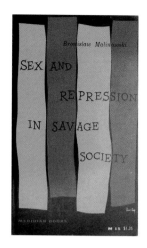

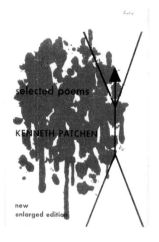

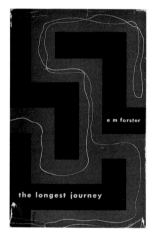

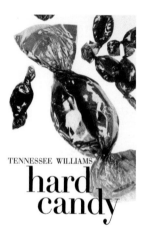

TOP ROW: *Stories of Artists and Writers*, Henry James, 1953

The Wanderer, Henri Alain-Fournier, 1946

Sex and Repression in Savage Society, Bronislaw Malinowski, 1955

BOTTOM ROW: *Selected Poems*, Kenneth Patchen, 1945

The Longest Journey, E.M. Forster, 1943

Hard Candy, Tennessee Williams, designed by Elaine Lustig Cohen

Elaine Lustig was only 28 years old in 1955 when her husband died. With no formal design education, she took over Alvin's studio and designed book covers, signage, and catalogs, developing her own style as she transitioned to her own studio. She later married book publisher Arthur Cohen, and together they founded Ex Libris, a rare book dealership specializing in the European avant-garde.

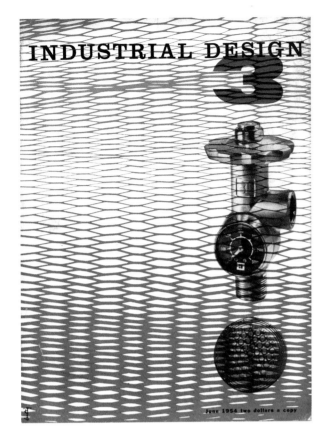

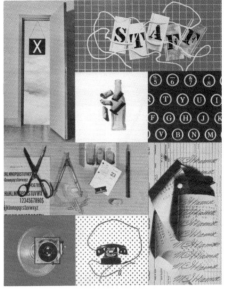

READ: *Born Modern: The Life and Design of Alvin Lustig,* by Steven Heller and Elaine Lustig Cohen
By Its Cover: Modern American Book Cover Design, by Ned Drew and Paul Sternberge

DO: Alvin Lustig made type an important part of the artwork for the book *Three Tragedies* when he drew the author's name in sand. For one of your projects, create "type" out of found materials or something from the natural world, photograph it, and incorporate it into your design.

ABOVE, LEFT: *Industrial Design* magazine cover, 1954

ABOVE RIGHT AND OPPOSITE: *Staff* magazine covers, 1944

staff

number 4 · june 20, 1944

CIPE PINELES

1908–1991 | BORN: Vienna, Austria | EDUCATION: Pratt Institute

Became the first female art director of a mass-market American magazine

Inducted into the New York Art Directors Club and elected to its Hall of Fame as the first woman

Hired fine artists to illustrate mainstream magazines

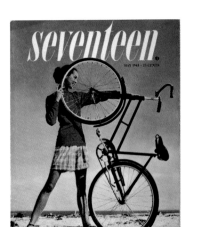

ABOVE: *Seventeen* cover, photograph by Francesco Scavullo, 1948

OPPOSITE: *Charm* cover, 1954

Today, women make up around half of the graphic design profession. But when Cipe Pineles was looking for her first design job, prospective employers were interested in her portfolio—until they learned that the unusual first name belonged to a woman.

She eventually became an assistant to Condé Nast's art director Mehemed Fehmy Agha in 1932, and would expand her role there over the next 15 years. Designing for magazines like *Vogue* and *Vanity Fair*, she learned all about editorial design, art direction, and European modernism. Agha pushed her to consistently outdo herself and to find inspiration in fine art. She became art director at *Glamour* in 1942, the first female to hold that position at a major American magazine.

She moved on to be art director at *Seventeen*, a magazine for teenage girls edited by Helen Valentine. While competing titles saw young women as frivolous husband hunters, *Seventeen* considered its readers smart and serious. By commissioning fine artists like Ad Reinhardt, Ben Shahn, and Andy Warhol to illustrate articles, Pineles rejected the idealized style typical of magazine illustrations at the time, and exposed her audience to modern art. As an artist herself, she was a hands-off art director. Her only request: that the artists produce illustrations that were as high in quality as their gallery work.

In 1950, Pineles became art director at *Charm*, a magazine targeting a new demographic: working women. She designed fashion spreads showing the clothes in use—at work, commuting, and running errands. "We tried to make the prosaic attractive without using the tired clichés of false glamour," she observed in a later interview. "You might say we tried to convey the attractiveness of reality, as opposed to the glitter of a never-never land."[8] Her work helped to redefine the look of women's magazines, while also furthering women's changing roles in society.

Beginning in 1961, Pineles worked independently for such clients as Lincoln Center for the Performing Arts. From 1962 until 1987, she taught editorial design at Parsons School of Design, and directed the design of the school's publications. Her approach to teaching was to focus on content, not style. During a career of many firsts, Cipe Pineles led with her work and she led by example.

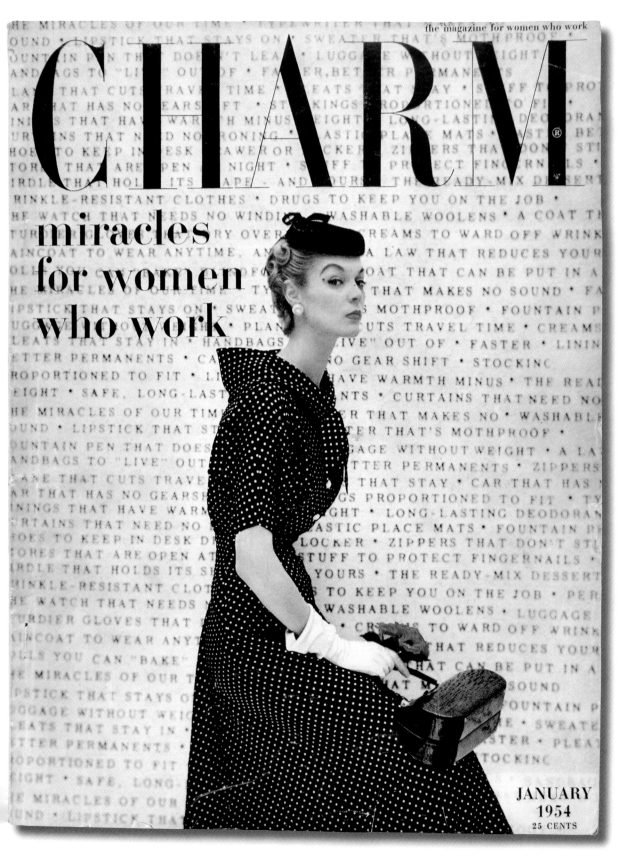

the magazine for women who work

CHARM

miracles
for women
who work

JANUARY
1954
25 CENTS

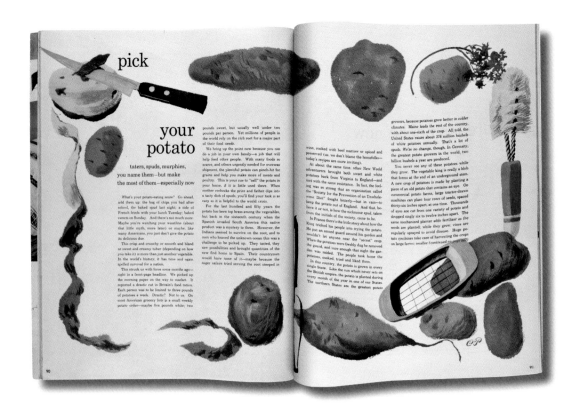

ABOVE: Spread from *Seventeen*, illustrated by Pineles, 1948

OPPOSITE: Fashion spread from *Charm*, 1957

DESIGNERS IN LOVE

Opposites don't always attract. Cipe Pineles was married to CBS Design Director William Golden, who lobbied for her induction into the Art Directors Club. After his premature death, she married information designer Will Burtin. Other design couples include Alexander Rodchenko and Varvara Stepanova, Charles and Ray Eames, Tibor and Maira Kalman, Massimo and Lella Vignelli, Seymour Chwast and Paula Scher (married, divorced, then remarried), Stephen Doyle and Gael Towey, Abbott Miller and Ellen Lupton, Rudy VanderLans and Zuzana Licko, Paul Sahre and Emily Oberman, Pum and Jake Lefebure, and Armin Vit and Bryony Gomez-Palacio.

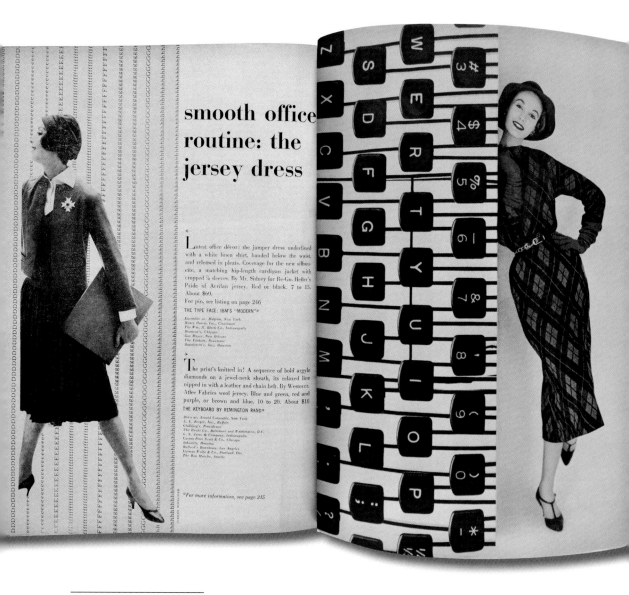

smooth office routine: the jersey dress

Latest office décor: the jumper dress underlined with a white linen shirt, banded below the waist, and released in pleats. Coverage for the new silhouette, a matching hip-length cardigan jacket with cropped ¾ sleeves. By Mr. Sidney for Re-Go. Heller's Pride of Acrilan jersey. Red or black. 7 to 15. About $60.

For pin, see listing on page 246

THE TYPE FACE: IBM'S "MODERN"*

Ensemble at: *Milgrim, New York*
Henry Harris, Inc., Cincinnati
The Wm. H. Block Co., Indianapolis
Bramson's, Chicago
Gus Mayer, New Orleans
The Fashion, Beaumont
Battelstein's, Inc., Houston

The print's knitted in! A sequence of bold argyle diamonds on a jewel-neck sheath, its relaxed line nipped in with a leather and chain belt. By Westover. Atlee Fabrics wool jersey. Blue and green, red and purple, or brown and blue. 10 to 20. About $18

THE KEYBOARD BY REMINGTON RAND*

Dress at: *Arnold Constable, New York*
L. L. Berger, Inc., Buffalo
Glidding's, Providence
The Hecht Co., Baltimore and Washington, D.C.
L. S. Ayres & Company, Indianapolis
Carson Pirie Scott & Co., Chicago
Sakowitz, Houston
Bullock's Downtown, Los Angeles
Lipman Wolfe & Co., Portland, Ore.
The Bon Marche, Seattle

*For more information, see page 245

READ: *Cipe Pineles: A Life of Design*, by Martha Scotford; *Women in Graphic Design 1890–2012*, edited by Gerda Breuer and Julia Meer

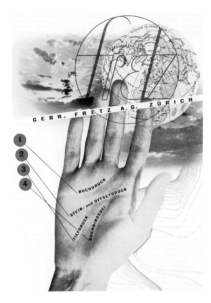

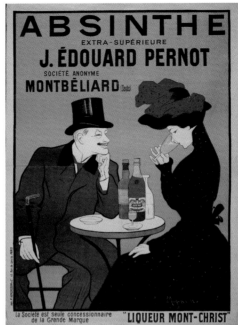

COLLECTING GRAPHIC DESIGN

Would you like to own one of the pieces shown in this book? You could. Posters, books, ads, and other printed ephemera are increasingly valued as collectible items. A collection can provide design inspiration, give a better understanding of history, and increase in value. It can be very expensive, but there are also very accessible ways of collecting iconic design pieces.

Investor Merrill C. Berman started collecting graphic design in the 1970s once he was priced out of the fine art market, and now likely has the most extensive private 20th-century design collection in the world. At the time he started, the art world looked down on commercial and political posters. Berman didn't begin his collection with the aim of selling it for future gain; rather, he embraced the challenge of creating a museum-worthy collection of modern graphic design, which nobody else was doing. Since he's not trained as a designer, he taught himself as he went along and learned from each piece. Berman's collection includes works by Herbert Bayer, E. McKnight Kauffer, Ladislav Sutnar and other notable designers featured in this book; he frequently loans items to museum exhibitions, helping the rest of us to learn as well. (View his collection at mcbcollection.com.)

How does one begin a design collection? It's not always easy, but there are four questions you should ask when considering a purchase:

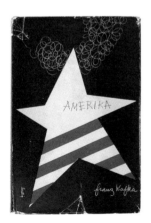

TOP, LEFT: Fretz brochure, designed by Herbert Matter, 1933.

TOP, RIGHT: Poster designed by Leonetto Cappiello, c. 1903.

ABOVE: Book cover by Alvin Lustig, 1946.

What do you like?

It's very simple: Buy what you like. You're going to live with it, so don't buy something you don't like just because you think it may increase in value. Is Art Nouveau your style, or Russian Constructivism? Or do you want an eclectic collection of pieces from different time periods and movements? If it's a poster you want to hang in your living room, color might be a factor. If it's for design inspiration, think about what you can learn from it.

Kind Company's Greg D'Onofrio, who curates a mid-20th century collection called Display, says, "We collect what we love. Ultimately, our collection becomes a valuable tool to design practice, education and research. It's not enough to own the object —it's also about what the object can teach us. Learning from our collection and sharing some of it online at thisisdisplay.org has made the experience of collecting worthwhile."

Look online, go to museums and galleries and vintage shops. Get a sense of what's out there and what you'd like to have for yourself.

Who's the designer?

Posters designed by Jules Cheret and Leonetto Cappiello are very popular, and it's fairly easy to find new, inexpensive reproductions of their original work. That popularity might make them seem a little common, though, so perhaps you want something different. Different can mean pricey. At the time of this writing, Herbert Matter's 1933 Fretz brochure recently sold at Swann Auction Galleries for $1,400, and El Lissitzky's *Beat the Whites with the Red Wedge* poster sold for $41,000. The Chisholm Larsson Gallery listed an Olivetti poster by Josef Müller-Brockmann for $650, and Milton Glaser's Bob Dylan poster for $350.

Have a smaller budget? Scout sellers on Etsy (like ProjectObject and New Documents) and eBay to find mid-century design ephemera ranging from paperback books to posters to postage stamps, at prices well under $100.

Is it rare?

Is it original, or a reprint? In most cases, the original will be worth something and the reprint will not. (For example, at the time of this writing, the Etsy shop New Documents listed two versions of Federico Garcia Lorca's *Three Tragedies*, with a cover designed by Alvin Lustig. The original 1947 hardcover was $149; the 1962 ninth-edition paperback with a slightly different design was $12.) If you're not looking at buying something as an investment, and just want to own something you like, that's fine—just decide that before you buy.

What's the condition?

Three things determine value: the designer, the rarity of the piece, and, as Scott Lindberg of New Documents says, "condition, condition, condition." Have the colors faded? Are there rips or stains? These are vintage pieces, after all, so expect some wear and tear. Aaron Cohen, who runs the Etsy shop ProjectObject, says "In order to be collectible, a piece can't simply be hard to find—but if it's popular, scarce and beautiful, then it's likely highly collectible. Then, of course, condition is a critical factor. When I have a mint copy of something, it is usually priced accordingly."

When asked about his biggest score, Cohen mentions Paul Bowles's personal copy of Franz Kafka's *Amerika*, designed by Alvin Lustig, as well as a rare holiday invitation Lustig designed for bookseller Jacob Zeitlin in 1937. Lindberg likes large collections, like a big pile of the Push Pin Graphic he recently acquired.

Before making any significant investments, learn all you can. And work with someone you can trust. If it seems too good to be true, it probably is.

BRADBURY THOMPSON

1911–1995 | BORN: Topeka, Kansas | EDUCATION: Washburn College

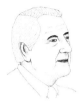

Recycled vintage elements in modern design

Designed and art directed 30-plus magazines

Developed new concept for the alphabet

Low budgets didn't limit Bradbury Thompson's creativity. Taking vintage letterpress type and found imagery, he used his background in printing and his deep knowledge of typography and color to develop projects that still look fresh today.

After graduating with a degree in economics, Thompson worked in the printing industry in his native Kansas. Always a fan of magazines growing up, he moved to New York and became art director at *Mademoiselle* (1945–59) and design director at *Art News* (1945–72). He designed for more than 30 other magazines during his career, including *Smithsonian* and *Business Week*.

But he is best remembered for his work with Westvaco (West Virginia Pulp and Paper Company). To promote the company's papers and printing processes, Thompson designed *Inspirations*, a magazine for design professionals. His big restriction: Use only existing imagery, borrowed or donated from printers, museums, and ad agencies. At a time when abstraction was popular in design, this could have easily resulted in work that looked old-fashioned. Not in Thompson's hands. He experimented with photographic reproduction techniques and printing processes. For example, he superimposed brightly colored dots on an old anatomical illustration, and broke photographs down into separate cyan, magenta, yellow, and black printing channels. By recycling the vintage pieces and combining them with bold colors, transparent layers, and dramatically scaled type, he showed how modern design could incorporate historic elements

Like Herbert Bayer, Thompson saw no need for both upper- and lowercase letters—asking, why does the lower-case "a" look different than the upper-case "A"? His solution? Alphabet 26, which used a single symbol to represent each letter; instead of using capitals, Thompson proposed setting the symbol at a larger size to begin sentences and proper nouns. Alphabet 26 wasn't a font, but rather a concept that could work with every typeface; while it generated mild interest, it was never widely adopted.

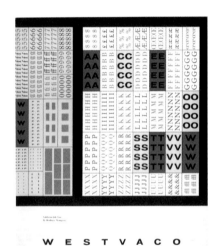

W E S T V A C O

Inspirations

208

ABOVE, OPPOSITE, AND OVERLEAF: Cover and pages from Westvaco *Inspirations,*1957, 1945, and 1958

Described as an elegant man with great taste and good manners, Thompson pursued a multi-disciplinary career. He designed more than 100 U.S. postage stamps, wrote *The Art of Graphic Design*, and taught at Yale University. In another example of combining the modern and historic, he designed the *Washburn College Bible*. He used classic type and artwork, but separated the text into phrases that ended at natural stopping points, giving it a more readable rhythm.

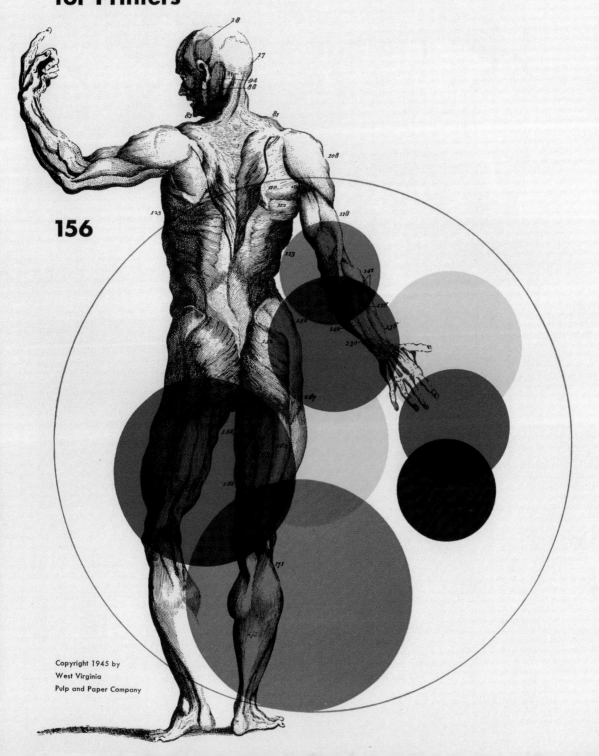

156

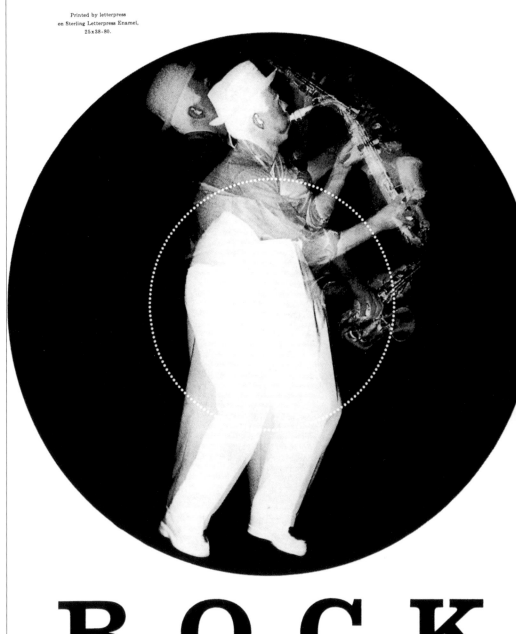

Printed by letterpress
on Sterling Letterpress Enamel,
25 x 38 - 80.

4188

R O C K

Photograph: Rollie Guild.
Engraving: Halftone, 120 line screen,
printed in three colors of ink.

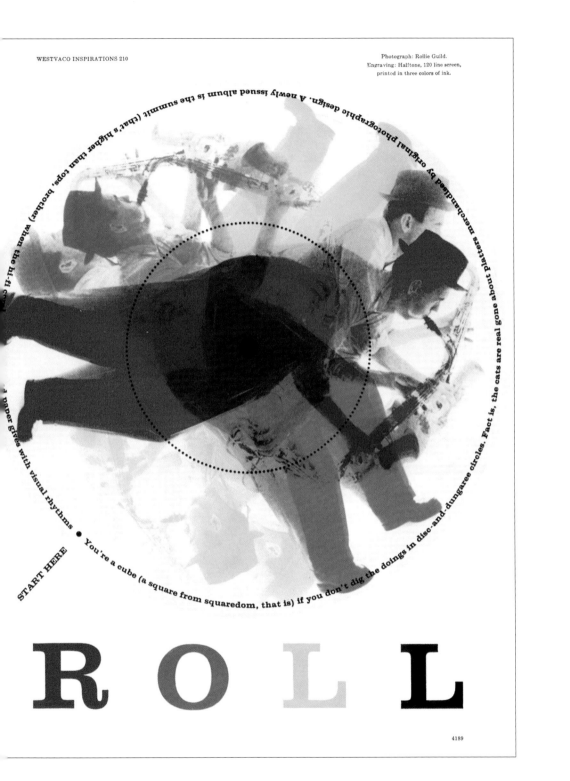

START HERE • You're a cube (a square from squaredom, that is) if you don't dig the doings in disc-and-dungaree circles. Fact is, the cats are real gone about platters merchandised by original photographic design. A newly issued album is the summit (that's higher than tops, brother) when the hi-fi [...] a paper gives with visual rhythms

ROLL

4189

ERIK NITSCHE

1908–1998 | BORN: Lausanne, Switzerland | EDUCATION: Collège Classique of Lausanne, Kunstgewerbeschule in Munich

Understood that design could shape a company's public image

Designed iconic scientific posters

Elevated the standard for nonfiction book design

Family friend Paul Klee inspired Erik Nitsche to become an artist. Nitsche dreamed of studying at the Bauhaus, but to his disappointment he didn't have the opportunity. He must have enjoyed hearing that László Moholy-Nagy later saw his work and wondered who this person was that was designing like the Bauhaus.

Nitsche immigrated to the United States in 1934, landing first in Hollywood and then moving to New York. After a productive period during which he illustrated magazine covers, designed movie posters and album covers, and created marketing materials for retailers, Nitsche began working with General Dynamics in 1955. It proved to be a case study in innovative corporate design.

Defense industry contractor General Dynamics wished to be seen as an agent of peace, rather than of weapons and war; executives gave Nitsche complete control to create a comprehensive new identity designed to shift public opinion. Since much of the company's work, like the first atomic submarine, was top secret, Nitsche used abstract symbols to express the concept of using military technology for peaceful ends. He designed a series of posters to represent the company at Geneva's International Conference on the Peaceful Uses of Atomic Energy (dubbed the "Atoms for Peace" conference). He combined vivid colors and

geometric forms with scientific imagery to develop designs that were bright and optimistic (two words that also describe Nitsche personally). It was a new way to present scientific information, and its influence can be seen in the space-age design style of the late 1950s.

To document the company's history, Nitsche designed *Dynamic America: A History of General Dynamics Corporation and Its Predecessor Companies*, a 420-page book packed with visuals. It raised the bar for nonfiction book design, and still inspires designers today. It also prompted Nitsche to publish his own books. In the 1960s and 70s, he developed a series of illustrated histories covering topics like transportation, communication, architecture, energy, music, medicine, astronomy, and photography. He hired writers for the text, but researched the images and designed the books himself. He made the historical visuals fresh and modern by using white space and combining images in new ways.

Nitsche also designed magazines, record covers, exhibitions, packaging, and signage. He moved around—Munich, Los Angeles, New York, Geneva, Connecticut—which he felt kept him creative. Business was not his strongest suit—he turned down the IBM identity design project that went to Paul Rand—but he was a confident designer who let his work do the talking.

OPPOSITE: Atoms for Peace/Solar Dynamics poster for General Dynamics, 1955

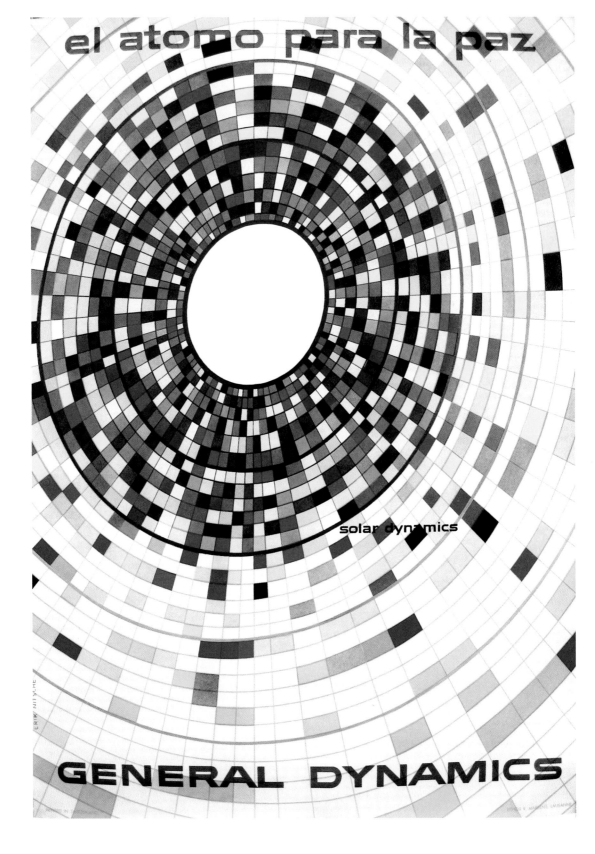

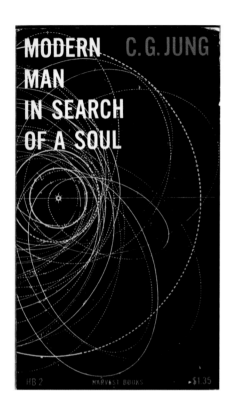

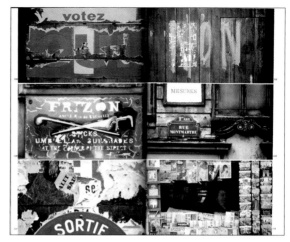

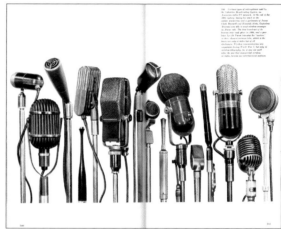

ABOVE: C.G. Jung book cover, 1933

RIGHT: Spreads from the book *A History of Communications*, Maurice Fabre, 1968

OPPOSITE: Posters for General Dynamics, 1955–1962

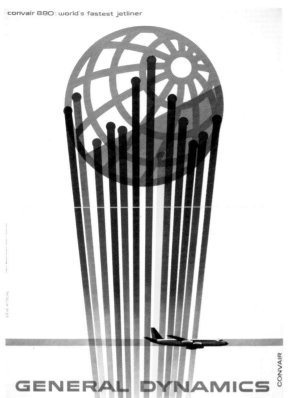

convair 880: world's fastest jetliner

GENERAL DYNAMICS

CONVAIR

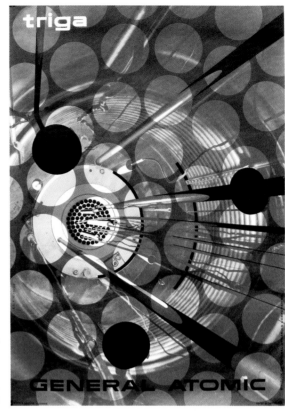

triga

GENERAL ATOMIC

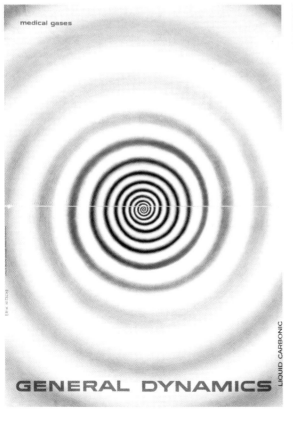

medical gases

GENERAL DYNAMICS

LIQUID CARBONIC

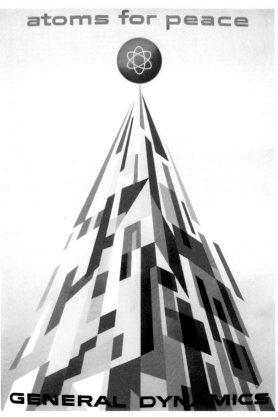

atoms for peace

GENERAL DYNAMICS

Kunstgewerbemuseum Zürich
Ausstellung

deFilm

10. Januar bis 30. April 1960

Offen: Montag 14-18, 20-22
Dienstag-Freitag 10-12, 14-18, 20-22
Samstag-Sonntag 10-12, 14-17

JOSEF MÜLLER-BROCKMANN

1914–1996 | BORN: Rapperswil, Switzerland | EDUCATION: University of Zurich, Zurich Gewerbeschule

Advocated the use of the grid, sans serif type, and objective photography

Founded *Neue Grafik* to promote Swiss Style

Wrote the first comprehensive history of graphic design

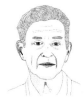

Josef Müller-Brockmann believed in rational, functional design. To achieve that, he used geometry, photography, and abstraction. And his favorite typeface: Akzidenz Grotesk.

The work and writing of Max Bill, an architect and designer who studied at the Bauhaus, influenced Müller-Brockmann and led him away from his illustrative beginnings. Bill developed Theo van Doesburg's idea of a universal visual language by using a modular grid—the underlying framework of columns and margins that guides the placement of text and images in a layout. It provides order, consistency, and flexibility, and helps to establish hierarchy. It continues to be an important tool today, especially in web design.

This grid-based approach to graphic design became the foundation of the International Typographic Style, or Swiss Style, and Müller-Brockmann was a key figure in this influential movement. He favored photography as a literal and unbiased alternative to hand-drawn illustration, which he considered too subjective and open to different interpretations from viewers. Müller-Brockmann stripped extraneous decoration from his design; every element in his layout had a purpose. Over time, his work grew increasingly abstract. For example, he designed a series of concert posters for Zurich's Tonhalle. There were no music notes or instruments. Geometric shapes and lines were placed on the grid, but were varied in position and scale to suggest movement and rhythm. The result was abstract, yet very musical.

Müller-Brockmann founded and co-edited the journal *Neue Grafik* (*New Graphic Designer*), to challenge the excessive and superficial design he was seeing at the time and to promote the Swiss Style. He also wrote the books *The Graphic Artist and his Design Problems* (1961) and *History of the Poster* (with Shizuko Müller-Yoshikawa, 1971). A third book, his *History of Visual Communication* (1971), was one of the first to summarize the history of graphic design. As an educator, he encouraged his students to be aware of the world outside of design, to become better problem solvers, and to always be self-critical.

Gestaltungsprobleme des Grafikers
The Graphic Artist and his Design Problems
Les problèmes d'un artiste graphique

ABOVE: *The Graphic Artist and his Design Problems* book cover, 1961

OPPOSITE: Der Film poster, 1960

"It's unfortunate that the Swiss Style is often pigeonholed as cold, sterile, and even corporate, when in fact Müller-Brockmann's work was quite vivid and expressive. If you take a look at his Musica Viva poster series for The Tonhalle Zürich, you'll see each design masterfully evokes the mood, feeling, tone, and harmony of the music that the poster is announcing."[9]

—Mike Joyce
Stereotype Design

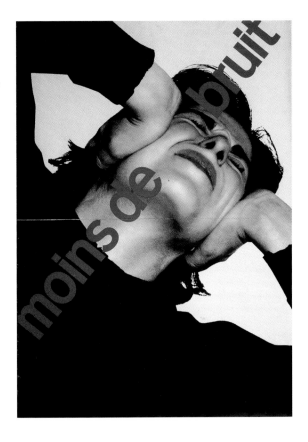

READ: *Grid Systems in Graphic Design*, by Josef Müller-Brockmann, a great how-to from the master himself.

SEE: Punk and indie rock posters for bands like Ramones, Pixies, and Yo La Tengo, have been redesigned in the Swiss Style (using only Akzidenz Grotesk) and are for sale at Swissted.com.

GET TO KNOW: Other noteworthy Swiss Style designers include Theo Ballmer, Karl Gerstner, Armin Hofmann, Ernst Keller, and Emil Ruder.

ABOVE: Weniger Lärm (Stop Noise Pollution) poster, 1960

OPPOSITE: Juni-Festwochen Zurich poster, 1957

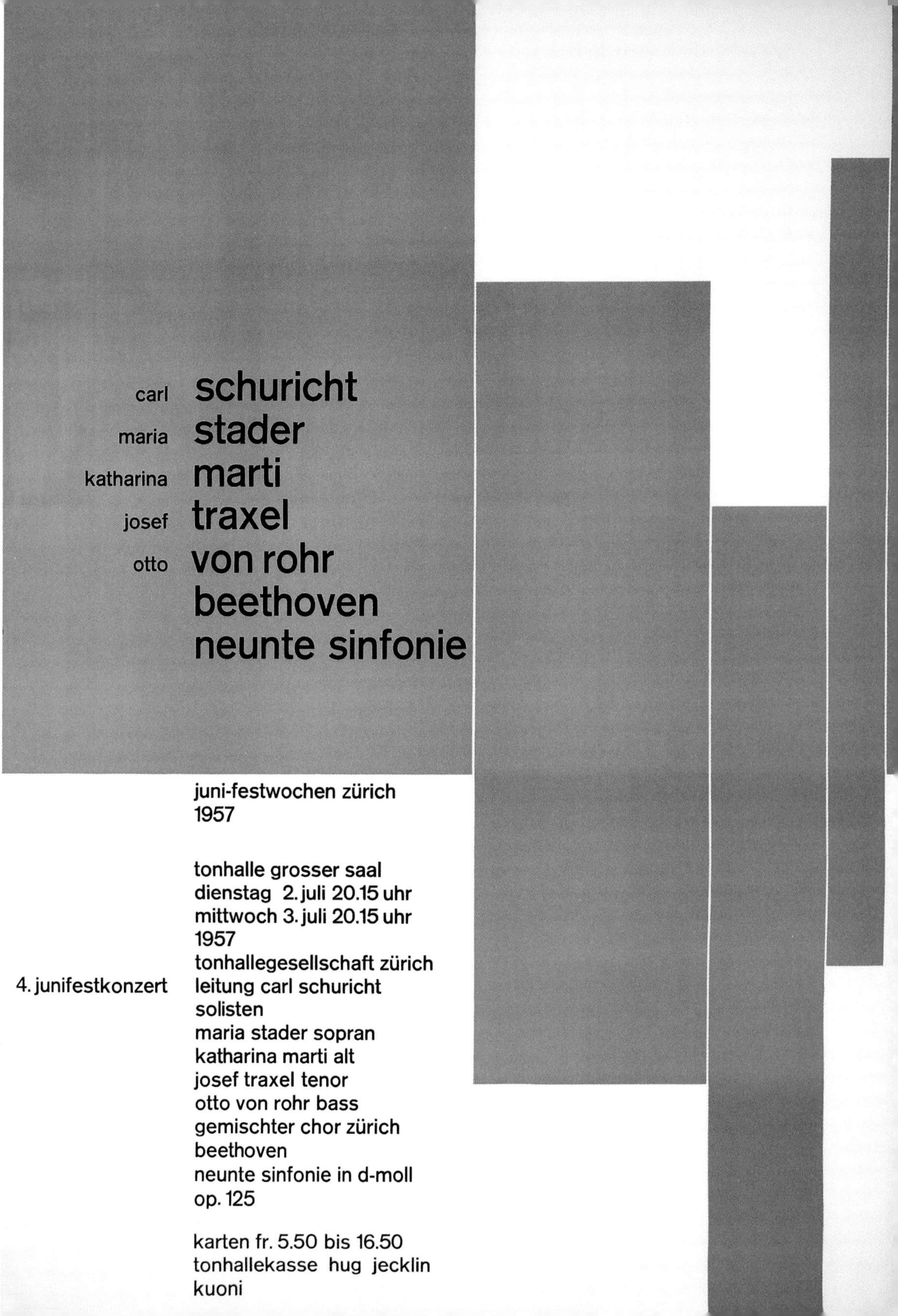

carl **schuricht**
maria **stader**
katharina **marti**
josef **traxel**
otto **von rohr**
beethoven
neunte sinfonie

juni-festwochen zürich
1957

tonhalle grosser saal
dienstag 2. juli 20.15 uhr
mittwoch 3. juli 20.15 uhr
1957
tonhallegesellschaft zürich
4. junifestkonzert   leitung carl schuricht
solisten
maria stader sopran
katharina marti alt
josef traxel tenor
otto von rohr bass
gemischter chor zürich
beethoven
neunte sinfonie in d-moll
op. 125

karten fr. 5.50 bis 16.50
tonhallekasse hug jecklin
kuoni

PAUL RAND

1914–1996 | BORN: Brooklyn, New York | EDUCATION: Pratt Institute, Parsons School of Design, Art Students League

Mastered corporate identity, advertising, and editorial design

Developed strong identity programs for major corporations

Influenced others through writing and teaching

Paul Rand said, "Visual communications of any kind, whether persuasive or informative, from billboards to birth announcements, should be seen as the embodiment of form and function: the integration of the beautiful and the useful."[10] It's not only about how it looks, or how it works, but about how it looks and works together.

Born Peretz Rosenbaum into an Orthodox Jewish family, Rand changed his name, thinking the name would hinder his career. Rand's art school education didn't cover graphic design, so he learned about the Bauhaus from European magazines and books. He found inspiration not in other designers, but in painters, like Pablo Picasso, Paul Klee, and Vassily Kandinsky, and the architect Le Corbusier. He combined these influences with his own wit and playfulness to develop a modern American visual language.

Early in his career, Rand worked in editorial design for *Esquire, Apparel Arts*, and the cultural journal *Direction*. In 1941, his collaboration with copywriter William Bernbach at the Weintraub Advertising agency effectively integrated art and copy in advertising—a marriage that continues today. Rand's book-cover designs typified his streamlined approach, featuring basic shapes, cutouts, and colors combined with simple sans serif type. To add warmth and authenticity, he'd sometimes incorporate his own handwriting.

Rand made his biggest mark in the area of corporate identity. One of his most famous logos was for IBM—a project that began as a collaboration with architect Eliot Noyes in 1956 and unfolded over more than 20 years. Rand knew the conservative company needed to be guided through a design progression. His first step was to tweak IBM's existing slab serif typeface, but it wasn't until 1972 that he incorporated the still-familiar horizontal stripes to better unify the three letters. In addition to the logo, he designed IBM's packaging, marketing materials, and annual reports. Rand was responsible for some of corporate America's most recognizable logos: Westinghouse, ABC, United Parcel Service, Yale University Press, Next Computers (for Steve Jobs), and Colorforms.

Design wasn't Rand's only talent. Perhaps more important: his skill in convincing corporate executives that design has value, and that it should evolve as companies grow and develop.

He railed against mediocrity, and he codified his approach and methodology in the classic book *Thoughts on Design.* (Unfortunately none of the books he authored remain in print.) He taught at Pratt Institute and Cooper Union before becoming a professor at Yale, where he spent 25 years. He worked hard up until the day he died, at age 82, and sacrificed much of his personal life for work. But, as he said, "Design is a way of life."

OPPOSITE: *Thoughts on Design* book cover, 1946

Thoughts on Design: Paul Rand

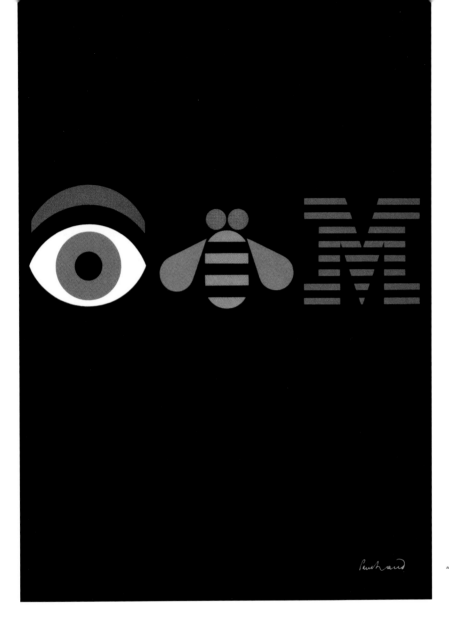

"Eye Bee M"
rebus poster,
1981

"At the very pinnacle of my graphic forefathers stands
the name of Paul Rand. Cantankerous, irascible, loving,
bristling with talent, brimming over with taste, and
endowed with invincible personal conviction—the original
and badass Rand showed the way."[11]

—George Lois

Effective use of the logotype:

The IBM logotype should not be viewed as a design encumbrance. Nor should it create the impression of having been dictated because of some company regulation. Its use should never appear arbitrary or forced

or as mere decoration in the absence of genuine ideas. A trademark is most effective when it serves the function assigned to it: to help identify a company or product.

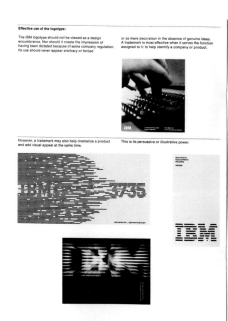

However, a trademark may also help dramatize a product and add visual appeal at the same time.

This is its persuasive or illustrative power.

It may serve as a decorative element, for instance, when used as a background in packaging, or wallcovering.

It may also function as a contrasting element and focal point.

Logotype design and variations:

Flexibility, versatility and adaptability are the principal considerations which determine the form of the IBM logotype. Its gestalt (configuration) is relatively simple, and it is designed to minimize problems of compatibility with other typefaces. To meet aesthetic and practical

requirements and to facilitate fabrication, several styles and weights were developed: solid, outline, and striped.

These choices give the designer sufficient latitude to select the form most suitable for a particular application.

IBM IBM IBM IBM IBM IBM

6

7

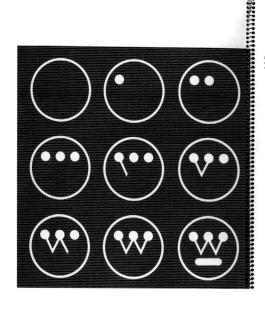

Left: Suggested use of circle W for TV animation and electric signs

The Circle W

The circle W is the key to Westinghouse's graphic design program. Every attempt should be made to place this symbol before the public in a manner commensurate with good design.

1: The circle W may be used in the following ways, in black and white, or in color:

 positive

 reverse wide border circle

 reverse narrow border circle

 reverse square

2: When the circle W is used three-dimensionally, the discs on top of the W should be flat, like a checker, and never concave or convex.

 three dimensional

ABOVE, TOP: The IBM Look, Corporate
Identification Design Guide Book, 1972

ABOVE: Westinghouse Graphics Identification
Manual, 1961

READ: *Paul Rand*, by Steven Heller and *Sparkle and Spin: A Book About Words*, by Ann and Paul Rand, one of three fun books for children illustrated by Rand and written by his second wife. *Designing Brand Identity: An Essential Guide for the Whole Branding Team*, by Alina Wheeler, explains the process from start to finish, illustrated by informative case studies.

DO: Paul Rand had a good way to test the effectiveness of a logo: Blur or distort it in some way. Is it still recognizable? Try this with one of your logo designs.

ABOVE: *Direction* magazine cover, 1940

OPPOSITE: Poster, 1970, featuring an illustration from 1957

The
Graphic art
of Paul Rand

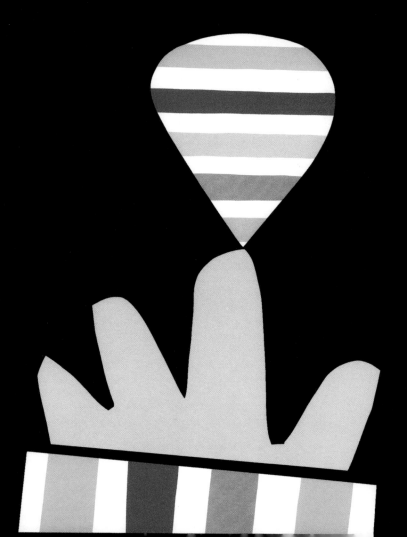

SAUL BASS

1920–1996 | BORN: The Bronx, New York | EDUCATION: Art Students League, Brooklyn College

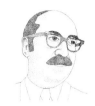

Pioneered the art of film title design

Developed comprehensive ad campaigns for movies

Designed many well-known corporate identity programs

"Bass fashioned title sequences into an art, creating in some cases a mini-film within a film. His graphic compositions in movement function as a prologue to the movie—setting the tone, providing the mood, and foreshadowing the action."[12]

—Martin Scorsese

OPPOSITE: *Vertigo* poster, 1958

Before Saul Bass, movie titles were considered so unimportant that theater curtains weren't pulled aside until they were over. When Otto Preminger's *The Man with the Golden Arm* was released in 1955, featuring Bass's minimal, animated title sequence, projectionists were actually instructed to open the curtain before the credits began.

Bass studied art in his native New York, learning about Russian Constructivism and the Bauhaus from his teacher György Kepes, who had studied under László Moholy-Nagy. He opened his own office in Los Angeles in 1952, where he designed print ads for movies. Director Otto Preminger hired Bass to design the poster for his 1954 film *Carmen Jones*; he liked it so much, he asked Bass to design the titles as well. Bass focused on two elements that symbolized the film: a rose and a flame, superimposed over each other.

That was a key element of Bass's work: Rather than spotlighting the movie's star, he would develop symbolic images to represent the film's meaning. For *The Man with the Golden Arm*, starring Frank Sinatra as a card dealer addicted to heroin, abstract paper cutouts enter the screen at different angles while the brassy score plays. At the end, the cutouts change into a distorted arm, the film's main symbol. For the first time, the title sequence set the mood and became part of the movie. Bass designed classic titles for *Psycho*; *It's a Mad, Mad, Mad, Mad World*; *Bonjour Tristesse*; *Vertigo*; *Grand Prix*; and *North by Northwest*. He continued designing for films into the 1980s and 90s, with titles for Martin Scorsese's *Goodfellas* and *Casino*, among others.

Bass also changed the way films were marketed. What other designers were doing for corporations, Bass was doing for movies, creating a comprehensive and consistent suite of materials, from on-screen titles, to posters, to advertising. Collaborating with his wife, Elaine, Bass also directed his own films, including the Academy Award-winning short *Why Man Creates*, and the feature-length *Phase IV*.

Bass brought that same iconic visual approach to his corporate identity work. He designed logos for Continental Airlines, Minolta, AT&T, Warner Communications, and others, some of which are still in use today.

JAMES STEWART
KIM NOVAK
IN ALFRED HITCHCOCK'S
MASTERPIECE

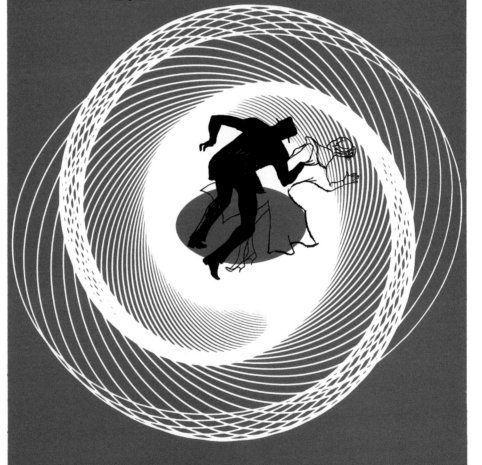

'VERTIGO'

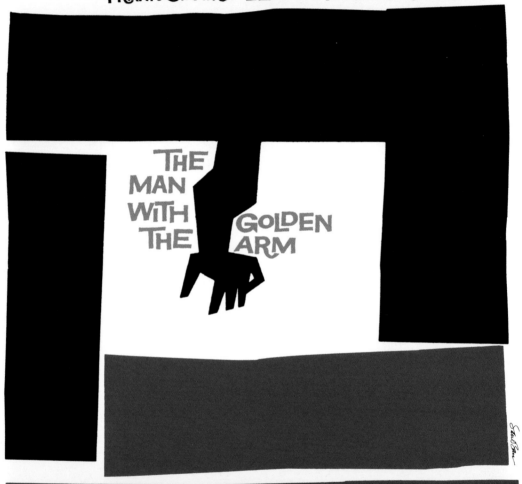

FRANK SINATRA · ELEANOR PARKER · KIM NOVAK

THE MAN WITH THE GOLDEN ARM

A FILM BY OTTO PREMINGER · FROM THE NOVEL BY NELSON ALGREN · MUSIC BY ELMER BERNSTEIN · PRODUCED & DIRECTED BY OTTO PREMINGER

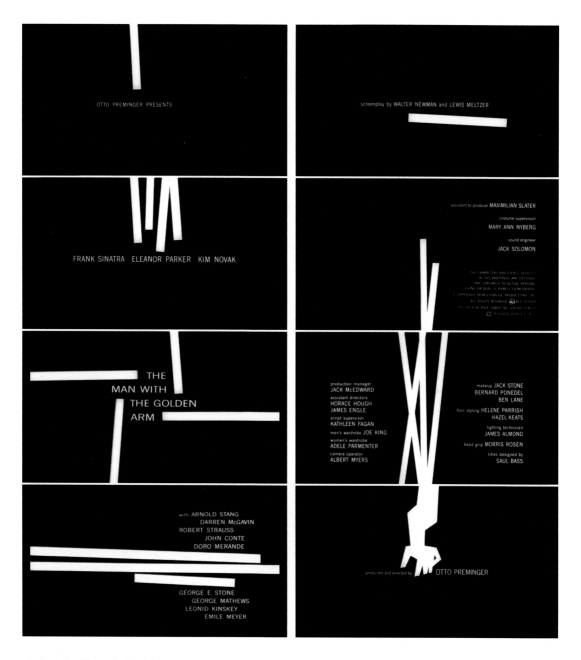

ABOVE: *The Man with the Golden Arm* film title stills, 1955

OPPOSITE: *The Man with the Golden Arm* poster, 1955

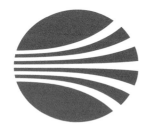

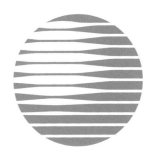

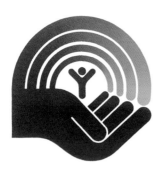

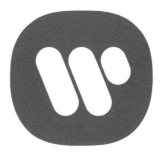

ABOVE: Logos for Continental, AT&T, United Way, and Warner Communications

OPPOSITE: Logos for Avery International, Girl Scouts, Alcoa, and United Airlines

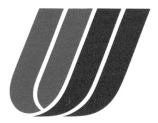

READ: *Saul Bass: A Life in Film and Design*, by Jennifer Bass and Pat Kirkham

GET TO KNOW: Other influential film title designers include Maurice Binder, Pablo Ferro, Kyle Cooper, Olivier Kuntzel and Florence Deygas, Danny Yount, and Gareth Smith and Jenny Lee.

GEORG OLDEN

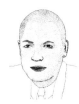

1920–1975 | BORN: Birmingham, Alabama | EDUCATION: Virginia State College

Pioneered on-air television graphics

Became the first notable African American graphic designer

Before Rosa Parks, Jackie Robinson, and Martin Luther King Jr. broke racial barriers, Georg Olden entered the traditionally white, male world of graphic design and became its first prominent African American practitioner.

Born in Alabama, Olden was the grandson of a slave who fought in the Civil War. During World War II, Olden left college to work as a graphic designer for the government's Office of Strategic Services. In a testament to the benefits of networking, Olden parlayed his contacts within the OSS to a job at CBS, in 1945.

TV was brand new then. Under the direction of William Golden, who designed the CBS eye logo, Olden was in charge of creating on-air titles for six shows. As a visual medium, TV was very limited: black and white, fixed proportions, and picture quality that made type look fuzzy. Olden put those limitations to work, though, by designing clean and simple titles that quickly communicated the gist of the show. He integrated type and images to create bold, graphic, and playful visuals. During Olden's 15 years at the network, he grew from a one-person department to leader of a 14-person creative team, as the number of TV sets in the United States increased from 16 thousand to 85 million. He moved into advertising in 1960, working first for the agency BBDO, then for McCann Erickson.

In 1963 Olden became the first African American ever to design a U.S. postage stamp when he was commissioned to mark the centennial of the Emancipation Proclamation, which freed the slaves still being held in the United States. The broken chain he designed was simple and direct, like his TV work. Olden attended a White House ceremony in which President John F. Kennedy introduced the stamp.

As one of the few blacks in the industry, Olden said he never felt racism. He believed that anyone with talent and hard work could achieve what he did. But in 1970, he was laid off from McCann Erickson, and pursued an unsuccessful lawsuit against the company for wrongful termination based on racial discrimination. He moved to California and worked several different jobs, even directing an episode of "The Mod Squad." Still upset about the layoff, he initiated a class action lawsuit against the agency along with others who felt they were victims of discrimination.

Right before that case went to trial, on January 25, 1974, Olden was shot to death. His live-in girlfriend was charged with his murder, but was later acquitted on the grounds of self-defense. But Olden's career as a talented and pioneering graphic designer outshines the circumstances of his death.

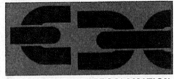

1863-1963 UNITED STATES 5 CENTS

EMANCIPATION PROCLAMATION

ABOVE:
Emancipation Proclamation centenary stamp, 1963

OPPOSITE, TOP:
On-air graphic, news programming, CBS

OPPOSITE, BOTTOM: Still from the title sequence for *Search for Tomorrow*, CBS, 1951

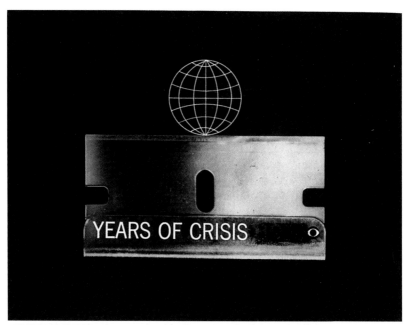

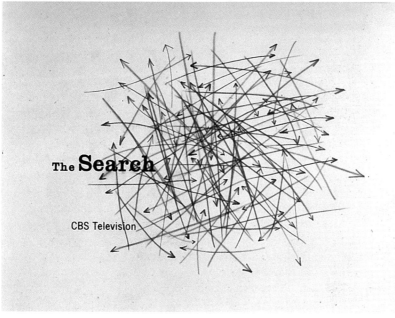

"As the first black American to achieve an executive position with a major corporation, my goal was the same as that of Jackie Robinson in baseball: to achieve maximum respect and recognition by my peers, the industry and the public, thereby hopefully expanding acceptance of, and opportunities for, future black Americans in business."[13]

—Georg Olden

READ: *TV by Design: Modern Art and the Rise of Network Television*, by Lynn Spigel, explores the role of modernism in network television in the 1950s and 60s.
Fly In the Buttermilk: Memoirs of an African American in Advertising, Design & Design Education, by Archie Boston

DO: The Organization of Black Designers (OBD) is a multicultural, multidisciplinary professional association of more than 10,000 members committed to the increased visibility, empowerment, and support of its membership. Learn more at obd.org

---

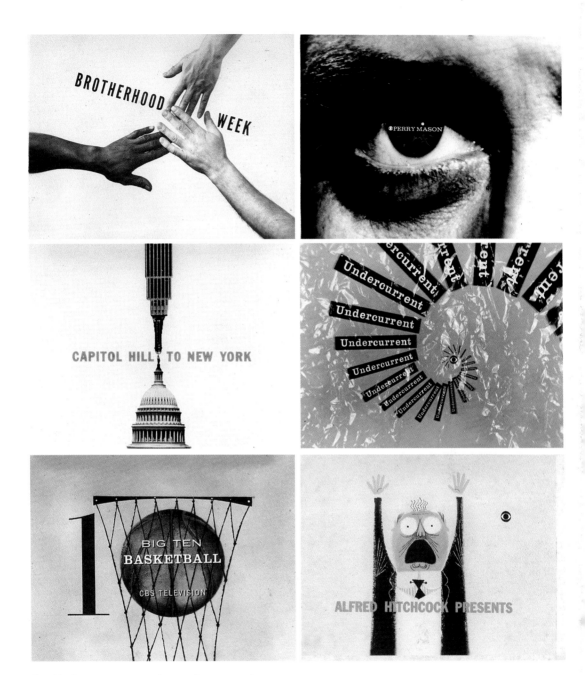

Graphics for news programming, sports programming, and stills from title sequences for the shows *Perry Mason* (1957), *Undercurrent* (1957), and *Alfred Hitchcock Presents* (1955), all for CBS

WILL BURTIN

1908–1972 | BORN: Cologne, Germany | EDUCATION: Handwerkskammer Köln, Kölner Werkschulen

Made complex information understandable through design

Advanced the understanding of science

Organized multidisciplinary conferences on communication

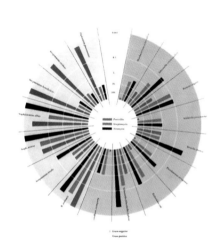

ABOVE: *Scope* magazine diagram, 1951

OPPOSITE: *Scope* magazine cover

Graphic design is usually not a matter of life and death. For Will Burtin, though, the lives of World War II combat fighters depended on the clarity and effectiveness of his design.

In his native Germany, Burtin was pressured to design Nazi propaganda for Adolf Hitler. Instead, he and his Jewish wife fled to the United States in 1938. It's said he never uttered another word in German.

Burtin was drafted into the U.S. Army in 1943, and designed gunnery-training manuals for air combat. The challenge was not only making complex information easy for soldiers to understand and remember, but also to consider how factors like time, motion, and judgment factored into the training. Burtin demonstrated that design can deliver important and useful information, and that its beauty lies in clarity and effectiveness. His well-designed manuals cut the Army's gunnery training time in half, and they set a pattern for his future work: thoroughly researching a complex subject and distilling it into a visual presentation.

Burtin was so talented that the publisher of *Fortune* magazine secured his early discharge from the Army because his work for the magazine would be in the country's best interest. Burtin brought elegant clarity to *Fortune*, designing easy-to-understand charts and graphs to present complex financial data. He did the same with medical information at *Scope*, the magazine for medical professionals from Upjohn Pharmaceuticals.

During his 30-year relationship with Upjohn, Burtin designed the company's identity, packaging, communication materials, and groundbreaking exhibits. To help people better understand the human cell, he designed a walk-through model, enlarged one million times, with pulsing lights powered by a mile of wiring. Around ten million people saw the exhibit as it traveled the United States.

Burtin also organized the multidisciplinary conferences Vision 65 and Vision 67, to address the challenges of mass communication and technology in the 1960s. Speakers included Josef Müller-Brockmann, Marshall McLuhan, Umberto Eco, Buckminster Fuller, Max Bill, and Wim Crouwel. Burtin always had good relationships with other designers. After his wife Hilda died, he married art director Cipe Pineles. And none other than Saul Bass gave the eulogy at Burtin's funeral.

SCOPE

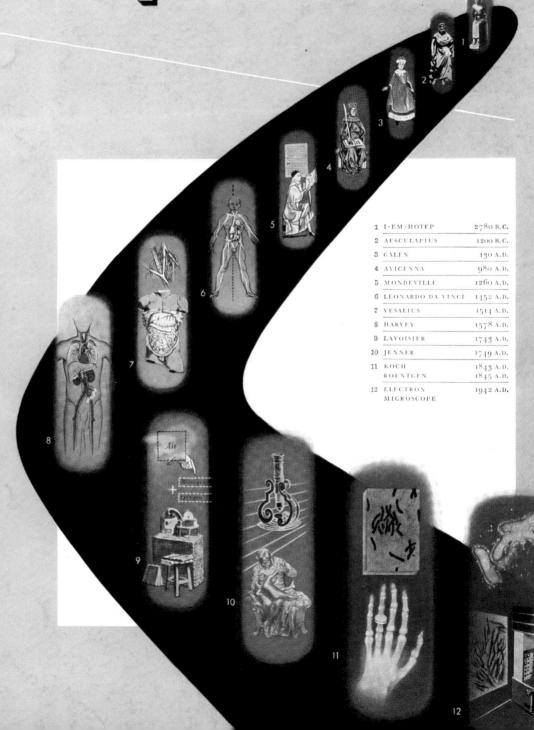

1	I-EM-HOTEP	2780 B.C.
2	AESCULAPIUS	1200 B.C.
3	GALEN	130 A.D.
4	AVICENNA	980 A.D.
5	MONDEVILLE	1260 A.D.
6	LEONARDO DA VINCI	1452 A.D.
7	VESALIUS	1514 A.D.
8	HARVEY	1578 A.D.
9	LAVOISIER	1743 A.D.
10	JENNER	1749 A.D.
11	KOCH	1843 A.D.
	ROENTGEN	1845 A.D.
12	ELECTRON MICROSCOPE	1942 A.D.

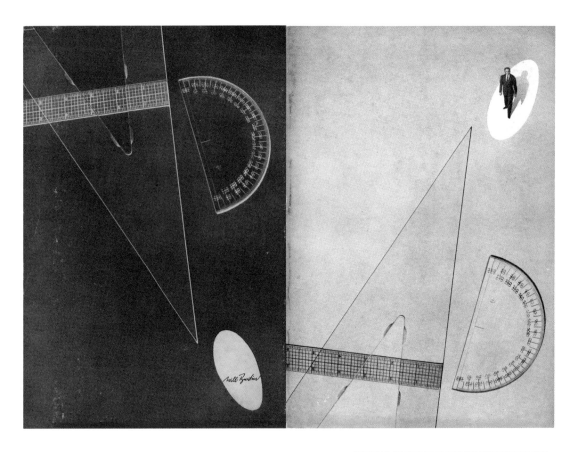

READ: *Design and Science: The Life and Work of Will Burtin*, by R. Roger Remington and Robert Fripp and *Visual Strategies: A Practical Guide to Graphics for Scientists and Engineers*, by Felice C. Frankel and Angela H. DePace, a useful handbook featuring several cases of contemporary design for science.

ABOVE: *A-D Graphic Design* magazine, front and back cover, 1942

OPPOSITE: The Brain exhibition, 1960

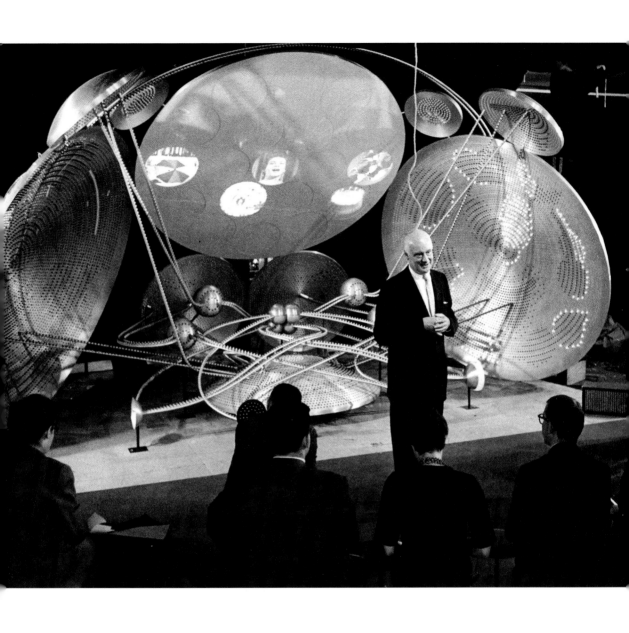

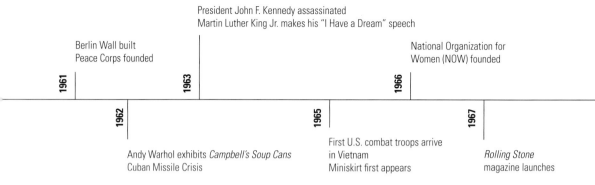

President John F. Kennedy assassinated
Martin Luther King Jr. makes his "I Have a Dream" speech

Berlin Wall built
Peace Corps founded

National Organization for
Women (NOW) founded

1961

1963

1966

1962

1965

1967

Andy Warhol exhibits *Campbell's Soup Cans*
Cuban Missile Crisis

First U.S. combat troops arrive
in Vietnam
Miniskirt first appears

Rolling Stone
magazine launches

LATE MODERN/POSTMODERN:
CHANGE SPARKS NEW FORMS OF EXPRESSION

The 1960s was a period of major social, political, and cultural upheaval around the world. People rebelled against restrictive norms. They wanted change and took action. Students and activists protested the Vietnam War. African Americans, fed up with being treated as second-class citizens, stood up for civil rights. Women rallied for equal pay at work, and gay people fought back against police harassment.

This emphasis toward action and activism filtered into graphic design, as well—with typography being a case in point. Developments in printing technology gave designers more control over their work: Instead of relying on a printer to compose type and position images in a layout, designers used rub-down type and photomechanical transfer to do it themselves. This DIY approach not only gave designers more freedom, but protest groups were able to get their messages out by using the new technologies to produce posters quickly and cheaply.

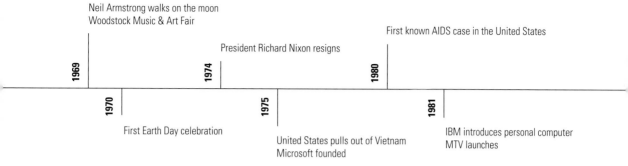

Neil Armstrong walks on the moon
Woodstock Music & Art Fair

First known AIDS case in the United States

President Richard Nixon resigns

1969

1974

1980

1970

1975

1981

First Earth Day celebration

United States pulls out of Vietnam
Microsoft founded

IBM introduces personal computer
MTV launches

Popular culture mixed with fine art to create Pop Art, a less serious movement. It was led by artists like Roy Lichtenstein and Andy Warhol, and incorporated advertising, comic strips, and product packaging into painting. Some graphic designers embraced this highbrow-lowbrow approach, which infused their work with fun and playfulness.

Even as the late modernists continued pushing the ideas of the movement, a new generation of designers began exploring different ways to communicate visually. Rather than strictly adhering to a rigorous set of rules, they embraced historical references and ornament, and blended different kinds of images and type styles. It was a looser, less formal approach that rejected rational order and yielded work that was more expressive, more personal.

For years, modernism had dominated graphic design. This new postmodern approach, which threw out the rule book and allowed for personal expression, brought new possibilities for communication and expression.

IVAN CHERMAYEFF AND TOM GEISMAR

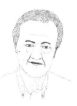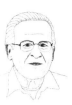

Ivan Chermayeff: 1932– | BORN: London, England | EDUCATION: Harvard University, the Institute of Design in Chicago, Yale University

Tom Geismar: 1931– | BORN: Glen Ridge, New Jersey | EDUCATION: Brown University, Rhode Island School of Design, Yale University

Design iconic logos and brand identities

Introduced abstract design in corporate identity in the United States

Design noteworthy exhibitions for major art and cultural institutions

In 1960, Chermayeff and Geismar proposed a radical idea: a corporate logo, for Chase Manhattan Bank, that was not based on letterforms or a recognizable image. Their design was simple—four wedges rotated around a square to form an octagon—but it met with resistance, because at that time no major American corporation had an abstract logo. And that's precisely why Chermayeff and Geismar's design worked; it stood out from the competition and became an identifying symbol inextricably associated with Chase. Soon, other corporations followed suit with abstract logos of their own.

But Chermayeff and Geismar haven't limited themselves to a particular style. For them, design is solving problems, and they pursue the best solution, regardless of form. They've designed more than 100 corporate identities, for clients such as NBC, PBS, Screen Gems, Barneys New York, Boston's MBTA, and Pan Am. They also create digital media and exhibitions, at venues like the well-known Ellis Island Immigration Museum and the John F. Kennedy Library. Their strength is in their ideas—and in their ability to sell those ideas.

Like Paul Rand, in the past they collaborated with architect Eliot Noyes on corporate identity work. As Noyes was designing modern service stations for Mobil Oil, Chermayeff and Geismar created a simple logo of geometric type to echo the circles and cylinders of the gas station designs. Thanks to a simple gesture—the setting of the "o" in red—the Mobil logo has remained iconic.

When asked about their influences, Tom Geismar said, "We spent a year together in the graduate graphic design department at Yale, at a time when even the term 'graphic design' was just coming into use. Among the visiting teachers were Lester Beall, Alexey Brodovitch, Leo Lionni, Alvin Lustig, and Herbert Matter. They are all rightful heroes to us, along with, and especially, Paul Rand, whose influence continues to evoke wonder."[14]

After graduating from Yale, Geismar designed exhibitions for the U.S. Army, and Chermayeff worked for Alvin Lustig. They opened their firm in 1958. Founding partner Robert Brownjohn left after two years, and Steff Geissbuhler was a partner from 1975 to 2005. More than 50 years after its start, the firm is still going strong; partner Sagi Haviv has joined the masthead, and the firm is now called Chermayeff & Geismar & Haviv. And they continue solving problems.

READ: *Identify*, by Ivan Chermayeff, Tom Geismar, and Sagi Haviv

OPPOSITE: Chase logo, 1961; Mobil logo, 1965; PBS logo

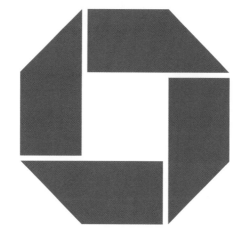

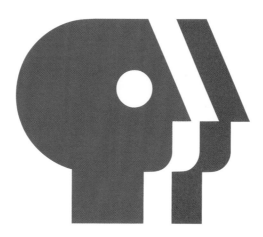

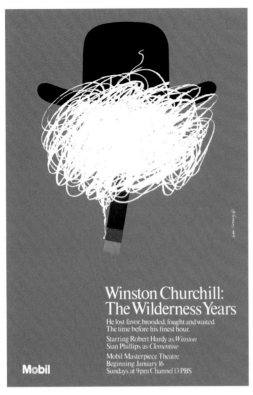

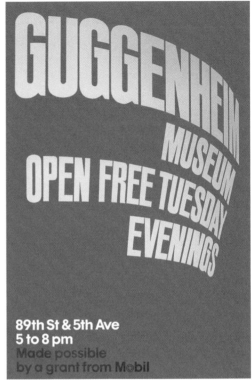

"There's a cleanliness and a simplicity to their work that just makes it look so easy, when in reality, consistently achieving consensus with a diverse range of clients is anything but."[15]

—David Airey

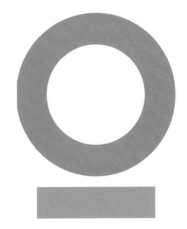

TOP, LEFT: Winston Churchill TV series poster, 1983

TOP, RIGHT: Guggenheim Museum poster, 1975

ABOVE: Conservation International logo, 2010

OPPOSITE: Signage for 9 West 57th Street, New York City, 1972

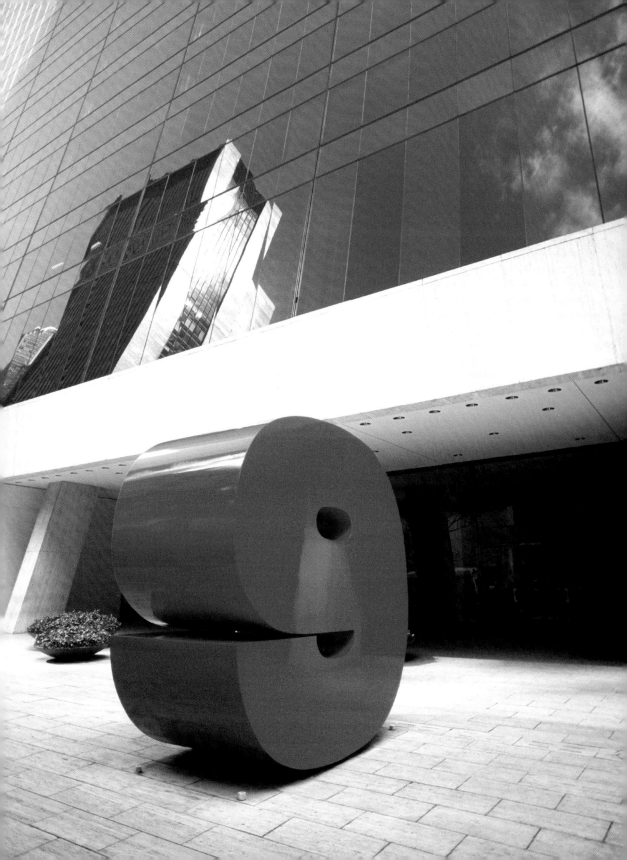

YUSAKU KAMEKURA

1915–1997 | BORN: Niigata Prefecture, Japan | EDUCATION: Institute of New Architecture and Industrial Arts, Tokyo

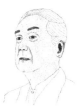

Combined European modernism with traditional Japanese aesthetics

Designed the first Olympics posters to use photography

Led and organized the Japanese graphic design profession

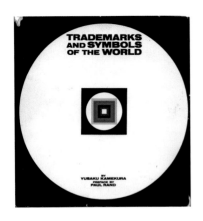

ABOVE: Book cover, 1965

OPPOSITE: Olympics poster, 1964

All eyes were on Japan during the summer of 1964. For the first time, the Olympics were to be held in an Asian country and broadcast in color. The people of Japan wanted to show the world that they had rebuilt after the devastation of World War II, that they were no longer the enemy, and that they were a force in the technology industry. Through the logo and dynamic posters he designed for the Games, Yusaku Kamekura showed the world that Japan was a force in the design world as well.

Kamekura studied the Bauhaus and Constructivism, and his work blended the functionality of these modern movements with the lyrical grace of traditional Japanese design. The result? A boldly minimal aesthetic that used color, light, geometry, and photography. He did more than design: His 1965 book, *Trademarks and Symbols of the World*, with a preface by Paul Rand, was a visual essay on the best logo designs. He was the editor of *Creation* magazine, which showcased design and art around the world. And, he apparently originated the phrase "corporate identity graphics."

Kamekura was a leader in Japanese design. He co-founded the Japanese Advertising Art Club, which raised the level of professionalism in Japanese design and helped creatives move beyond the country's traditional handmade approach. He was a founder and managing director of the Japan Design Center, connecting designers with corporate leaders.

His legacy lives on through the Yusaku Kamekura Design Award, presented annually to the *Graphic Design in Japan* competition award winner. He continues to represent design excellence not just in Japan, but also all over the world.

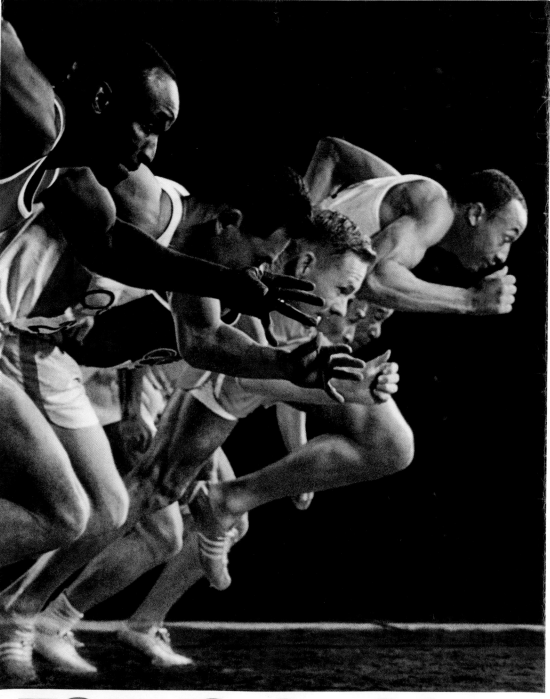

TOKYO ● 1964

Art Direction & Layout
Yusaku Kamekura
Photo Direction
Jo Murakoshi
Photograph
Osamu Hayasaki
Printed by
Toppan Printing Co. Ltd.
Japan

GET TO KNOW: Other influential designers from Japan include Masuda Tadashi, Tadanori Yokoo, Ikko Tanaka, Takenobu Igarashi, Shigeo Fukuda, and Koichi Sato.

READ: *White,* by Kenya Hara, a brief book about Japanese aesthetics, emptiness, purity, and simplicity.

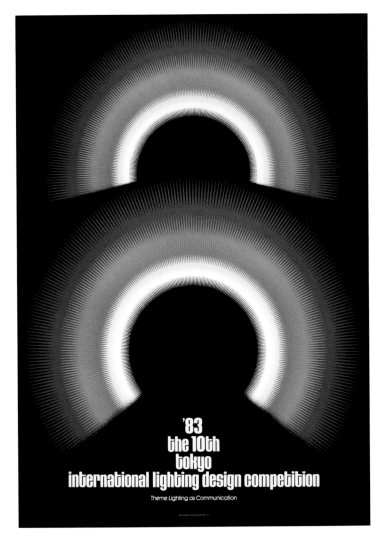

ABOVE AND OPPOSITE: Posters, 1983

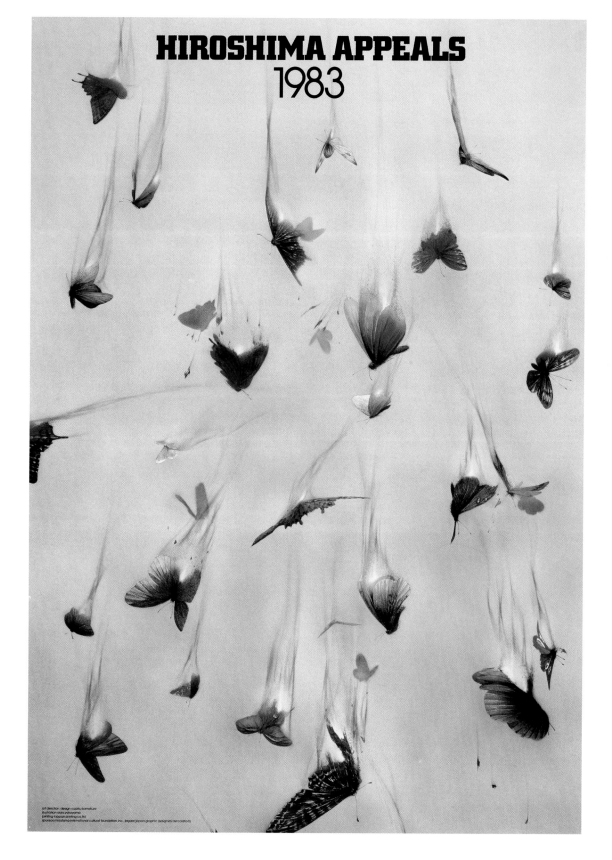

HIROSHIMA APPEALS
1983

art direction: design-yusaku kamekura
illustration-akira yokoyama
printing-toppan printing co.,ltd.
sponsors-hiroshima international cultural foundation, inc., jagda (japan graphic designers association)

U&lc.

Aa Bb Cc Dd Ee Ff Gg Hh Ii Jj Kk Ll Mm Nn Oo Pp   Qq Rr Ss Tt Uu Vv Ww Xx Yy Zz 1234567890 & Æ Œ $ ¢ £ % !? ( ) [ ]

UPPER AND LOWER CASE, THE INTERNATIONAL JOURNAL OF TYPOGRAPHICS   PUBLISHED BY INTERNATIONAL TYPEFACE CORPORATION, VOLUME FIVE, NUMBER ONE, MARCH 1978

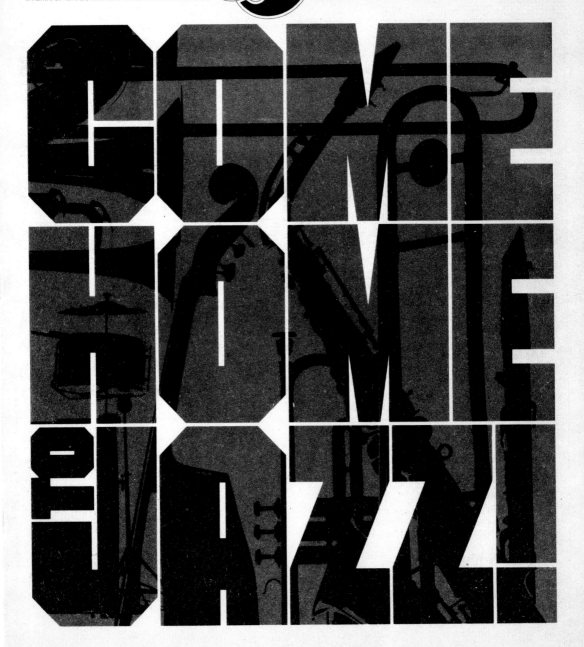

HERB LUBALIN

1918–1981 | BORN: Brooklyn, New York | EDUCATION: The Cooper Union

Mastered expressive typography and type as image

Rejected rational modernism

Established an influential type foundry

Although he is celebrated for his lively type, Herb Lubalin didn't consider himself a typographer; the term felt too mechanical. Instead, he said, he designed with letters. He rejected the rules of traditional typography and the rigors of modernism to create type that was more expressive. He manipulated letterforms, incorporated flourishes, and added a dose of humor. Type became more than a medium for setting text; type became image.

Changes in technology helped. Phototypesetting, a process of projecting type onto film for printing, gave designers in the 1960s much more freedom than setting metal type. This enabled Lubalin to experiment with big changes in scale and unusual letterspacing. He co-founded International Typeface Corporation (ITC) in 1970 to produce typefaces for the new technology, and sought to compensate type designers fairly with royalties and copyright protection. To promote ITC's products, Lubalin edited and designed the journal *U&lc*, which became a respected source for inspiration and information.

Lubalin began his career in advertising, spending 20 years at the agency Sudler & Hennessey, Inc. He established his own studio in 1964 and worked with different partners over the years. Throughout the 1960s, Lubalin collaborated with publisher Ralph Ginzburg on three progressive magazines that reflected the changing sexual and political culture of the era: *Eros*, *Fact*, and *Avant Garde* (whose logo later became a typeface). Accordingly, Lubalin's designs were looser and more experimental than traditional periodicals.

Lubalin died in 1981, but there has been a renewed interest in his work as designers move beyond simple and clean in a search for new means of expression.

LEFT: Preparation H ad

OPPOSITE: *U&lc* magazine cover, 1978

LICK HEMORRHOIDS WITH PREPARATION H

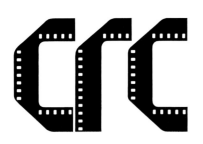

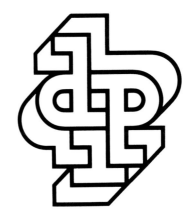

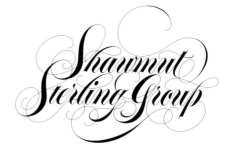

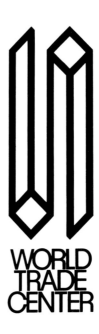

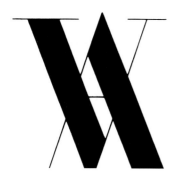

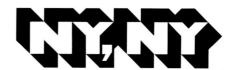

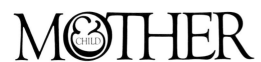

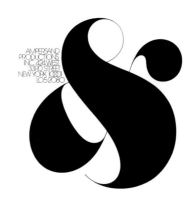

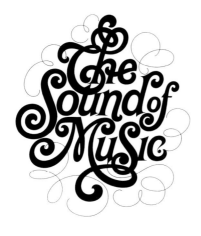

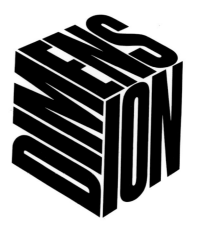

ABOVE AND OPPOSITE: Logos

fact

JANUARY-FEBRUARY 1964   VOLUME ONE, ISSUE ONE • $1.25

Bertrand Russell considers *Time* magazine to be "scurrilous and utterly shameless in its willingness to distort." **Ralph Ingersoll:** "In ethics, integrity, and responsibility, *Time* is a monumental failure." **Irwin Shaw:** *Time* is "nastier than any other magazine of the day." **Sloan Wilson:** "Any enemy of *Time* is a friend of mine." **Igor Stravinsky:** "Every music column I have read in *Time* has been distorted and inaccurate." **Tallulah Bankhead:** "Dirt is too clean a word for *Time*." **Mary McCarthy:** "*Time*'s falsifications are numerous." **Dwight Macdonald:** "The degree of credence one gives to *Time* is inverse to one's degree of knowledge of the situation being reported on." **David Merrick:** "There is not a single word of truth in *Time*." **P. G. Wodehouse:** "*Time* is about the most inaccurate magazine in existence." **Rockwell Kent:** *Time* "is inclined to value smartness above truth." **Eugene Burdick:** *Time* employs "dishonest tactics." **Conrad Aiken:** "*Time* slants its news." **Howard Fast:** *Time* provides "distortions and inaccuracies by the bushel." **James Gould Cozzens:** "My knowledge of inaccuracies in *Time* is first-hand." **Walter Winchell:** "*Time*'s inaccuracies are a staple of my column." **John Osborne:** "*Time* is a vicious, dehumanizing institution." **Eric Bentley:** "More pervasive than *Time*'s outright errors is its misuse of truth." **Vincent Price:** "Fortunately, most people read *Time* for laughs and not for facts." **H. Allen Smith:** "*Time*'s inaccuracies are as numerous as the sands of the Sahara." **Taylor Caldwell:** "I could write a whole book about *Time* inaccuracies." **Sen. John McClellan:** "*Time* is prejudiced and unfair."

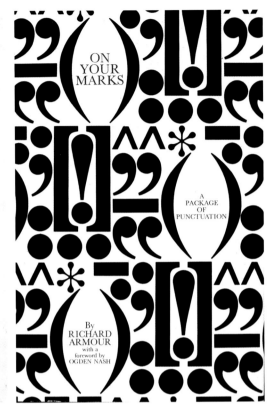

READ: *New Ornamental Type: Decorative Lettering in the Digital Age,* by Steven Heller and Gail Anderson, to see more recent examples of expressive typography.

SEE: The Herb Lubalin Study Center of Design and Typography, at the Cooper Union in New York, collects Lubalin's work, including sketches, drafts, and finished pieces. It's free and open to the public by appointment. Online, see lubalincenter.cooper.edu

---

ABOVE, LEFT: *Fact* magazine cover, 1964

ABOVE, RIGHT: Cover for book on punctuation, 1969

OPPOSITE: Avant Garde type specimen poster

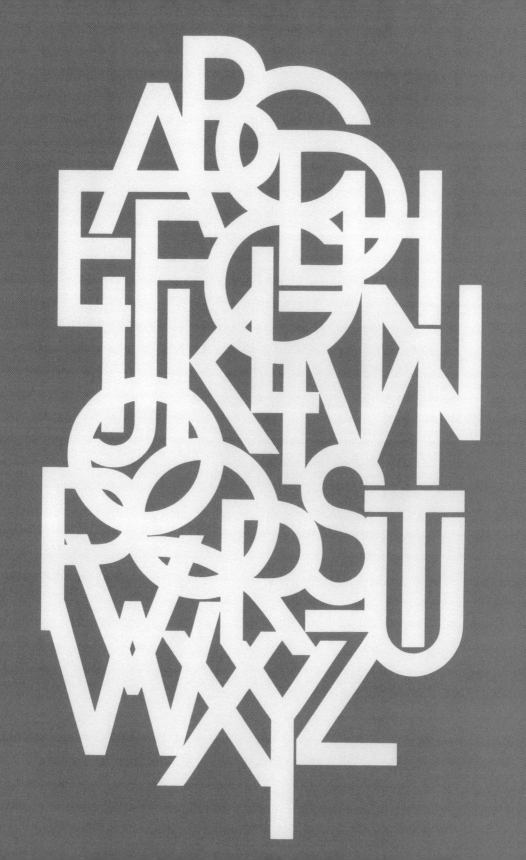

GASTROTYPOGRAPHICALASSEMBLAGE

When CBS moved into its new headquarters in 1965, the company's vice president and creative director, Lou Dorfsman, proposed a typographic solution to decorating a 33-foot wall in the cafeteria: cover the wall with food-related words, rendered in 3D in different typefaces. Herb Lubalin and Tom Carnase created the custom type for more than 1,400 hand-milled wood letters, which were painted white and displayed both horizontally and vertically.

In the 1990s, CBS dumped the wall during a redesign, and it was saved and stored by designer Nick Fasciano. Atlanta nonprofit The Center for Design Study, led by Rick Anwyl, acquired it and spent years restoring the panels to their former glory. In 2014 it will go on permanent display at The Culinary Institute of America, in Hyde Park, New York.

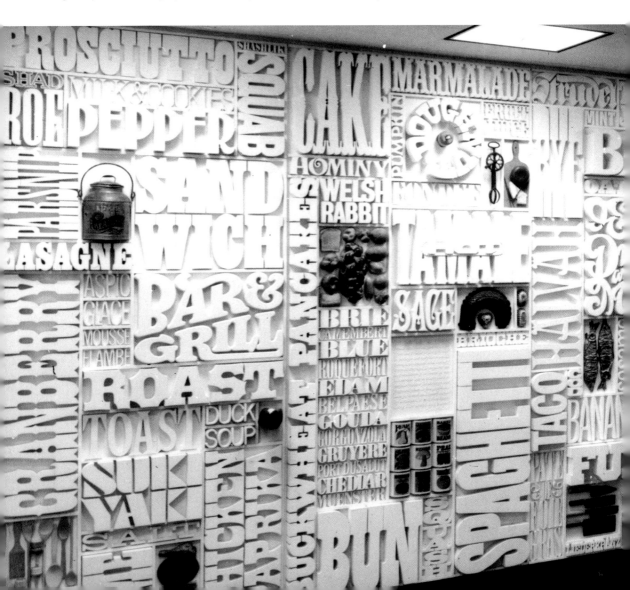

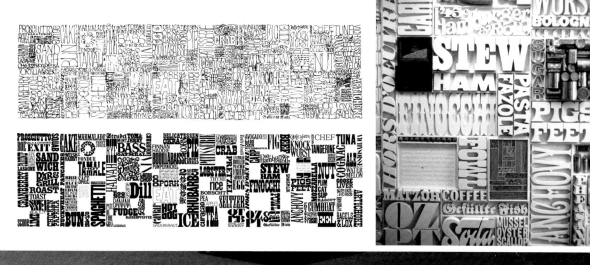

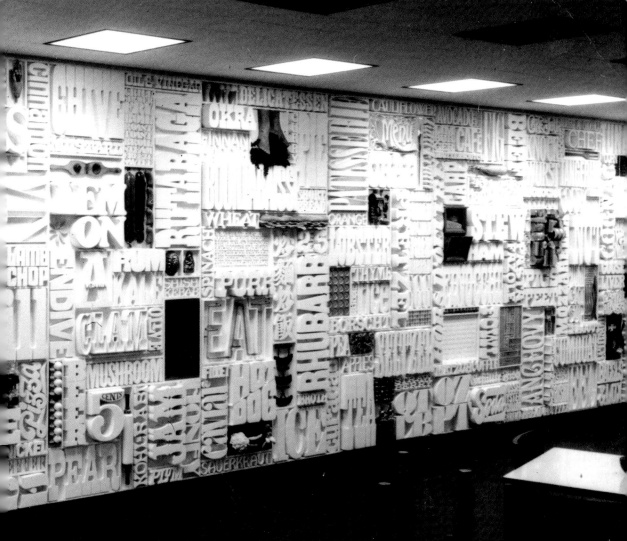

SEYMOUR CHWAST

1931– | BORN: Bronx, New York | EDUCATION: The Cooper Union

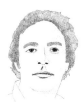

Combines illustration and design

Incorporates historic styles

Co-founded Push Pin Studios

Inspired by comic books, Victorian type, and Walt Disney, Seymour Chwast merged illustration and design in a big departure from modernism. He revived historic styles and blended them in a fresh way, creating fun and expressive visuals.

To attract clients for freelance projects at the beginning of their careers, Chwast and his Cooper Union friends Edward Sorel, Reynold Ruffins, and Milton Glaser published the *Push Pin Almanack*, an ambitious recurring promotional piece that focused on a different theme with each issue. More important than exhibiting their drawing skills, it showed the importance of ideas in design and illustration. It was so successful that Chwast, Glaser, and Sorel went into business together full-time, forming Push Pin Studios in 1954. Ruffins joined a year later; both he and Sorel had left by 1960.

The studio became well known for its eclectic and playful posters, ads, and covers for books, records, and magazines. The *Almanack* became the *Push Pin Graphic*, and its themes ranged from social and political issues to popular culture. When Glaser left the studio in 1974, Chwast carried on, renaming it Pushpin Group in 1981, and continued to collaborate with other designers and illustrators. He also branched out into publishing to create the kind of playful books that he liked, for both children and adults.

Recently, Chwast transformed classic literature like Dante's *Inferno* and *The Canterbury Tales* into graphic novels. His sense of design still comes into play: He doesn't just draw scenes, but works at pacing and surprise. When asked what keeps him working after all these years, he replies, "I like to draw."[16]

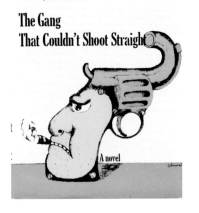

Jimmy Breslin

The Gang
That Couldn't Shoot Straight

A novel

ABOVE: Book cover, 1969

OPPOSITE: Antiwar poster, 1967

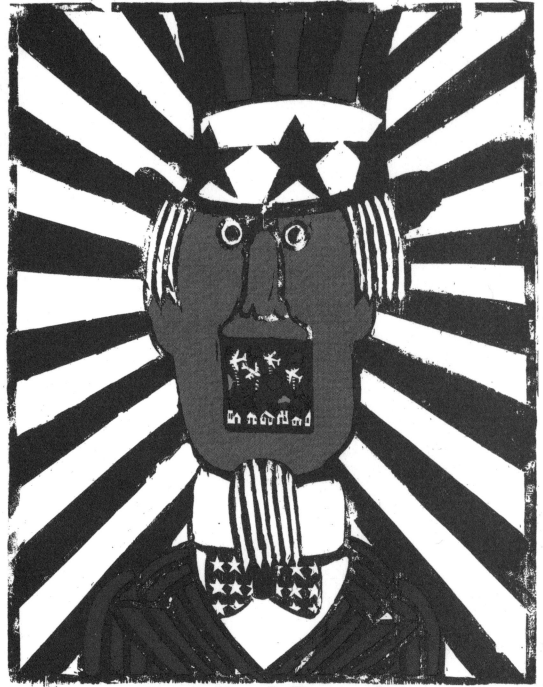

End Bad Breath.

READ: *Seymour: The Obsessive Images of Seymour Chwast,* by Seymour Chwast

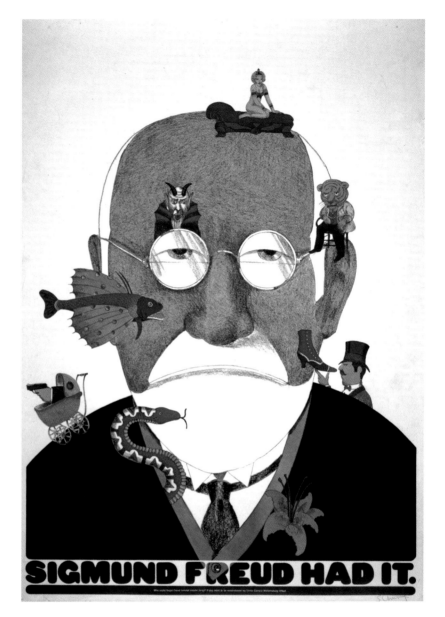

ABOVE: Poster

OPPOSITE: Book cover, 1969

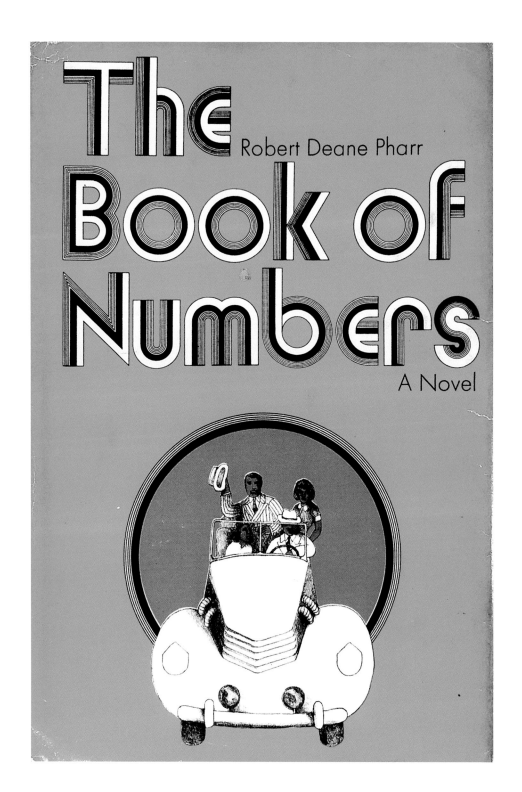

The Book of Numbers

Robert Deane Pharr

A Novel

MILTON GLASER

1929– | BORN: New York, New York | EDUCATION: The Cooper Union, New York, and the Academy of Fine Arts, Bologna, Italy

Blended historic styles to move past modernism

Designs iconic logos, posters, magazines, and restaurants

Influences others through writing and teaching

Studying under painter Giorgio Morandi in Italy transformed Milton Glaser's views on design. He learned to respect the past and to draw inspiration from ideas and movements that actually came *before* the Bauhaus. Glaser had nothing against modernism; he just felt it had run its course for innovation and expression. Instead, he embraced historical styles, ornament, and complexity.

Upon his return to the United States, Glaser teamed with Seymour Chwast, Reynold Ruffins, and Edward Sorel to form Push Pin Studios, the influential collaborative famous for its eclectic illustration and storytelling. For Glaser, Push Pin was fun—a place where the Cooper Union alumni could re-create their school experience. In 1974, Glaser left to start his own studio, as he felt Push Pin was so well known that it had become a style in itself, limiting his creative potential.

In 1966, Glaser designed a poster that was included with Bob Dylan's *Greatest Hits* album: a simple silhouette of the singer/songwriter's profile, inspired by a Marcel Duchamp self-portrait, brought to life with a rainbow of curls and a custom typeface. The album sold millions of copies, making the poster one of the most widely distributed in history (though Dylan himself apparently never liked it).

The 1970s brought financial crisis and high crime rates to New York. The state wanted to attract tourists and raise morale among residents. Glaser designed the simple I (Heart) NY logo, by now so familiar that it feels like it has always existed, pro bono. (Although he didn't make money from it, someone did and still is—it would have cost a ridiculous amount to publish it in these pages.) As someone who believes in being active in his community, Glaser has said he is proud to be part of a movement that transformed the city and state that he calls home.

One of Glaser's many strengths is his versatility. He founded *New York* Magazine with journalist Clay Felker in 1968, art directing it for nine years. It became the blueprint for city magazines all over the country. To make a federal building in Indianapolis more inviting, Glaser designed *Color Fuses*, a mural wrapping around the building that explores the interaction of light and color. His love of food led to graphic and interior design projects for several restaurants, including Windows on the World at the World Trade Center. He has also designed packaging and store environments for supermarkets, like Grand Union, making product information clearer and helping people better navigate through the store.

His teaching and writing have contributed greatly to the field. He still works today, and credits his longevity to his love for design and his ability to feel what Alexey Brodovitch always wanted: He can still be astonished.

OPPOSITE: Bob Dylan poster, 1966

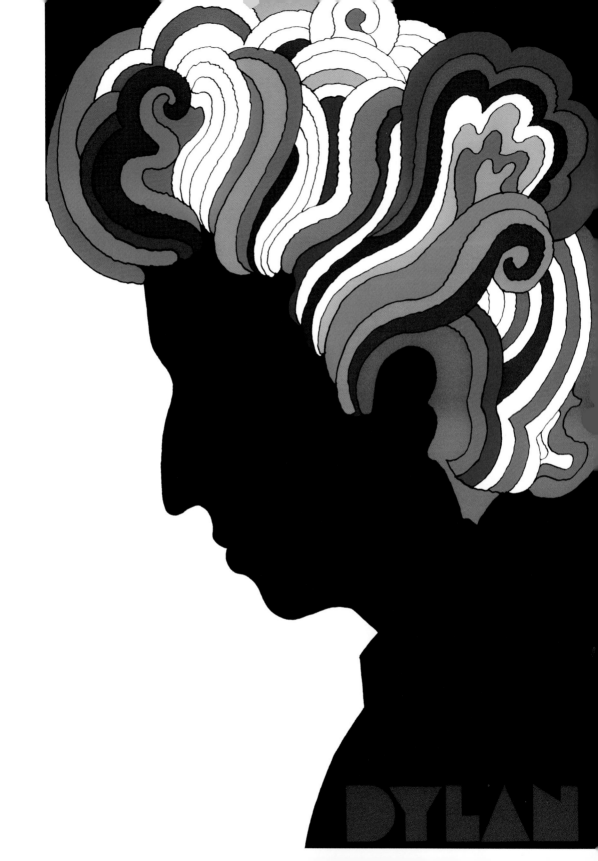

"Less is not necessarily more.
Just enough is more."[17]

—Milton Glaser

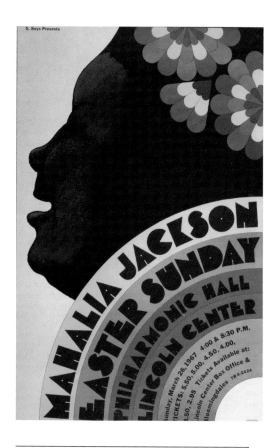

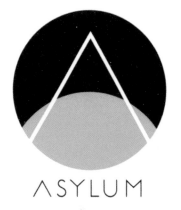

READ: *Milton Glaser: Graphic Design* and *Art is Work*, two career overviews published 25 years apart

WATCH: *Milton Glaser: To Inform and Delight*, a documentary on Glaser's career and everyday life

SEE: Milton Glaser Design Study Center and Archives, at 380 Second Avenue in New York City, preserves the work of Glaser and other designers affiliated with the School of Visual Arts, and is accessible to researchers and designers by appointment. Online, go to Glaserarchives.org

ABOVE: Mahalia Jackson poster, 1967

ABOVE, RIGHT: Identity for Asylum Records, 1983

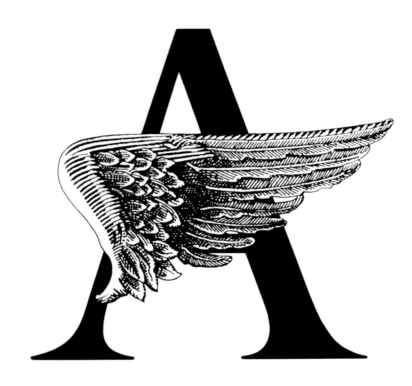

ABOVE: Logo for the play
Angels in America, 1993

OPPOSITE: School of Visual
Arts poster, 1996

Art is...

WHATEVER

 Note To the Viewer:

I thought I might use a visual cliché of our
time, Magritte's Everyman, to express the
idea that Art has mystery, continuity and
history. I am also convinced that in an era
of computer manipulation surrealism has
become banal, a shadow of its former self.
The phrase "Art is whatever" expresses
the current inclusiveness that surrounds art
making; a sort of "it ain't what you do, it's
the way that you do it" notion. The shadow
of Magritte's man falls across the central
part of the poster, a poetic event that occurs
as the shadow man isolates the word "hat"
hidden in the word "whatever". The four
hats shown in the poster suggest how Art
might be defined: as the thing itself, the
word for the thing, the shadow of the thing
and the shape of the thing . . . . Whatever.

Milton Glaser

 School of VISUAL ARTS

SVA

**APRIL 1968
PRICE $1**

Esquire

THE MAGAZINE FOR MEN

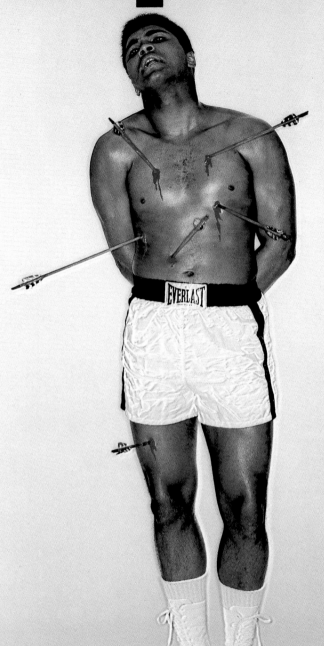

The Passion of Muhammad Ali

GEORGE LOIS

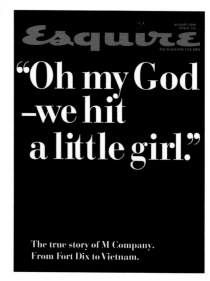

1931– | BORN: Bronx, New York | EDUCATION: Pratt Institute

Designed iconic and controversial magazine covers
Developed advertising campaigns for top brands

"I'm not a designer. I'm a communicator."[18] George Lois has communicated for many brands, like MTV, Stouffer's Lean Cuisine, Aunt Jemima, and Jiffy Lube. He's an advertising man.

Lois's advertising work caught the eye of *Esquire* magazine editor Harold Hayes in 1962, a period of major change around the world. *Esquire* featured great writers, like Truman Capote, Gay Talese, and Tom Wolfe, covering politics, racism, and popular culture. *Esquire's* covers weren't as strong as its content; they were designed by committee and looked like every other magazine. Lois knew that the package had to be as least as good as what was inside. Although he was busy running his own ad agency, Papert Koenig Lois, he was willing to take on the cover design job, as long as he could do it his way.

Lois's goal was to create covers so compelling they would stop people on the street and make them buy the magazine. The first cover he designed—featuring the African American boxer Sonny Liston as Santa Claus—sparked controversy. In the early stages of the Vietnam War, people in the United States were not yet aware of the war's brutality and problems. Based on an interview in the magazine, Lois designed a cover that needed no image, just a quote from a horrified U.S. soldier when he saw the aftermath of an attack: "Oh my God—we hit a little girl." It was a big wake-up call to the nation, and protests followed soon, as people learned more about the war. When heavyweight champion boxer Muhammad Ali refused to join the army on religious grounds (he had recently converted to Islam), Lois posed him as the Christian martyr St. Sebastian, known for surviving an attempted execution by arrows. Lois designed 92 covers for Esquire that captured the era's changing times—many of which angered advertisers and subscribers.

Lois continues in advertising, always pursuing what he calls the "Big Idea." He believes a million dollars can become 10 million if an idea cuts through the clutter and reaches people. He developed the "I want my MTV" campaign, even convincing Mick Jagger to appear in an ad for free. He has authored several books, including *Damn Good Advice (For People with Talent!): How to Unleash Your Creative Potential by America's Master Communicator*. When asked for tips for young designers, he said, "My advice is to read *Damn Good Advice* and then read it again, and again, just as I read *Thoughts on Design* by Paul Rand when I was 14 years old."[19]

ABOVE AND OPPOSITE: *Esquire* covers, 1968 and 1966

READ: *George Lois: On His Creation of the Big Idea*, by George Lois

DO: Pick up a copy of your favorite magazine, select a memorable or emphatic quote from one of the articles, and create a compelling cover using just those words.

WIM CROUWEL

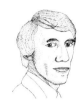

1928– | BORN: Groningen, The Netherlands | EDUCATION: Minerva Academy, Groningen

Designed radical typeface for computer use

Co-founded influential multidisciplinary design studio

Developed grid system for museum communications

The Netherlands is a small country, but it's had a big impact on design. Wim Crouwel's typographic work is a good example of Dutch design at its best: clean and functional, like the work of his forefather Theo van Doesburg—yet progressive and surprising.

In the 1960s, Dutch graphic designers usually worked solo, and companies with large projects hired firms outside the country. In order to attract those large projects, Crouwel and four partners, with a range of experience in graphic and industrial design, formed Total Design. It was the country's first multidisciplinary studio, where teams handled complex two- and three-dimensional projects. Private corporations, government agencies, and arts organizations hired Total, and their designs for postage stamps, airport signage, and museum posters made a distinct mark on the country's visual culture.

Crouwel had an uncanny sense of how computers would influence design and vice versa, and he created a groundbreaking typeface to work with this emerging technology. At the time, dot-matrix printers and computer screens couldn't reproduce traditional type with curved letterforms. Starting with the Swiss typographic grid, Crouwel based letters on the rectangle, using only vertical, horizontal, and diagonal lines. The result was 1967's New Alphabet, so radical in appearance that it was almost abstract. It was never meant to be used; it was just an experiment. Crouwel must have been surprised to see the New Alphabet used on the cover that Peter Saville designed for New Order's *Substance* album 20 years later.

Still, that concept influenced his future work, like his poster for *Vormgevers* (Designers), for which he hand-rendered the lettering based on squares in a visible grid. Crouwel developed a system for Amsterdam's Stedelijk Museum where each piece—posters, brochures, advertisements—used the same grid. Although these pieces promoted art exhibits, they never depicted the art itself. The type-centric design and common grid unified the museum's communications, yet the system was flexible enough to remain fresh and interesting.

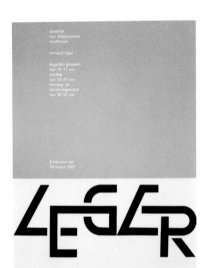

ABOVE: Leger poster, 1957

OPPOSITE: New alphabet, 1967

Hans Rudi Erdt, A. M. Cassandre, and especially Josef Müller-Brockmann are big influences on Crouwel's work, and in turn, Crouwel remains a prevalent figure in the design world—in 2013, he was celebrated with a retrospective at London's Design Museum. Crouwel inspires young designers, including Philippe Apeloig and Spin, who created a series of posters based on the grid he developed for the Stedelijk Museum.

neu alphabet

a	een	une	eine
possibility	nodelijkheid	possibilité	nodlichteit
for	voor	pour	für
the	de	le	die
new	nieuwe	développement	neue
development	ontwikkeling	nouveau	entwicklung

an
introduction
for
a
prodrugged
typography

augustus

2	3	4	5	6	7	1
9	10	11	12	13	14	8
16	17	18	19	20	21	15
23	24	25	26	27	28	22
30	31					29

zondag / maandag / dinsdag / woensdag / donderdag / vrijdag / zaterdag

---

READ: *Dutch Graphic Design: A Century*, by Kees Broos and Paul Hefting

GET TO KNOW: Additional influential Dutch designers include H.N. Werkman, Piet Zwart, Gert Dumbar, Jan van Toorn, Irma Boom, and Experimental Jetset.

ABOVE: Calendar, 1964

OPPOSITE: Stedelijk Museum poster, 1968

stedelijk museum amsterdam
5 april t/m 23 juni 1968

vorm
gevers

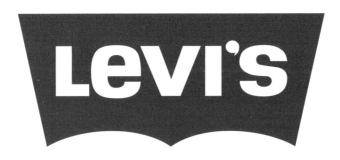

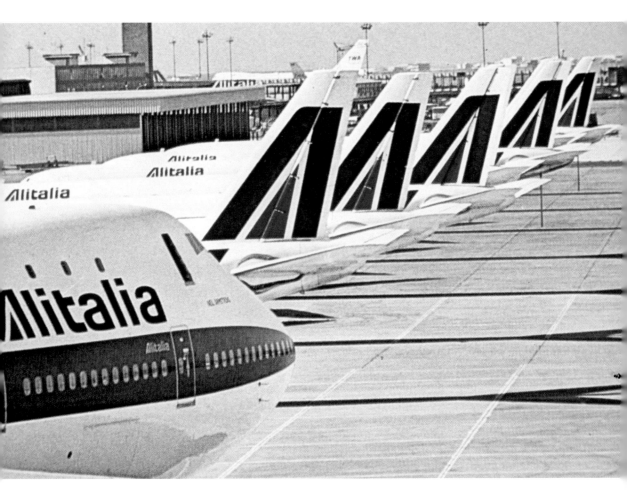

WALTER LANDOR

1913–1995 | BORN: Munich, Germany | EDUCATION: Goldsmith College School of Art at London University

Pioneered design based on consumer research

Built one of the world's largest brand design agencies

Walter Landor believed in designing for the consumer, not for award shows or for his peers. He constantly sought ways to better understand his audience, by testing package designs right on grocery-store shelves and asking shoppers directly for their opinions. He based design decisions on these early forms of consumer research—and built one of the world's most successful branding agencies as a result.

Landor was an industrial designer in London who came to New York in 1939 to attend the World's Fair. He traveled to San Francisco and fell in love with the city, and stayed there to teach at California College of Arts and Crafts (now California College of the Arts), where he fell in love with his student and future wife, Josephine. She was his only associate when he started his firm in their small apartment.

The agency grew, and in 1964 moved to the *Klamath*, a ferryboat docked at San Francisco's Pier 5. That creative use of space enhanced the firm's reputation and provided it with room to grow into large corporate identity projects. It also accommodated a photo studio and mock store for market research. (The *Klamath* also hosted many Friday night parties for designers and media types, along with occasional guests like Andy Warhol and members of the Grateful Dead.)

Landor didn't think of design as art. It was communication. The days of store clerks recommending products had passed—he knew that the package itself must send the message through strong shelf impact. Seeking emotional connections between brands and consumers, Landor preferred warmer, more accessible designs over the cooler Swiss modernism that was popular at the time.

Brands as diverse as Levi's, Coca-Cola, Bank of America, Alitalia, and the World Wildlife Fund benefited from Walter Landor's expertise. Young & Rubicam bought Landor Associates in 1989, but the founder's legacy of research and strategy lives on.

READ: *A Designer's Research Manual: Succeed in Design by Knowing Your Clients and What They Really Need*, by Jenn and Ken Visocky O'Grady; *Packaging Essentials: 100 Design Principles for Creating Packages*, by Sara Roncarelli and Candace Ellicott

GET TO KNOW: Other big brand design and strategy agencies include Lippincott, Wolff Olins, Siegel + Gale, Interbrand, Sterling Brands, and FutureBrand.

Landor Associates continues without its founder, and still designs iconic brands. In 1994, designer Lindon Leader transformed Federal Express into FedEx, a nickname and verb customers had already been informally using. The logo appears to be simply typographic, but the negative space between the "E" and "x" forms a subtle arrow—a great way to imply speed and motion without being too obvious.

OPPOSITE: Levi's logo, 1968

Alitalia identity, 1969

OTL AICHER

1922–1991 | BORN: Ulm, Germany | EDUCATION: Academy of Fine Arts, Munich

Designed grid-based pictograms

Co-founded influential design school

"Otl Aicher's work is part of my childhood memories. While for most people it must look cold, geometrical, stark, that's not the case for me. His work comes with romantic overtones, which makes it so special to me."[20]

—Jan Wilker,
karlssonwilker inc.

DOWNLOAD: Fifty transport pictograms to communicate information, such as departing flights, baggage claim, and restrooms, developed by AIGA and the U.S. Department of Transportation, are free to use: aiga.org/symbol-signs.

OPPOSITE: Munich Olympics pictograms, 1972

Systems were crucial in the work of Otl Aicher. He designed comprehensive identity systems for companies such as Lufthansa German Airlines, Braun, and chemical company BASF. He developed an integrated design education system, and created a system of simplified pictograms that became an international visual language that's still used today.

In 1936, the Olympics were held in Berlin, Germany. Hitler was gaining power, and saw the games as an opportunity for Nazi propaganda. When the Olympics returned to Germany in 1972, organizers hoped to move past the "Nazi Olympics" and show the world a bright and happy face.

Otl Aicher and his design team developed colorful posters and a logo based on the sun. To transcend language barriers among the international audience, Aicher relied on visuals rather than text as much as possible. He developed a system of pictograms to identify the different sports and to provide general wayfinding information. He reduced the human image to the simplest of geometric forms, yet kept it recognizable. Aicher wasn't the first to design pictograms for the Olympics. But he was the first to base each one on a grid, establishing a unity of form lacking in earlier, more illustrative versions. Unfortunately, the Munich Games were not happy: Eleven Israeli athletes were killed by members of Black September, a Palestinian terrorist group.

With Swiss designer Max Bill, Aicher co-founded and taught at the Ulm School of Design (Hochschule für Gestaltung) in Ulm, Germany in 1953. The curriculum was based on the Bauhaus, but it expanded to include science and semiotics, the study of signs and symbols. Aicher didn't just want to train successful designers, he wanted to educate responsible citizens who would change the world through their work. Over time, Aicher's designs, including posters to promote events and lectures at the school, became more abstract, focusing on color, pattern, and geometry.

Inspired by the development of phototypesetting, Aicher designed two typefaces, including Rotis, which bridged serif and sans serif fonts. He named this type family, which includes semi sans and semi serif styles, after the town where he lived and worked.

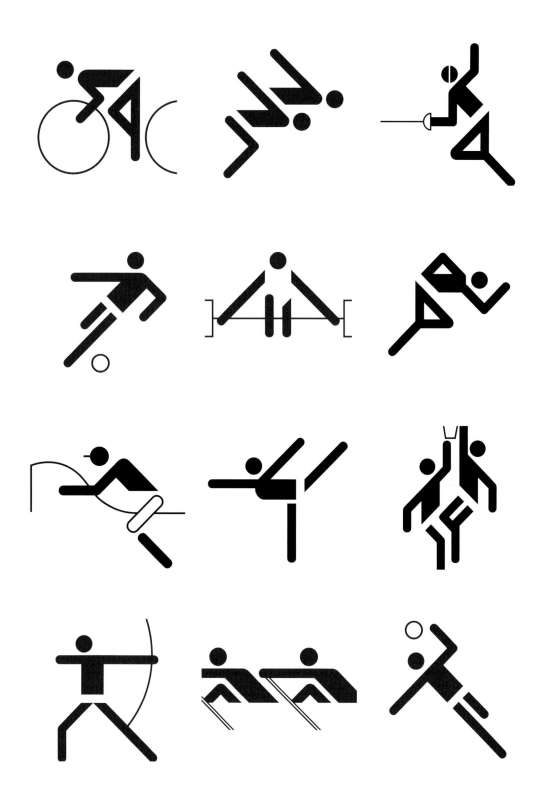

MICHAEL VANDERBYL

1947– | BORN: Oakland, California | EDUCATION: California College of Arts and Crafts (later California College of the Arts)

Expanded graphic design into multiple disciplines

Helped establish San Francisco as a design hub

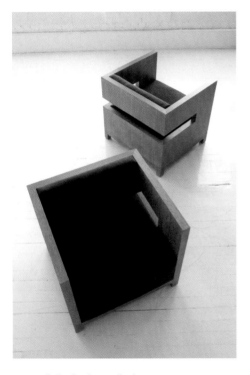

ABOVE: Bolier furniture collection

OPPOSITE: Poster, 1979

Graphic design isn't all that Michael Vanderbyl does—he also designs furniture, showrooms, and products—but graphic design *informs* everything he does. He proves that if you can design, you can design anything.

Vanderbyl started his design firm in San Francisco in 1973. His early graphic design work combined simple typography with playful postmodern elements like pastel palettes, diagonals, textures, and patterns. Design rode a wave of prominence in San Francisco in the 1980s, and Vanderbyl was an energizing force behind it.

His 1979 poster for California Public Radio is a perfect example, with its clean horizontal lines, symbolic geometric shapes enhancing a silhouette of a face, and a repeating scribble representing radio waves. The design was simple, yet warm and expressive.

Vanderbyl was always intrigued by three-dimensional work (even though he was once told he wasn't smart enough to be an architect). When one of his major clients didn't have the budget to hire an architect, Vanderbyl stepped in to design a product showroom. His graphic-design background led the way, as he looked at the project like a life-size brochure, with an emphasis not on the space, but on the products. Vanderbyl's product-oriented solution stood out, and he gained more work designing showrooms.

Vanderbyl is now Dean of Design at his alma mater, California College of the Arts. He encourages his students to really listen to the problem at hand, which will guide them to an appropriate solution. He is also a fan of self-doubt, as it means one is still learning as a designer.

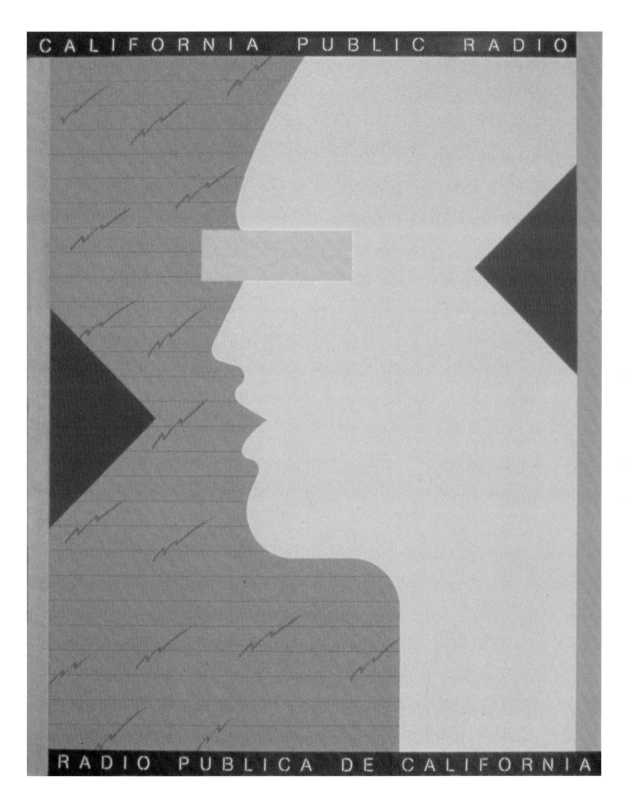

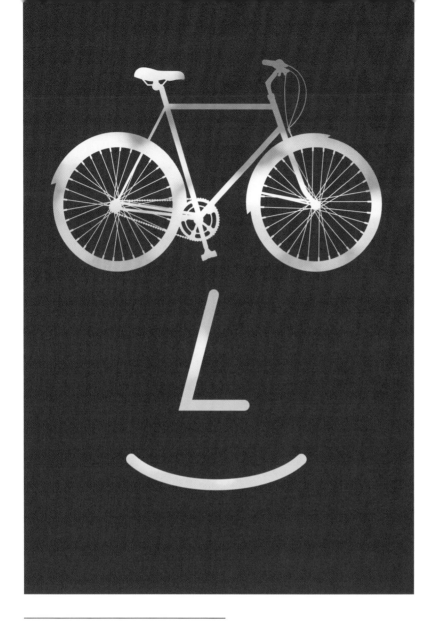

GET TO KNOW: "The Michaels"—San Francisco designers who gained prominence in the 1980s and '90s and share a first name: Cronan, Mabry, Manwaring, and Schwab

ABOVE: Poster for an organization that advocates reclaiming public spaces for bicycles, 2013

OPPOSITE: Teknion showrooms in Montreal and Chicago

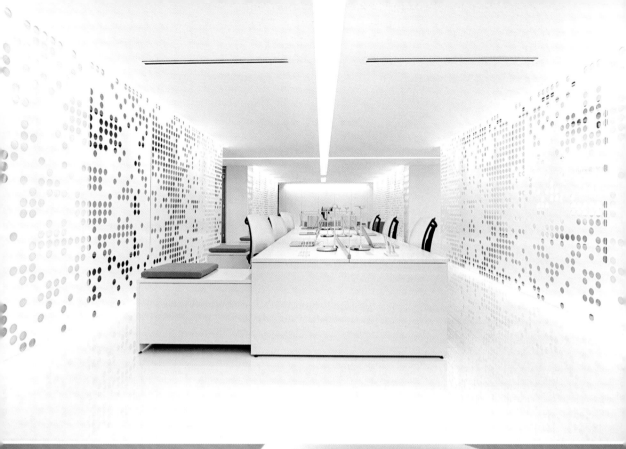

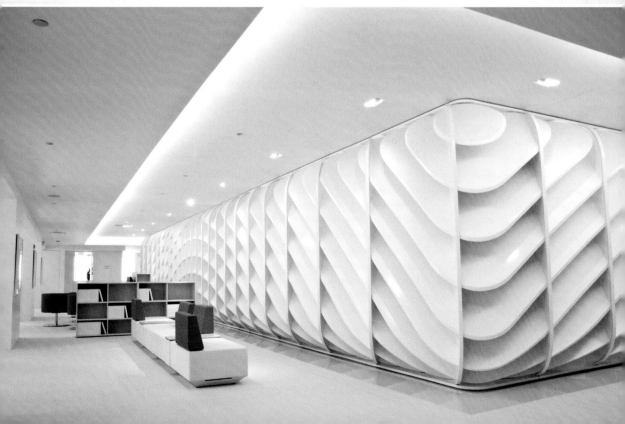

PETER SAVILLE

1955– | BORN: London, England | EDUCATION: St. Ambrose College, Manchester Polytechnic (later Manchester Metropolitan University)

Designed influential album covers

Focused on conceptual imagery to make an emotional connection between bands and their fans

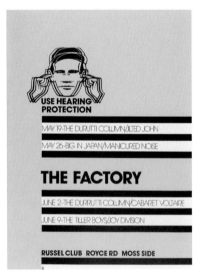

ABOVE: Poster, 1978

OPPOSITE: New Order's *Power, Corruption & Lies* album cover, 1983

While punk and disco dominated the 1970s music scene, Peter Saville was listening to experimental and electronic bands, like Roxy Music and Kraftwerk. So it's not surprising that this British designer deployed his talents in the music world.

In 1978, British journalist Tony Wilson hired Saville to design a poster promoting his Manchester music club, The Factory. An anarchic punk-rock aesthetic dominated gig posters and album covers at the time, but Saville was instead influenced by early-modern typographers like Jan Tschichold and Herbert Bayer; his first poster for The Factory, based on an industrial warning sign, is ordered and simple.

Wilson and Saville co-founded Factory Records, an independent label where freedom (in both the music and the design) ruled. As art director working with bands like Joy Division, Saville was able to design without creative, budgetary, or time constraints (a situation that probably doesn't exist anywhere today). In 1979, he moved to London and worked for DinDisc, where he enjoyed the same artistic liberty. There, he met future business partner Brendan Wickes and photographer Trevor Key, who challenged Saville to use new techniques in photography and printing.

By the early '80s, Saville had moved beyond his early modern influences and into classical and historic references. His 1983 album cover for New Order's *Power, Corruption & Lies* featured a painting of roses by artist Henri Fantin-Latour juxtaposed with a grid of colored squares representing the band's name and album title (a decoder on the back of the jacket revealed the meaning). It was much more evocative than a portrait of the band and connected with listeners in a deeper way. Just as fashion allows like-minded people to connect with each other by dressing in a certain way, Saville's designs drew music fans together with the bands they love.

Saville went on to design album covers for mainstream acts, such as Wham! and Peter Gabriel, before briefly becoming a partner at Pentagram Design and working with ad agency Frankfurt Balkind. He continues to work for clients like Whitechapel Art Gallery, fashion designer Stella McCartney, and the city of Manchester, as well as to design his personal art projects.

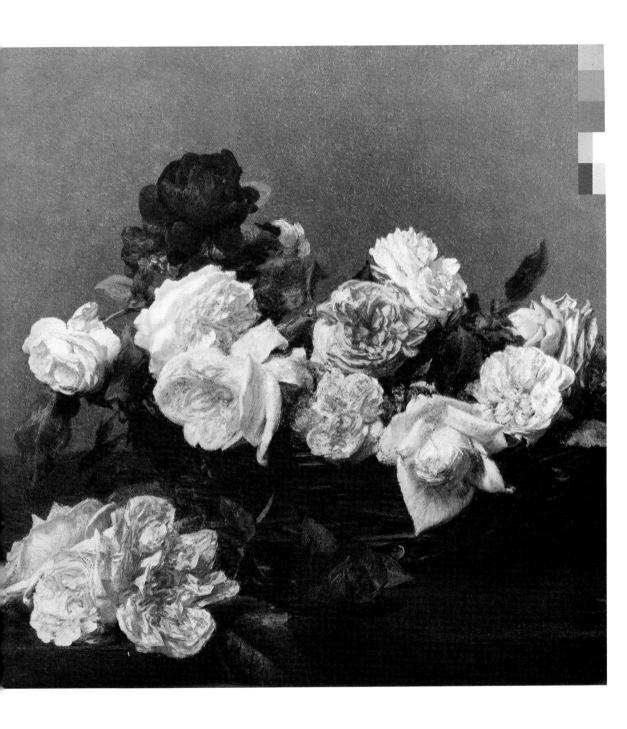

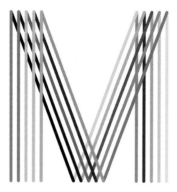

WATCH: *24 Hour Party People*, a
2002 comedic docudrama with an
entertaining take on the Factory
Records story and the Manchester,
England, music scene.

ABOVE: City of Manchester identity, 2005

RIGHT: Joy Division's *Unknown Pleasures*
album cover, 1979

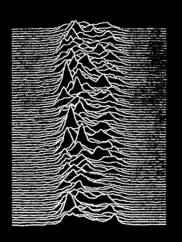

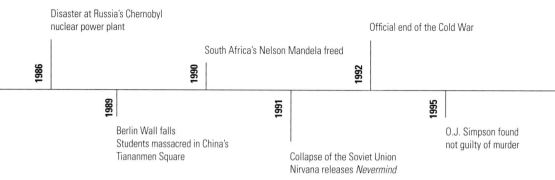

Disaster at Russia's Chernobyl nuclear power plant

Official end of the Cold War

South Africa's Nelson Mandela freed

1986 **1990** **1992**

1989 **1991** **1995**

Berlin Wall falls
Students massacred in China's
Tiananmen Square

Collapse of the Soviet Union
Nirvana releases *Nevermind*

O.J. Simpson found
not guilty of murder

THE DIGITAL ERA: THE COMPUTER CHANGES EVERYTHING

Apple Inc. launched the Macintosh personal computer in 1984. It was more user-friendly than other PCs—and with its desktop publishing software, graphical user interface, and mouse (all novel at the time), the Mac was uniquely geared to designers. Compared to what we can create on the computer today, the original Macintosh, with only 128k, had limited capabilities. At the time, though, it opened up so many new possibilities.

Of course, using a computer didn't automatically make designers better at their craft. Instead, the new technology gave them more control and sped up their exploration process. As with anything unfamiliar, the Mac sparked debate among designers during this time: While some saw the computer as simply another tool for creating work, like a drawing pen, others saw its potential as a medium in itself.

Emerging digital technology also changed typography, exploding the number of typefaces available and giving designers the tools to create and distribute their own fonts. Some digital typefaces were updated versions of classics, while others were brand new: type that was made for low-resolution screens, and type that was less functional and more illustrative. It was easier to break the rules.

As computers spread from education and business into the home, the general public took an increased awareness of and interest in graphic design, as people began picking

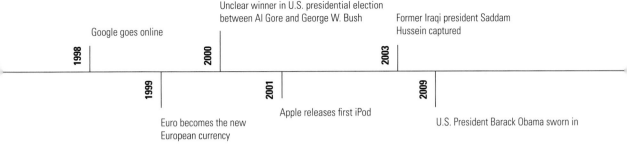

Google goes online

1998

1999

Euro becomes the new
European currency

Unclear winner in U.S. presidential election
between Al Gore and George W. Bush

2000

2001

Apple releases first iPod

Former Iraqi president Saddam
Hussein captured

2003

2009

U.S. President Barack Obama sworn in

out fonts and colors as they made their own flyers, scrapbooks, and invitations. The line between the professional designer and the hobbyist began to blur.

In the 1990s, designers like David Carson broke all the rules as they played with image distortion, type legibility, and basic hierarchy. Why not make page numbers the most prominent part of a layout? Why not set an entire article in a symbol font that the reader will have to decipher? There was a refreshing jolt of youthful experimentation as people moved past the limits of the rational and functional.

Finally, the computer offered something brand new: interactivity. With the rise of the Internet, social media, and mobile applications, the user gained control over how, when, and where they accessed information. For the first time, designers could shape different experiences for different people.

Of course, technology wasn't the only new development during this era: Design education programs expanded and became more rigorous. Design writing evolved into its own discipline, as practitioners took matters into their own hands to write articles, books, and criticisms that brought new perspectives to the design canon. And designers were—and are—affected and influenced by social, political, and cultural changes as they explored new ways to engage their audiences.

Today, people all over the world can communicate with each other like never before. The digital revolution continues, and design is sure to play a significant role in shaping the future.

APRIL GREIMAN

1948– | BORN: New York, New York | EDUCATION: Kansas City Art Institute, Allgemeine
Kunstgewerbeschule (General Arts Trade School) in Basel, Switzerland

Pioneered computer technology as a design tool

Established New Wave design in the United States

April Greiman uses different words to describe what she does: "hybrid imagery," "transmedia," "visual communication." But not "graphic design." She feels the term refers exclusively to print, and her work combines elements from different types of media. Greiman thinks in terms of space when she designs, not in terms of a page. This is probably why designing digitally has been such a good fit for her.

New Wave typographer Wolfgang Weingart encouraged Greiman, while in graduate school at Basel, to break free from a grid-based approach to design—to layer type, to float it in space, to make it illegible. She brought this knowledge to New York and, after growing frustrated by the rigid limitations imposed by East Coast clients, she moved in 1976 to Los Angeles and opened a studio. She began teaching at California Institute of the Arts (CalArts) in 1982 and gained access to the school's computers and video equipment.

The new technology opened so many possibilities for Greiman, enabling her to combine print, video, and type into multiple layers that were previously impossible to create. She felt strongly that these new tools weren't just a means to arrive at the same old solutions, but that they should lead us to explore ideas and create something new.

When Greiman designed an issue of *Design Quarterly* for the Walker Art Center in 1986, she blew up the traditional magazine format, creating a 2-foot-by-6-foot folding collage that combined a nude portrait of the designer overlaid with multiple layers of images and text. While the fact that Greiman used a computer to create the work hardly seems noteworthy today, consider that the computer had one megabyte of RAM and a monochrome 9-inch display. Greiman built the collage on the computer and output letter-size pages on her dot-matrix machine, then directed the magazine's printer to assemble the pages and photograph the entire composition. Greiman wasn't just tinkering with the computer; she was exploring the idea of making sense, touching on philosophy and physics. Like much of Greiman's work, the project wasn't just about technology, it was personal.

Greiman's list of influences is well-rounded: Among them are her former teachers Armin Hofmann and Wolfgang Weingart, singer/songwriter/poet Leonard Cohen, theoretical physicist David Bohm, psychiatrist Carl Jung, and spiritual leader the Dali Lama.

As the world continues to change, so does Greiman. More recently, she's been creating web design, branding, signage, and public art, and consulting on color, finishes, and textures for architectural projects. She continues to teach, and believes in always being open to new ways of doing things.

OPPOSITE: *Your Turn My Turn*, 3-D poster, 1983

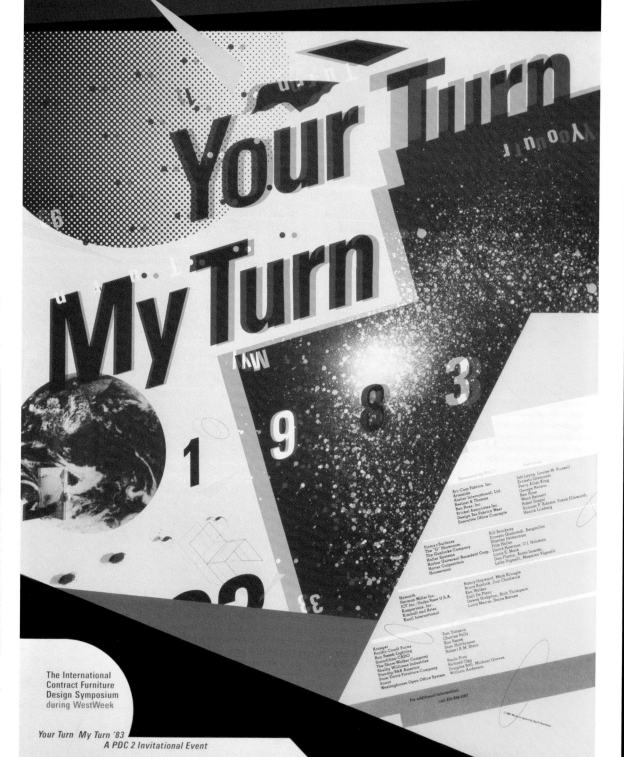

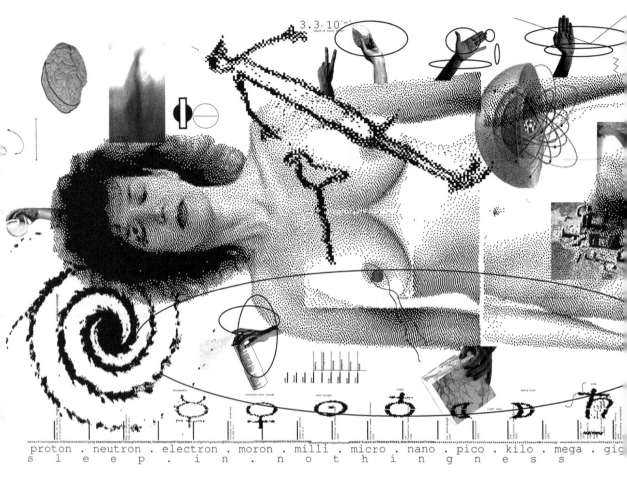

proton . neutron . electron . moron . milli . micro . nano . pico . kilo . mega . gig

s l e e p . i n . n o t h i n g n e s s

"Does It Make Sense?" *Design Quarterly*, 1986

"Do what you love to do, with a vengeance.

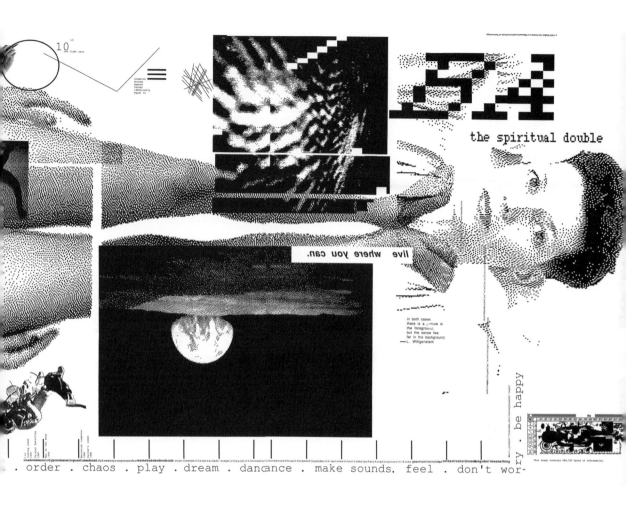

the spiritual double

live where you can.

in both cases
there is a picture in
the foreground,
but the sense lies
far in the background.
— L. Wittgenstein

. order . chaos . play . dream . dance . make sounds. feel . don't wor-

It's not WHAT YOU DO but WHO YOU ARE."[21]

—April Greiman

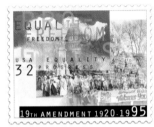

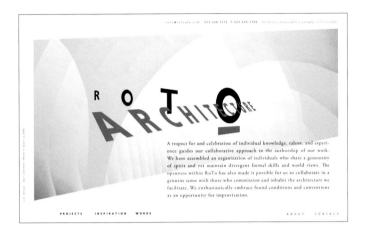

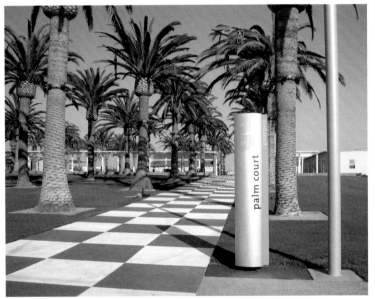

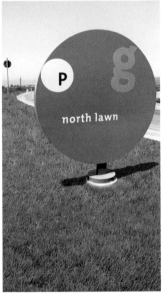

STAY: Miracle Manor Retreat Bed and Breakfast in Desert Hot Springs, California, is a mid-century modern spa/motel near Joshua Tree National Park owned by Greiman and her husband, architect Michael Rotondi.

TOP, LEFT: 19th Amendment commemorative stamp, U.S. Postal Service, 1995

TOP, RIGHT: Roto Architects website, 2008

ABOVE: Color, branding, and signage for the Great Park of Irvine, CA

OPPOSITE: *Hand Holding a Bowl of Rice*, mural, Wilshire Vermont Station, Los Angeles, 2007

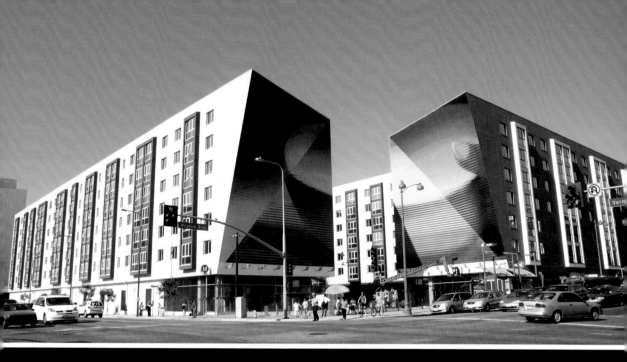

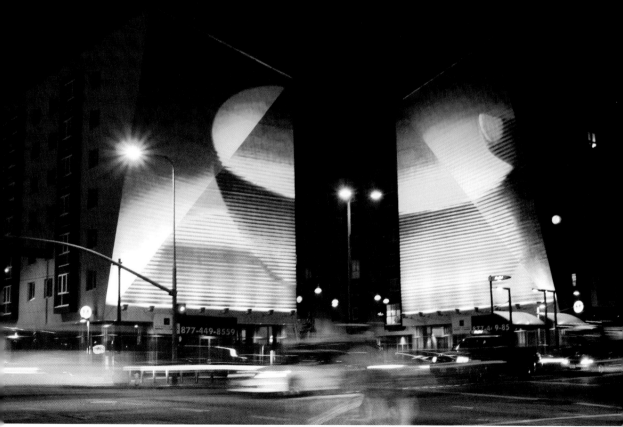

RUDY VANDERLANS
AND ZUZANA LICKO

Rudy VanderLans: 1955– | BORN: Voorburg, The Netherlands | EDUCATION: Royal Academy of Art, The Hague, The Netherlands; University of California at Berkeley

Zuzana Licko: 1961– | BORN: Bratislava, Czechoslovakia | EDUCATION: University of California at Berkeley

Founded experimental design journal

Designed groundbreaking digital typefaces

Embraced new design tools

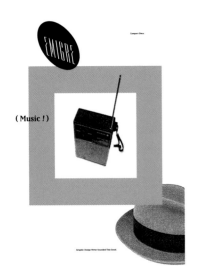

(Music !)

ABOVE: Emigre music poster

OPPOSITE: Oakland type specimen, now part of the Lo-Res type family

Apple broke new ground in 1984 when it introduced the Macintosh computer. Designers Rudy VanderLans and Zuzana Licko did the same (albeit on a much smaller scale) with *Emigre* magazine.

While many designers initially resisted the computer, VanderLans and Licko embraced it, though in different and complementary ways: VanderLans liked the freedom it gave him in designing layouts, while it gave Licko a disciplined method for designing type.

VanderLans studied design in The Netherlands and worked at Total Design. But he was more attracted to the expressive work of Herb Lubalin and Milton Glaser than to the Dutch modernists. He went on to study photography at UC Berkeley, where he met Licko, his future wife and business partner, as she studied graphic communications.

Emigre magazine quickly became a forum for designers, especially those interested in experimentation and technology. It featured in-depth articles and visual essays, in layouts that broke all the rules—with varying type sizes, overlapping layers, text columns crashing into each other, and distorted letterforms, all techniques that the Mac made easier. VanderLans and Licko sold their type designs to fund the magazine (which meant they didn't have to cater to advertisers).

The typefaces were an important part of the magazine's design as well. After the first two issues, the magazine was set exclusively in Emigre fonts. Licko began with rough, pixilated typefaces, like Oakland, and progressed to more versatile fonts, like the popular Mrs. Eaves. Emigre Fonts also carried select designs by Barry Deck, Jonathan Barnbrook, Elliot Earls, Bob Aufuldish, and Ed Fella, among others.

The magazine ceased publication in 2005, but Licko continues designing fonts, and VanderLans designs the type specimens. They also sell books, ceramics, and collectible items.

ABCDEFGH
IJKLMNOPQR
STUVWXYZ
abcdefgh
ijklmnopqr
stuvwxyz
0123456789

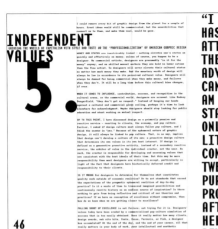

"I AM A HAPPY INVALID AND IT HAS REVOLUTIONIZED MY WHOLE ATTACK. MY BACK IS TURNED ON THE MORE BANAL KIND OF ADVERTISING, AND I HAVE CANCELED ALL COMMISSIONS AND AM RESOLUTELY SET ON STARVING. I SHALL UNDERTAKE ONLY THE SIMPLE CHILDISH LITTLE THINGS THAT CALL FOR COMPROMISE WITH THE UNIVERSAL TWELVE-YEAR-OLD MIND OF THE PURCHASING PUBLIC AND I WILL PRODUCE ART ON PAPER AND WOOD AFTER MY OWN HEART WITH NO HEED TO ANY MARKET. REVOLUTION, STARK AND BRUTAL." — W.A. DWIGGINS

LEFT: *Emigre* magazine spreads: Number 43, Number 49

OPPOSITE: *Emigre* magazine covers: Number 19, Number 33, Number 53, Number 64

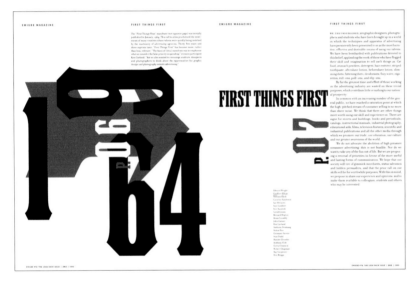

READ: *Merz to Emigre and Beyond: Avant Garde Magazine; Design of the Twentieth Century*, by Steven Heller

GET TO KNOW: Other influential type designers include Morris Fuller Benton, Matthew Carter, William Addison Dwiggins (see page 60), Tobias Frere-Jones, Adrian Frutiger, Eric Gill, Jonathan Hoefler, Paul Renner, Erik Spiekermann, Jan Tschichold (see page 64), Carol Twombly, and Herman Zapf.

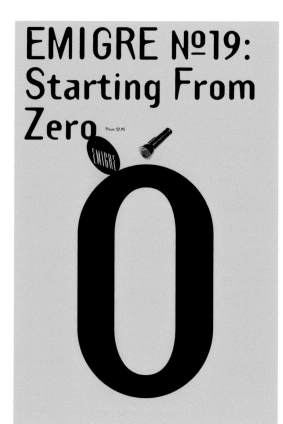

EMIGRE Nº19:
Starting From
Zero

Price: $7.95

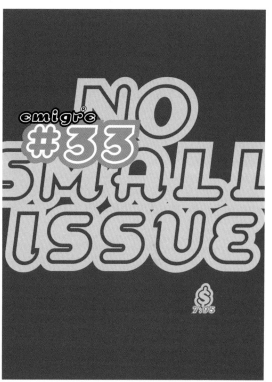

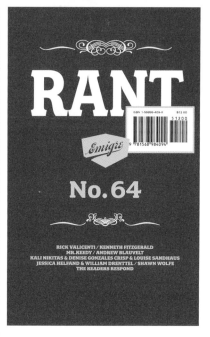

GRAPHIC

DESIGN

INCL.

EMIGRE No.53 / WINTER 2000 / PRICE 7.95

EDWARD FELLA

1938– | BORN: Detroit, Michigan | EDUCATION: Cranbrook Academy of Art

Created handmade lettering and design

Taught design for 25 years

Embraced American vernacular in his work

"Do something you haven't done before,"[22] Ed Fella would tell his students. It's great advice for expanding one's horizons, and it also describes Fella's career.

For almost 30 years, Fella worked in commercial design in Detroit, growing frustrated all the while by the lack of personal expression in his work. At age 47, he quit and went to graduate school at Cranbrook, where Katherine and Michael McCoy's innovative design program enabled him to explore and ask questions without real-world limitations.

After Cranbrook, Fella moved west to teach at California Institute of the Arts (CalArts), and his design work was anything but commercial. He collaged pieces of found imagery with hand-drawn type, creating designs influenced by Dada and Surrealism. He traveled cross-country every summer, photographing quirky signs along the way. Many graphic designers take such photos, but Fella incorporated that vernacular into his work in a meaningful way: one that breaks the rules and appreciates everyday beauty. In an age of computer-generated design, Fella works entirely by hand.

Although he retired from teaching in 2013, Fella's influence in formal exploration and in expressive and playful typography will continue through the students he taught over 25 years. Consistently described as "nice" and "generous," Fella is also a great photographer who loves to read, and who encouraged his students to be curious about the world. He also encourages people to understand history and to participate in design discourse, saying, "It's all the difference between an amateur and a professional, a hack and a master!"[23]

ABOVE: Detroit Focus Gallery flyer, 1989

OPPOSITE: Lecture poster

SLIDE LECTURE

ED

EXIT-LEVEL·DESIGNER

FELLA

HISTORY,
COMMERCIAL
ART ART AND
THE AMERICAN
VERNACULAR"

PRESENTED BY

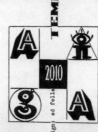

ARIZONA
STATE
UNIVERSITY

TEMPE·AZ

TUESDAY 7:30 PM
FEBRUARY 16 TH
LIFE SCIENCES
CENTER ROOM 191

AIGA
2010

design by ed fella

READ: *Fingerprint: The Art of Using Hand-Made Elements in Graphic Design*, by Chen Design Associates, to see examples of contemporary designers who have incorporated the handmade into their work.

DO: Tackle your next design project entirely by hand from concept to finished work, using found imagery, your own photography, hand-lettering, and other analog elements. How does working by hand change your thinking?

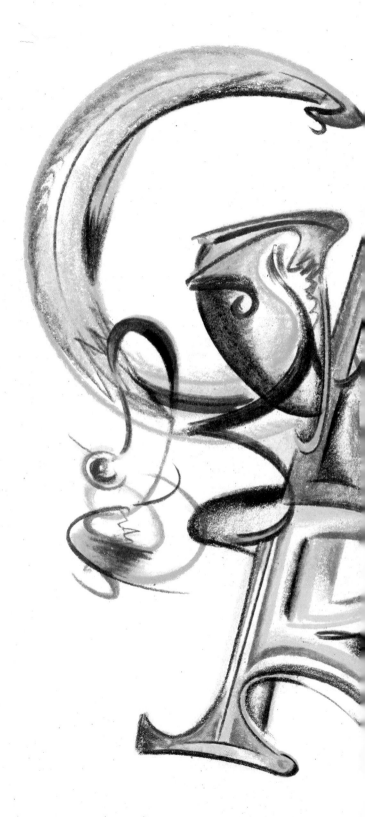

Lettering for *The New York Times Book Review*, 1999

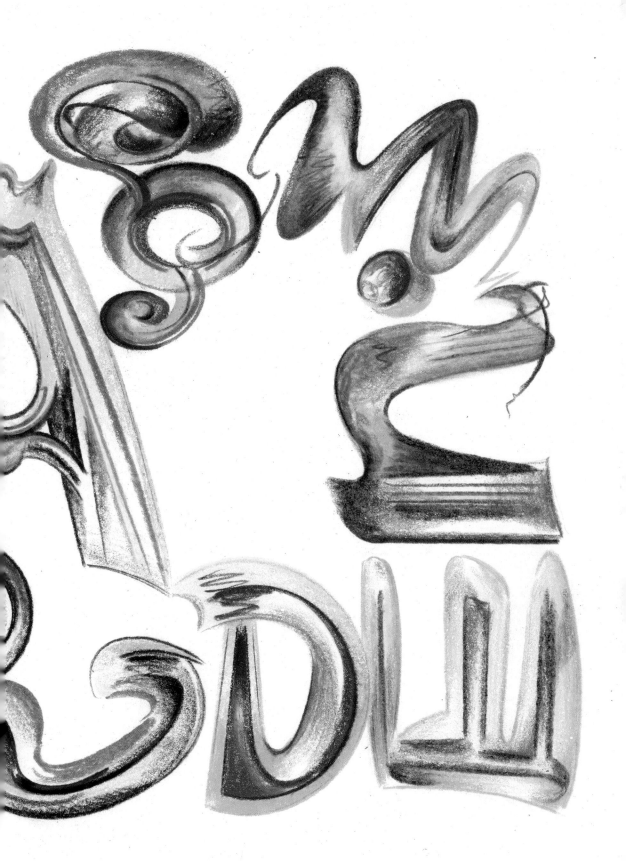

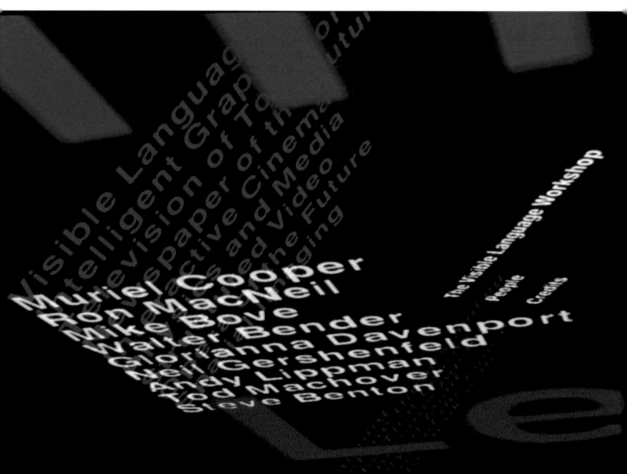

MEDIA

Visible Language Workshop
Visible Language Graphics of
Intelligent Graphic Tools
Television of Tomorrow
Newspaper of the Future
Interactive Cinema
Movies and Media
Images and Video
Movies of the Future
Imaging Changing

The Visible Language Workshop

People

Credits

Muriel Cooper
Ron MacNeil
Mike Bove
Walter Bender
Glorianna Davenport
Neil Gershenfeld
Andy Lippman
Tod Machover
Steve Benton

MURIEL COOPER

1925–1994 | BORN: Brookline, Massachusetts | EDUCATION: The Ohio State University and the Massachusetts College of Art (later Massachusetts College of Art and Design)

Pioneered design for the screen

Blended graphic design and computer science

Designed important books about the design profession and its practitioners

Muriel Cooper had two design careers: first as a print designer and second as a groundbreaking digital designer. Both revolved around the Massachusetts Institute of Technology (MIT), and both were based on her quest to make static media more dynamic.

MIT's Office of Publications hired Cooper in 1952 and continued working with her after she established her own studio. She then became art director for MIT Press, where she designed classic books, such as Hans Wingler's *Bauhaus*. She designed the first edition of *Learning from Las Vegas*; authors Robert Venturi, Denise Scott Brown, and Steven Izenour hated what she did, but many graphic designers loved it.

Cooper took her first computer class at MIT in 1967, and it bewildered her. However, she could see the computer's potential in the creative process, and soon began the second phase of her career: applying her design skills to computer screens. With Ron MacNeil, Cooper co-founded the research group Visible Language Workshop in 1975, which later became part of MIT's Media Lab. Cooper didn't write code, but she didn't need to; she was the designer and the thinker. She knew what she wanted visually, and encouraged her students to use technology to present well-designed information.

Cooper presented the group's research at the influential TED5 (Technology, Entertainment, Design) conference in 1994. For the first time, computer graphics were shown in three transparent dimensions, which moved, changed sizes, and shifted focus, instead of the standard Microsoft Windows interface of opaque panels stacked like cards. She made a big impact: Even Microsoft founder Bill Gates was interested in her work. Unfortunately, she died soon after of a heart attack, but her legacy in interactive design continues.

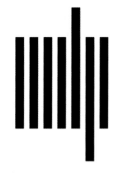

"Muriel Cooper taught me that design had very little to do with how you make something, and instead *why* you make something."[24]

—John Maeda

ABOVE: MIT Press logo

OPPOSITE, TOP: Image rendered as soft type, MIT Media Lab's Visible Language Workshop

OPPOSITE, BOTTOM: "Information Landscape," MIT Media Lab's Visible Language Workshop, 1994

STEVEN HELLER

1950– | BORN: New York, New York

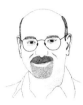

Wrote hundreds of books and articles about design

Co-founded innovative educational programs

Art directed *The New York Times* Book Review

GET TO KNOW: Other design writers include Michael Bierut, Ralph Caplan, William Drenttel, Peter Hall, Jessica Helfand, Richard Hollis, Ellen Lupton, Philip B. Meggs, Rick Poynor, Kerry William Purcell, Alston Purvis, Adrian Shaughnessy, Alice Twemlow, Lorraine Wild, and Veronique Vienne.

READ: *Writing and Research for Graphic Designers: A Designer's Manual to Strategic Communication and Presentation*, by Steven Heller

LISTEN: Podcasts of Heller's SVA lectures are available, as are other presentations and discussions. Go to hellerbooks.com or download them from the Apple Store.

OPPOSITE: Some of the more than 100 books written by Heller

While researching this book, it's been difficult for me to find source material that was *not* written by Steven Heller. Thirty years ago, there were very few books on graphic design. Heller has since authored or co-authored more than 100 titles, educating readers about the power of graphic design.

Heller wasn't the first one to write about design, of course, but he's the most prolific. Through his writing, he teaches, he connects, he criticizes, and he celebrates. Heller has brought a deeper understanding of design not only to students and practicing designers, but also to the public (including clients). Thanks to him, it's now easier to explain what we do for a living to our families. It seems that an author who writes 100 books on one subject would repeat himself. Not Steven Heller: His titles range from how-tos and histories to biographies and design criticism. Heller's output continues apace: He contributes to publications both online and off, including *Print* magazine, *Design Observer*, AIGA's online journal, and *The New York Times* Book Review.

Heller began his career as a practitioner, and he worked as an art director for *The New York Times* for more than 30 years. But at his core, Heller is an educator: writing, teaching, and lecturing about design. In 1998, he co-founded the Designer as Author MFA program at the School of Visual Arts in New York, which he co-chairs with Lita Talarico. The entrepreneurial program guides students beyond being service providers, to become, in fact, their own clients—to not only design content, but to create it. As someone who generously shares what he knows, he also co-founded SVA's MFA Design Criticism (D-Crit) program, with Alice Twemlow, for the study of design writing, research, and criticism, as well as the MFA Interaction Design program, with Liz Danzico.

"Among my peers," Heller says, "Rick Poynor is excellent, Michael Bierut is lyrical, Karrie Jacobs is powerful and Ralph Caplan is sublime."[25] But he's mostly inspired by writers who tackle other subjects and genres: art critic Arthur Danto, columnist Frank Rich, and novelists Philip Roth, T.C. Boyle, and Paul Auster. It's hard to imagine a design practitioner today who hasn't read—and learned from—Steven Heller.

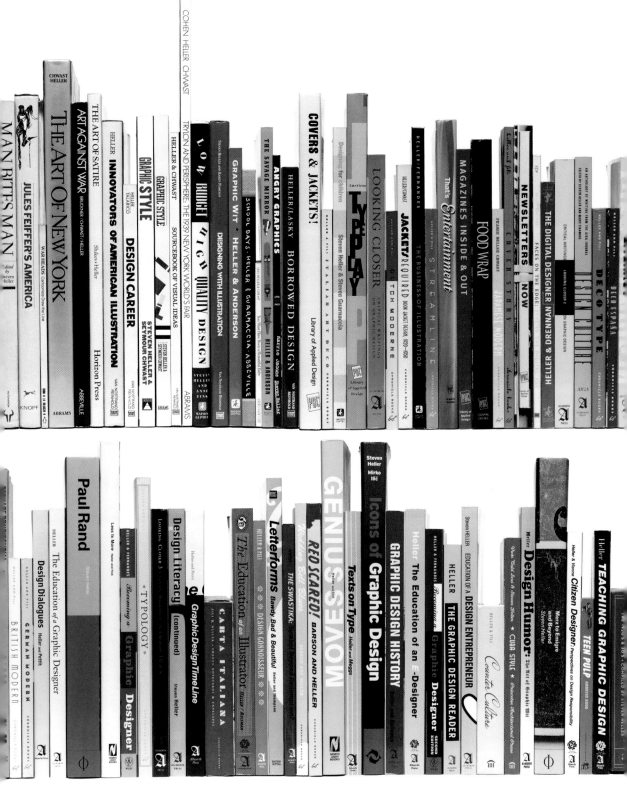

STEPHEN DOYLE

1956– | BORN: Baltimore, Maryland | EDUCATION: The Cooper Union, New York

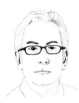

Experiments with typography

Harnesses color's power to connect and communicate

Balances art and commerce

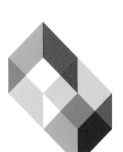

THECOOPERUNION

ABOVE: Logo for The Cooper Union, at its 150th anniversary

OPPOSITE: 19th Amendment anniversary installation in New York's Grand Central Terminal

A master of type, color, and dimension, Stephen Doyle is equally at home working on massive commercial projects and on small, quietly beautiful artistic experiments. He built a career on designing for major brands, and more recently has become something of a sculptor, creating dimensional illustrations out of paper, wood, and found objects.

After art directing *Esquire* and *Rolling Stone*, Doyle landed at the influential M&Co., whose founder, Tibor Kalman, shaped his creative approach. In 1985, Doyle, Tom Kluepfel and William Drenttel launched Drenttel Doyle Partners, a hybrid design and advertising agency that worked with top clients, including *Spy* magazine, IBM, and Champion Paper. Drenttel left in 1997, and the studio carried on as Doyle Partners.

Doyle's packaging for Martha Stewart's line of home goods sold at mass-market retailer Kmart remains among his most high-profile work. And for good reason: Doyle used clean typography, bright colors, and beautiful photography to create a unified and instantly identifiable brand that included thousands of products. The packaging—and the products themselves—proved that high-quality design could appeal to everyday shoppers seeking everyday goods.

A regular contributor to *The New York Times*, Doyle creates illustrations that focus on a single word that he constructs (using materials like wood, water, or paper) and transforms (by bending, twisting, or breaking). The images are consistently visually arresting; more important, they force the viewer to think. Doyle furthers his experiments with type and meaning in his free time, cutting text from books and building elaborate paper sculptures.

Among his influences, Doyle praises M&Co. and Kalman, who, he says, created a "kind of 'un-design' underground that attempted to play with the vernacular and mess with the context of things. This uniquely New York school of thought took a very antithetical approach to the high-falutin' and the overly-intellectual design approach. At M&Co., real text and real context were actually being smacked together in a real-world context, resulting in work that came to life with raw ideas, positioning them (us), in hindsight, as 'constructionists' swimming upstream against the current of 'deconstructivists' which was the mode du jour."[26]

Doyle's humor and enthusiasm are evident in his work, and he seems to enjoy himself most when he doesn't know what he's doing. That uncertainty keeps his ideas fresh—each project is different; so is each solution.

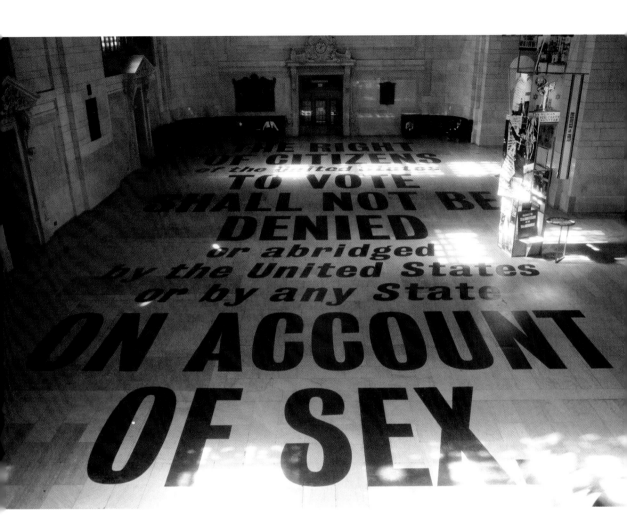

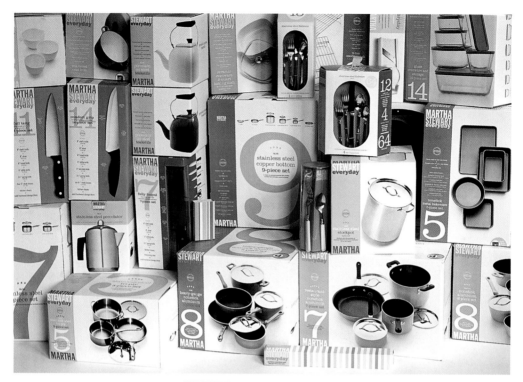

GET TO KNOW: Tibor Kalman and the work he did at M&Co and *Colors* magazine.

SEE: The Type Directors Club promotes excellence in typography in print and on screen. The organization holds annual competitions, publishes books, hosts exhibitions, and offers classes and lectures. Visit tdc.org

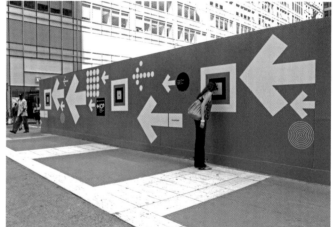

ABOVE, TOP: Packaging for Martha Stewart Everyday products in Kmart

ABOVE: Construction site fence housing a mini-photo exhibition through peepholes, International School of Photography

OPPOSITE: Poster for The Academy of American Poets, 2011

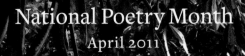

National Poetry Month
April 2011

BRIGHT
OBJECTS
HYPNOTIZE
THE MIND

from
"A Word with You," by Elizabeth Bishop

Academy of American Poets
poets.org

Poster by Stephen Doyle   Photograph by Victor Schrager   Additional support for this poster was provided by the American Booksellers Association and the National Council of Teachers of English. Paper provided by New Page and Lindenmeyr/Sappi. Special thanks to Let There Be Neon.

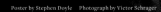

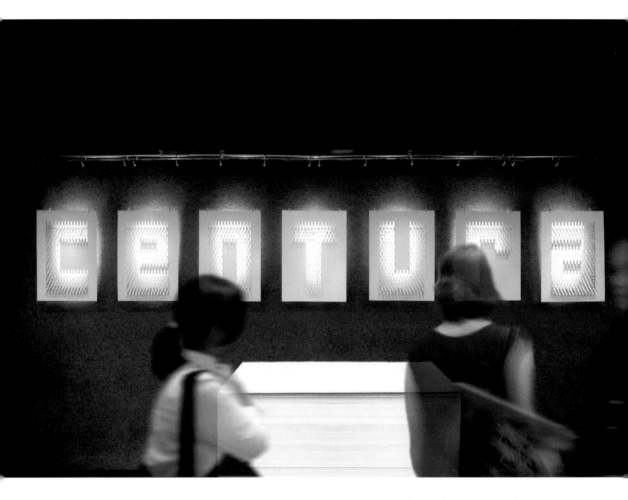

ABOVE: Signage for a paper trade show

OPPOSITE: Illustration for *The New York Times* about computers misinterpreting information

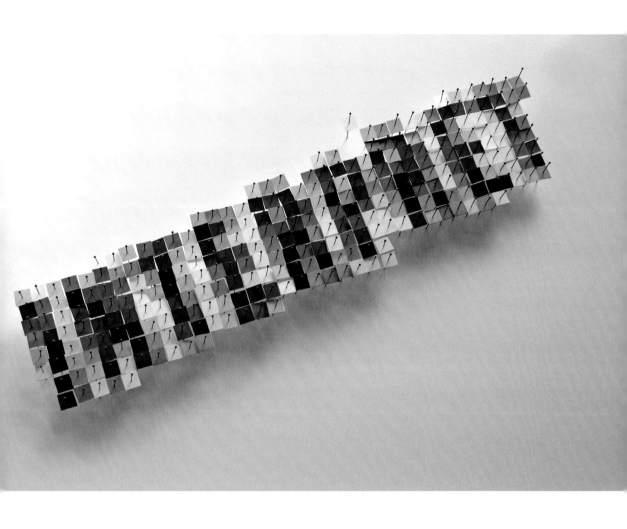

PAULA SCHER

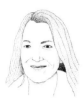

1948– | BORN: Washington, DC | EDUCATION: Tyler School of Art, Philadelphia

Illustrates with typography

Designs distinctive identities for cultural institutions and corporations

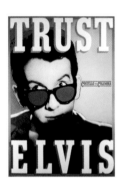

ABOVE: "Trust Elvis" poster for CBS/Columbia Records, 1981

OPPOSITE: Season campaign poster for The Public Theater, 1995
Photo: Carol Rosegg

As a design student, Paula Scher couldn't get the hang of working with type, of formally positioning words and letters in a layout. (She's hardly the first—or last—design student to struggle through typography class.) Then her teacher, Stanislas Zagorski, suggested that she think of type in a more conceptual way, using it as the main image in her work, to communicate visually as well as verbally. That simple direction helped Scher establish herself as a master of persuasive, expressive, even aggressive type.

As art director at CBS Records and Atlantic Records during the 1970s, Scher worked on big-budget album covers, but she found the small-budget projects more interesting, because they required her to create her own artwork. Because she hated the sterility of the typeface Helvetica, she experimented with older type styles—art deco, mid-century modern, constructivism—and combined them. Not because she was a postmodernist, but because she wanted to create something more expressive than Helvetica.

After a few years in a partnership with editorial designer Terry Koppel, Scher joined the influential studio Pentagram as partner in 1991. Three years later, she took on a defining project: a new identity for New York City's Public Theater (formerly known as Shakespeare in the Park). Director George Wolfe wanted a visual identity that looked nothing like Shakespeare, and Scher designed exactly that: a big, bold typographic language that was loud and urban and distinctive. Scher's street posters for the show *Bring in Da Noise, Bring in Da Funk* pushed this in-your-face style even further, with brash type that actually looked noisy. Scher's design became so popular that it changed theater advertising, as more groups tried to capture the youthful vigor of her work for the Public.

Scher is a very intuitive designer—her first or second idea is usually her best. That doesn't mean it's easy: For her, the best way to grow as a designer is to take on projects for which she's not qualified. After making a big splash with the Public, she was approached to design architectural signage for other performance venues. She had no experience in that field, but the work forced her to think in new ways; her fresh approach resulted in innovative and successful signage for projects such as Symphony Space and Jazz at Lincoln Center.

As someone who worked with her hands in the days before the computer, she misses the craft of making something. When she's not designing for CitiBank or the Metropolitan Opera or Bloomberg, she paints large-format typographic maps.

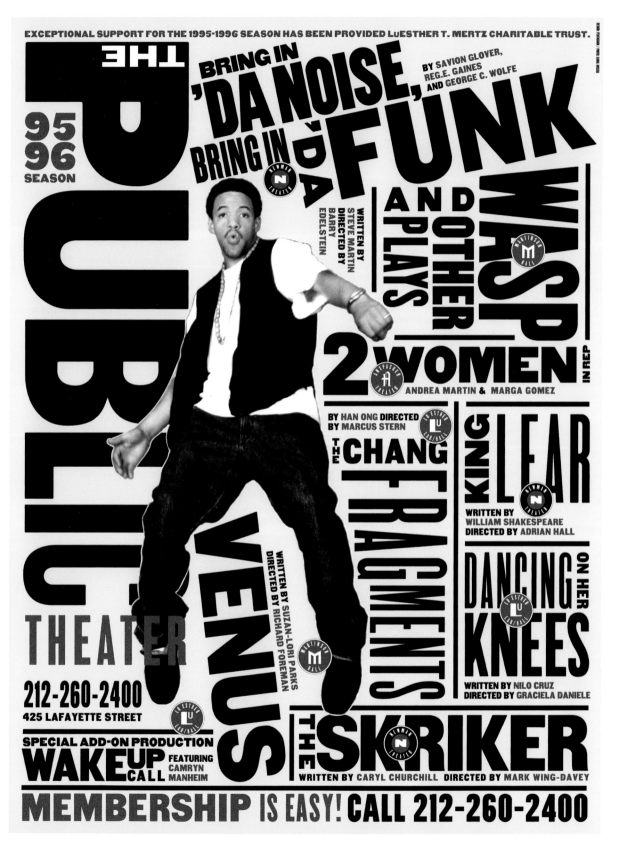

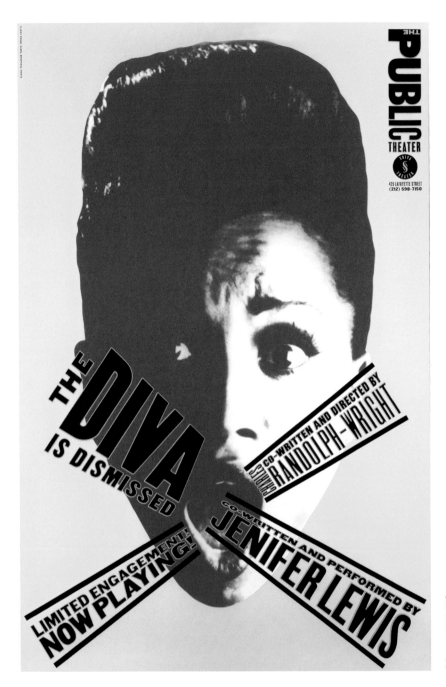

ABOVE: "The Diva Is Dismissed" poster for The Public Theater, 1994

OPPOSITE: Ballet Tech poster, 1997

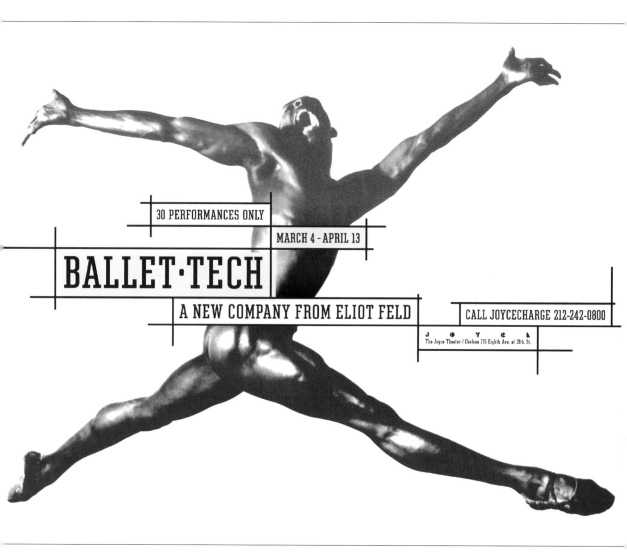

30 PERFORMANCES ONLY

MARCH 4 - APRIL 13

BALLET·TECH

A NEW COMPANY FROM ELIOT FELD

CALL JOYCECHARGE 212-242-0800

J O Y C E
The Joyce Theater / Chelsea 175 Eighth Ave. at 19th. St.

Pentagram is a multidisciplinary design collective owned by partner designers, with offices in New York, London, San Francisco, Austin, and Berlin. There isn't much they can't do, with graphic designers, architects, interior designers, and product designers on board. Each partner must be an active designer as well as a good business-person. Pentagram began in 1972 when Crosby/Fletcher/Forbes added two new partners and named themselves after a five-pointed star. In 2013, there were 19 partners, among them Michael Gericke, Luke Hayman, Angus Hyland, Natasha Jen, Abbott Miller, Emily Oberman, Eddie Opara, Woody Pirtle, DJ Stout, and Lisa Strausfeld.

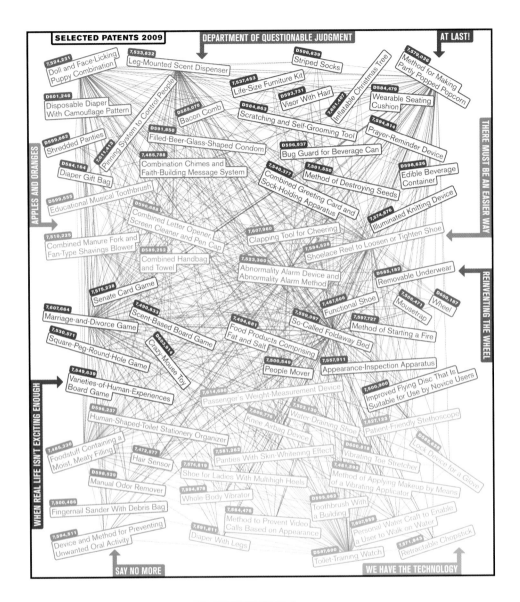

The diagram labels include:

SELECTED PATENTS 2009 | **DEPARTMENT OF QUESTIONABLE JUDGMENT** | **AT LAST!**

APPLES AND ORANGES — THERE MUST BE AN EASIER WAY — REINVENTING THE WHEEL — WHEN REAL LIFE ISN'T EXCITING ENOUGH — SAY NO MORE — WE HAVE THE TECHNOLOGY

(Patent entries include: Doll and Face-Licking Puppy Combination; Leg-Mounted Scent Dispenser; Striped Socks; Method for Making Partly Popped Popcorn; Disposable Diaper With Camouflage Pattern; Life-Size Furniture Kit; Visor With Hair; Wearable Seating Cushion; Bacon Comb; Scratching and Self-Grooming Tool; Inflatable Christmas Tree; Prayer-Reminder Device; Shredded Panties; Filled-Beer-Glass-Shaped Condom; Pinning System to Control People; Combination Chimes and Faith-Building Message System; Bug Guard for Beverage Can; Diaper Gift Bag; Method of Destroying Seeds; Edible Beverage Container; Educational Musical Toothbrush; Combined Greeting Card and Sock-Holding Apparatus; Illuminated Knitting Device; Combined Letter Opener, Screen Cleaner and Pen Cap; Clapping Tool for Cheering; Shoelace Reel to Loosen or Tighten Shoe; Combined Manure Fork and Fan-Type Shavings Blower; Combined Handbag and Towel; Abnormality Alarm Device and Abnormality Alarm Method; Removable Underwear; Senate Card Game; Functional Shoe; Mousetrap; Wheel; Marriage-and-Divorce Game; Scent-Based Board Game; So-Called Foldaway Bed; Method of Starting a Fire; Square-Peg-Round-Hole Game; Food Products Comprising Fat and Salt; Crazy-Mouse Toy; People Mover; Appearance-Inspection Apparatus; Varieties-of-Human-Experiences Board Game; Improved Flying Disc That Is Suitable for Use by Novice Users; Human-Shaped-Toilet Stationery Organizer; Passenger's Weight-Measurement Device; Water-Draining Shoe; Patient-Friendly Stethoscope; Foodstuff Containing a Moist, Meaty Filling; Knee Airbag Device; Hair Sensor; Vibrating Toe Stretcher; Lock Device for a Glove; Manual Odor Remover; Panties With Skin-Whitening Effect; Shoe for Ladies With Multihigh Heels; Method of Applying Makeup by Means of a Vibrating Applicator; Fingernail Sander With Debris Bag; Whole-Body Vibrator; Toothbrush With a Building; Method to Prevent Video Calls Based on Appearance; Personal Water Craft to Enable a User to Walk on Water; Device and Method for Preventing Unwanted Oral Activity; Diaper With Legs; Toilet-Training Watch; Retractable Chopstick)

ABOVE: "Selected Patents, 2009" diagram for *The New York Times* magazine, 2009

OPPOSITE: Environmental graphics for the New Jersey Performing Arts Center (NJPAC), 2001
Photo: Peter Mauss/Esto

READ: *Maps*, by Paula Scher; *Graphic Design and Architecture, A 20th Century History*, by Richard Poulin, for examples of environmental design and typography in architecture.

WATCH: Artist Series, a group of short films directed by the late web designer/filmmaker Hillman Curtis, includes Paula Scher, David Carson, Milton Glaser, and Stefan Sagmeister.

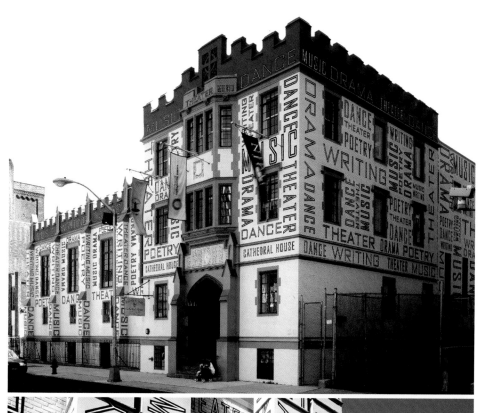

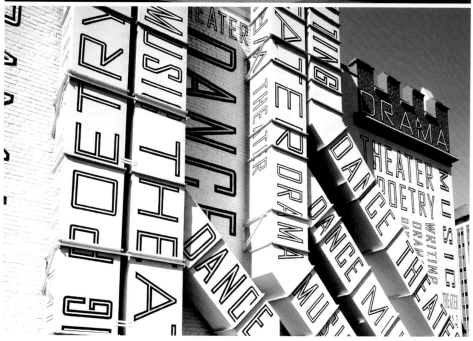

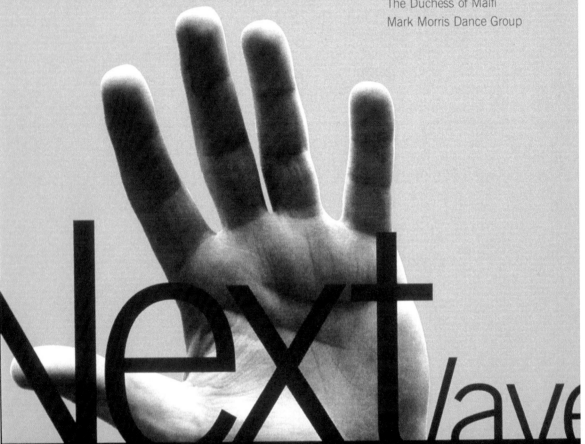

Brooklyn
Academy
of
Music

The Next Wave
Festival 1995
Alice
Artists in Action
Alternative Jazz
Salome
Nine Songs
The Passion of Joan of Arc
From Gospel to Gershwin
Brooklyn Philharmonic Orchestra
Kronos Quartet
Chinoiserie
The Whispers of Angels
The Duchess of Malfi
Mark Morris Dance Group

Next
Wave

BAM 1995 Next Wave Festival is sponsored
by Philip Morris Companies Inc.

MICHAEL BIERUT

1957– | BORN: Cleveland, Ohio | EDUCATION: University of Cincinnati's College of Design, Architecture, Art, and Planning

Designs bold identities

Co-founded online forum for design

"I admire creative people who don't wait for inspiration or strokes of genius, but who can simply show up for work every day and do the best they can," says Michael Bierut of his creative influences. "My favorite example is the Motown songwriting team Holland-Dozier-Holland. They had no idea they were making timeless contributions to popular culture, but rather were just grinding out song after song for the Four Tops, the Supremes, and the Vandellas. Yet what they created have touched millions and millions of people."[27]

The above quote speaks to Bierut's work ethic and his ability to make design and creativity understandable. It makes sense that he uses music to illustrate a point: Like many other designers, it was a love of album covers that led him to graphic design. After an internship at Boston public TV station WGBH under Chris Pullman, Bierut worked for design legend Massimo Vignelli for 10 years. In 1990, he became a partner at the New York office of Pentagram.

For avant-garde performance space Brooklyn Academy of Music (BAM), Bierut developed a simple yet bold visual language of large cropped type, suggesting something exciting beyond the horizon. The identity remains one of the most recognizable in New York City.

Bierut excels as an identity designer, developing comprehensive brands from the ground up as well as consulting with companies that need a refreshed look. Luxury retailer Saks Fifth Avenue had used several logos over the years and wanted something new. Bierut looked back through the brand's history and found a cursive logo from 1973, drawn by Tom Carnase (and part of an earlier identity designed by Vignelli). To freshen it up, Bierut placed the logo into a square, then broke that square into several smaller squares that could be rotated and arranged to create hundreds of different patterns. The ever-changing new look references the store's long heritage, while looking fresh and modern.

Bierut's friendly and approachable nature fosters a sense of community among designers through his involvement and leadership in the AIGA, the professional association for design. He also writes for design publications, and is a critic at the Yale School of Art. In 2003, along with William Drenttel, Jessica Helfand, and Rick Poynor he co-founded the website *Design Observer*, which has become a forum for designers of all disciplines.

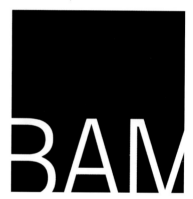

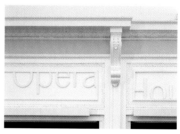

ABOVE AND OPPOSITE: Identity, signage and poster for the Brooklyn Academy of Music, 1995

OVERLEAF: Environmental graphics for The New York Times Building, 2007
Photo: Peter Mauss/Esto

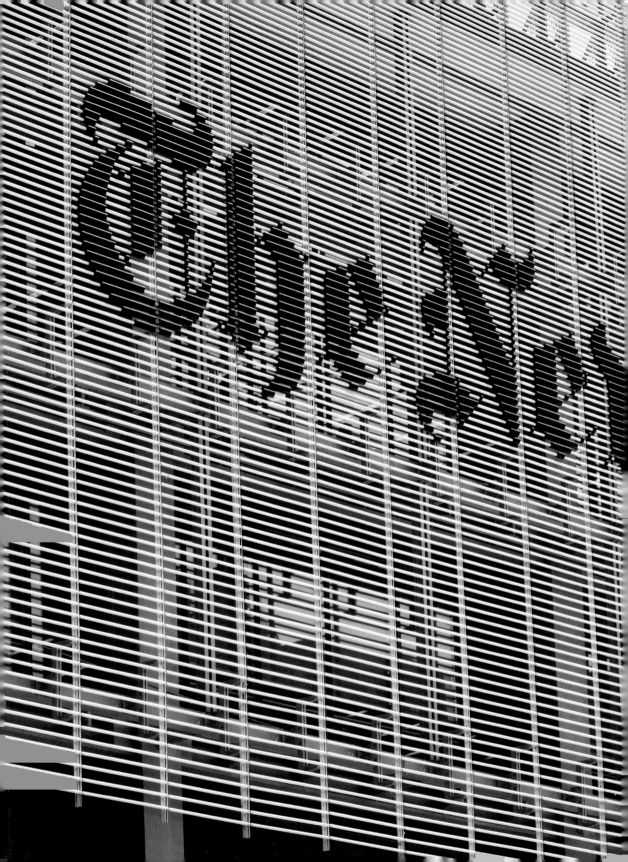

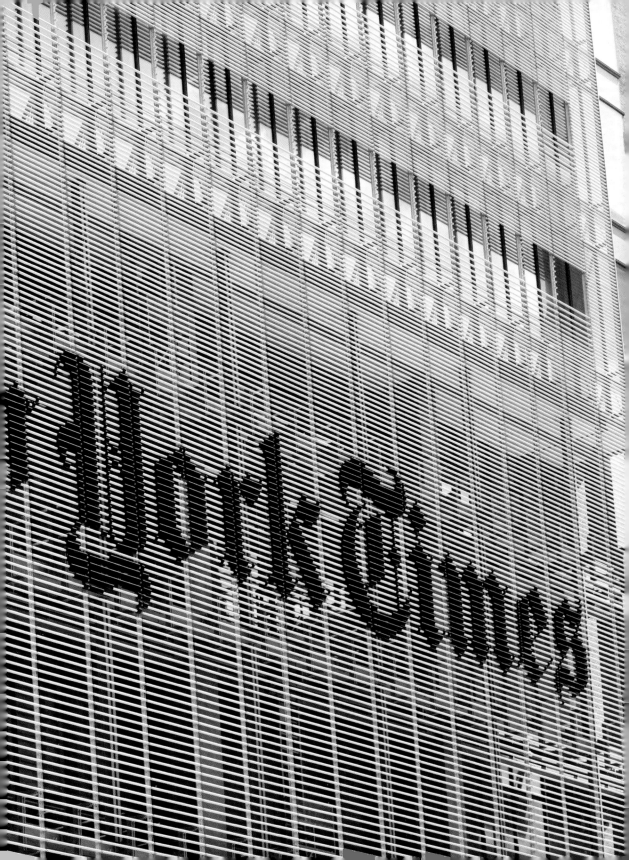

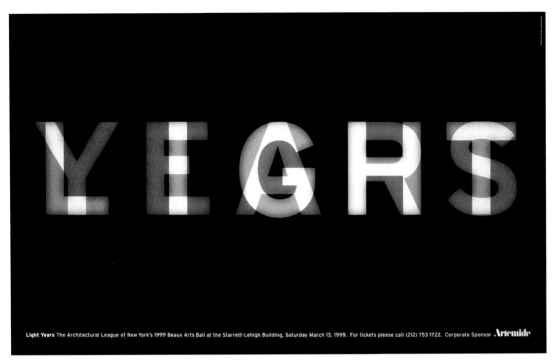

Light Years The Architectural League of New York's 1999 Beaux Arts Ball at the Starrett-Lehigh Building, Saturday March 13, 1999. For tickets please call (212) 753 1722. Corporate Sponsor **Artemide**

ABOVE: Poster for The Architectural League of New York's Beaux Arts Ball, 1999

RIGHT: Poster for the AIGA National Design Conference, 2001

OPPOSITE: Identity and shopping bags for Saks Fifth Avenue, 2006

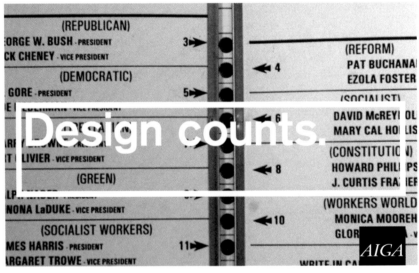

READ: *Seventy-Nine Short Essays on Design*, by Michael Bierut; *Design Observer* at http//:designobserver.com

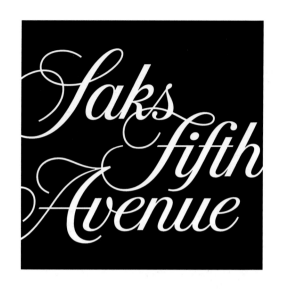

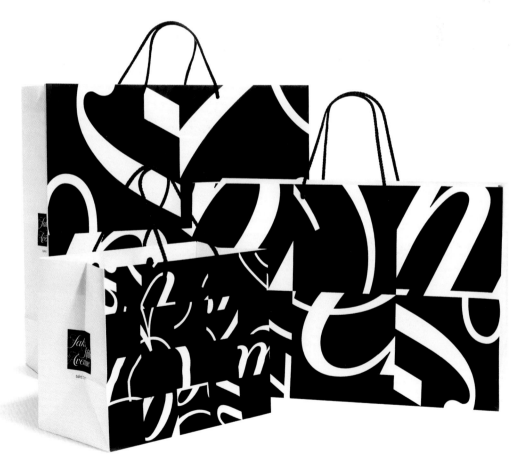

JOHN MAEDA

1966– | BORN: Seattle,Washington | EDUCATION: Massachusetts Institute of Technology, Cambridge, Massachusetts; University of Tsukuba Institute of Art and Design, Japan

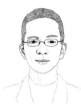

Combines design and technology

Advocates computer knowledge for designers

Leads well-known design college

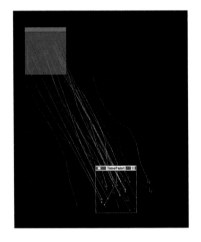

ABOVE: Time Paint software for Macintosh, 1994

OPPOSITE: One of ten poster designs for Japanese type foundry Morisawa, 1996

John Maeda was a computer science grad student at MIT on his way to becoming a user interface designer. Then he read *Thoughts on Design*, by Paul Rand—an experience that shifted the course of Maeda's career.

Maeda took a humbling message from Rand's book: Understanding the computer did not necessarily make one a good designer. Encouraged by his professor Muriel Cooper, Maeda decided to study graphic design in Japan, where he added traditional design skills and concepts to his knowledge of computers.

Maeda then returned to MIT to teach, and founded the Aesthetics and Computation Group at the Media Lab. It was there that Maeda, who as a child excelled at both math and art (though his father only bragged about the math part), explored the area where design and technology meet. For Maeda, the computer is a tool and a medium. Through the Media Lab, Maeda created digital experiences like The Reactive Square, in which shapes responded to sound, and Time Paint, a time-based program of flying colors. His Design by Numbers project (no longer active) encouraged designers and artists to learn computer programming.

In his quest to educate, Maeda writes books, too: *The Laws of Simplicity* outlines his hopes that technology will simplify, rather than complicate, our lives. In 2008, Maeda became president of Rhode Island School of Design. As an educator, he considers creative thinking equally important as technical capability in developing the leaders of tomorrow. To the emphasis on science, technology, engineering, and math (STEM) throughout the country's educational system, Maeda proposes adding an A for Art, to create STEAM. His goal? Not to make the world more high-tech, but to make it more humane.

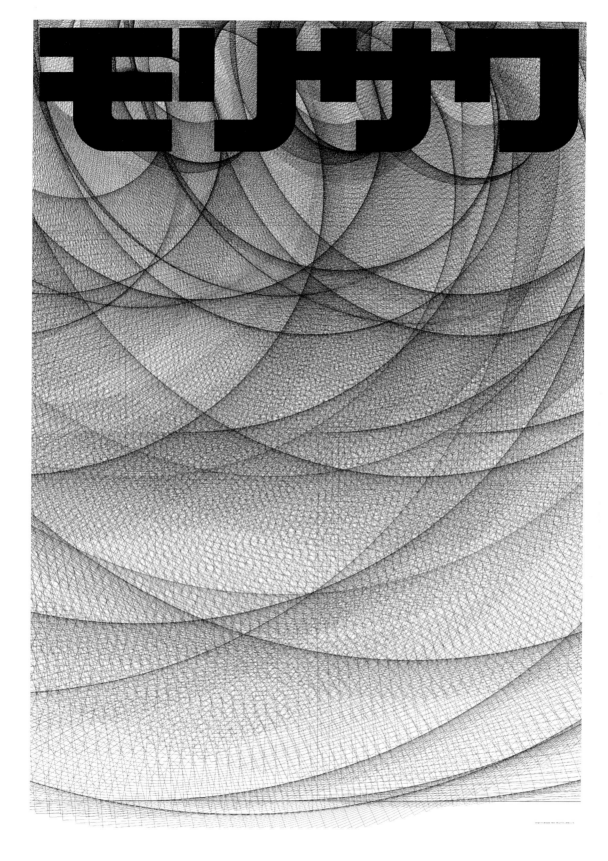

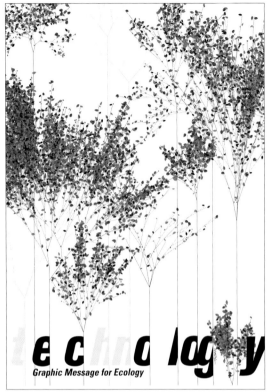

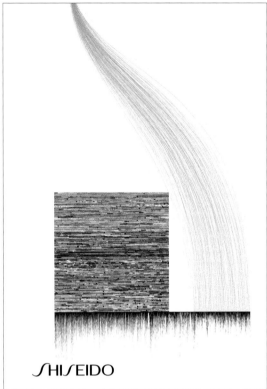

READ: *The Laws of Simplicity*, by John Maeda

GET TO KNOW: Other influential digital designers include: Jake Barton, Scott Dadich, Joshua Davis, Jason Fried, Ji Lee, Jason Santa Maria, Lisa Strausfeld, Khoi Vinh, and Robert Wong.

ABOVE, LEFT: Exhibition poster for Ginza Graphic Gallery, 2002

ABOVE: Shiseido poster celebrating 30 years of commercial films, 1995

OPPOSITE: MIT Math Department poster, 1998

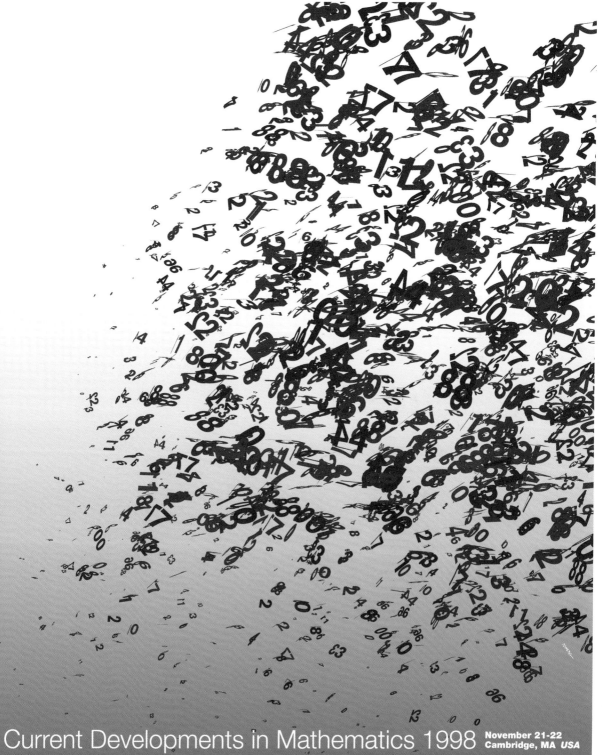

Current Developments in Mathematics 1998

**November 21-22
Cambridge, MA *USA***

**American Academy of Arts and Sciences, Cambridge, MA / Inquiries Harvard Mathematics Department (617) 495-1980
Organized by David Jerison, I.M. Singer, Daniel Stroock (MIT) + Barry Mazur, Wilfried Schmid, Shing-Tung Yau (Harvard)**

http://www.math.harvard.edu/cdm98

STEFAN SAGMEISTER

1962– | BORN: Bregenz, Austria | EDUCATION: University Applied Arts, Vienna, Austria; Pratt Institute, New York

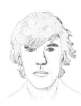

Designed innovative CD packaging

Takes sabbaticals to experiment

Pushes and provokes with his work

Legendary designer Tibor Kalman once told his young protégé, "Stefan, this is terrible, just *terrible*. I am so disappointed."[28] Even at its worst, Stefan Sagmeister's work is remarkable. And Kalman—his criticism notwithstanding—remains a big influence for Sagmeister.

Stefan Sagmeister doesn't see a new project as just another job; he sees an opportunity to create something magnificent. He pushes beyond the functional to develop designs that consistently provoke a reaction.

After working at ad agency Leo Burnett's design group in Hong Kong, Sagmeister joined Kalman's M&Co in New York in 1993. Although his tenure there was brief, his boss taught him to take risks and to explore different design disciplines. But, Sagmeister recalls, "It was, more than anything else, his incredible salesmanship that set his studio apart from all the others. There were probably a number of people around who were as smart as Tibor (and there were certainly a lot who were better at designing), but nobody else could sell these concepts without any changes, get those ideas with almost no alterations out into the hands of the public. Nobody else was as passionate."[29]

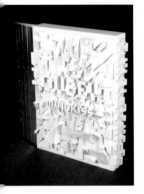

ABOVE: *Art of Oubey*, artist monograph, in 3-D molded slipcase

OPPOSITE: AIGA Detroit lecture poster, 1999

When Sagmeister launched his own studio that same year, he wanted to focus on design for music. Business was slow, so he designed a CD for a friend's band (which was called H.P. Zinker), with a special red jewel box that concealed a "secret" image on the inside cover. The design trick worked: Major record labels noticed Sagmeister's innovative package, and he went on to design for top artists, including Lou Reed, Pat Metheny, David Byrne, and the Rolling Stones.

Not shy about using his body to make a point, Sagmeister appeared nude on a postcard to announce his new studio. He also photographed himself in his underwear before and after he ate 100 different kinds of junk food, showing what a 23-pound weight gain looks like. For a poster promoting an AIGA event, he had the type carved into his torso by an assistant. It was a pretty shocking image, and the entire design industry noticed.

As music downloads became more common, CD packaging jobs dwindled, forcing Sagmeister to rethink his business. He began looking for ways to incorporate meaning into his work, and took a yearlong sabbatical to explore and experiment. He returned refreshed and inspired, and he continues to regularly schedule extended time off.

In 2012 Sagmeister added Jessica Walsh as his partner—in a nod to the firm's first promo, they announced the partnership with a postcard featuring a nude double portrait. The two continue pushing boundaries and balancing commercial projects with self-directed work.

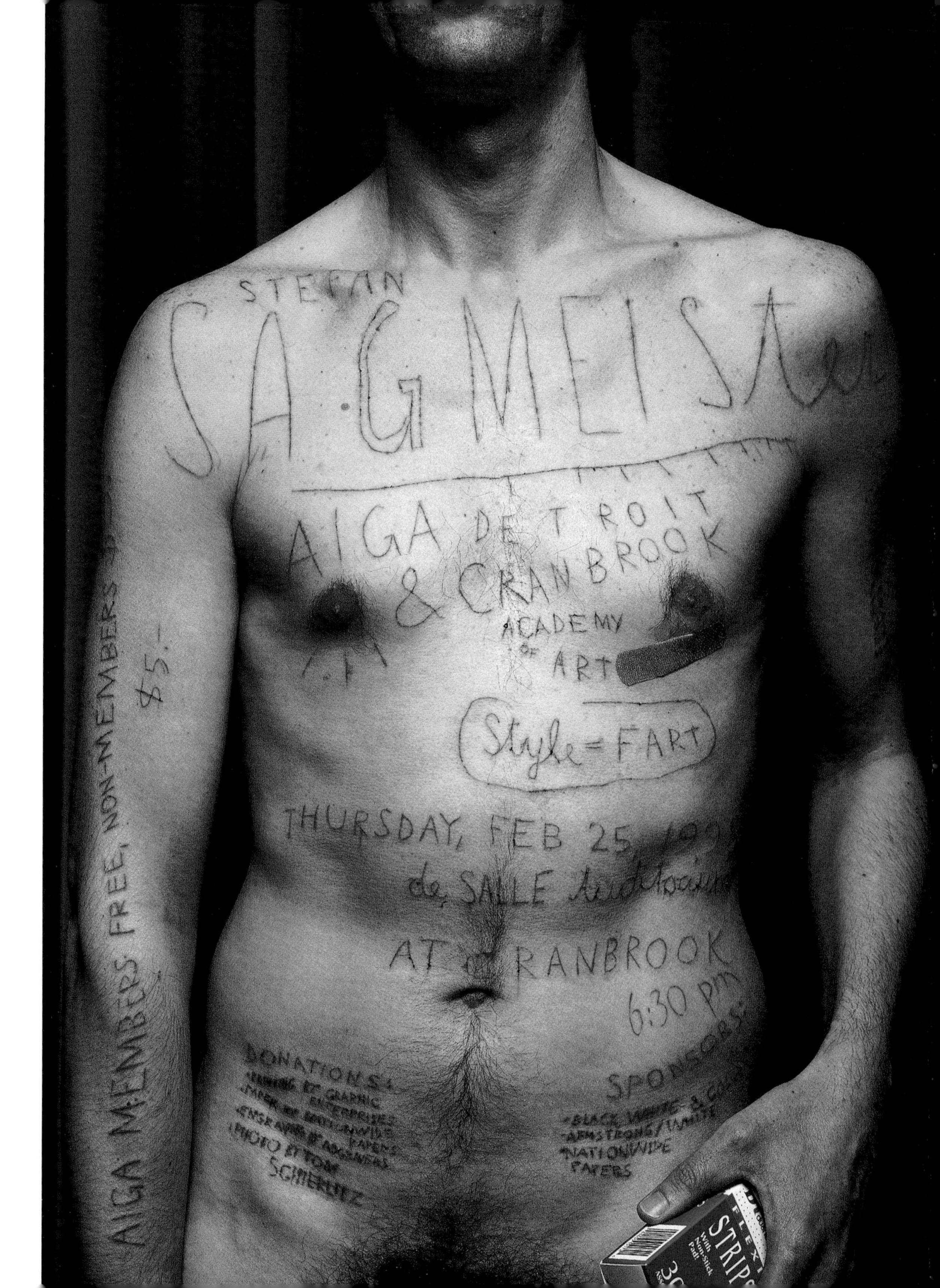
STEFAN
AIGA DETROIT
& CRANBROOK
ACADEMY
OF ART
Style = FART
THURSDAY, FEB 25,
AT CRANBROOK
6:30 pm
DONATIONS:
SPONSORS:
AIGA MEMBERS FREE, NON-MEMBERS $5.-
STRIPS

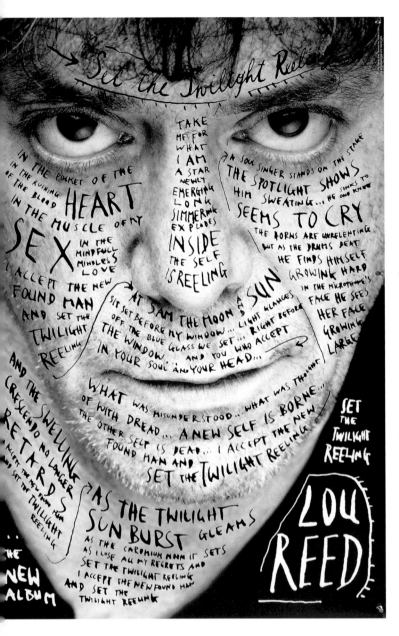

READERS: *Things I Have Learned in My Life So Far* and *Made You Look*, both by Stefan Sagmeister (the latter features an outer case that reveals a hidden image, similar to Sagmeister's CD slipcover for H.P. Zinker). Both books are out of print but available from online booksellers.

ABOVE: Lou Reed *Set the Twilight Reeling* poster, 1996

OPPOSITE: Levi's billboard, 2010

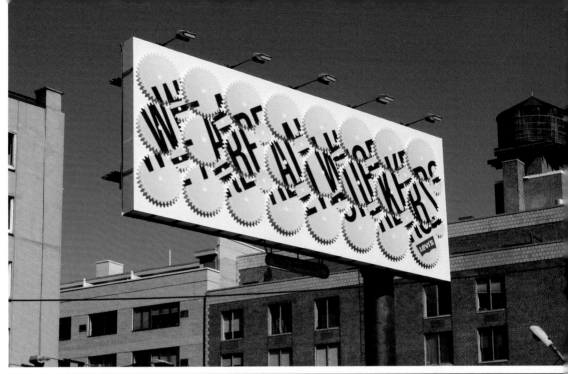

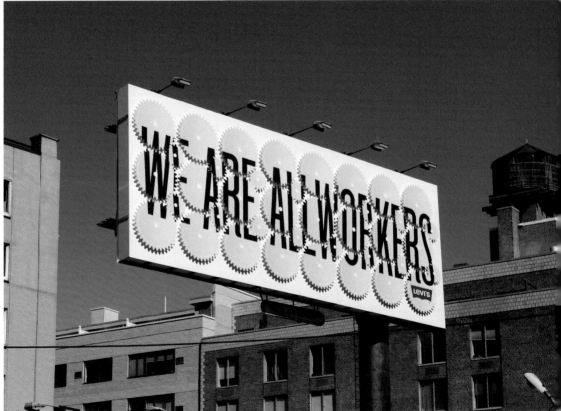

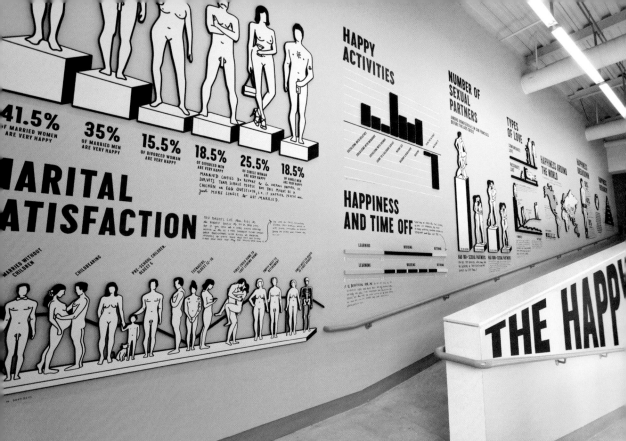

HAPPY ACTIVITIES

NUMBER OF SEXUAL PARTNERS

TYPES OF LOVE

HAPPINESS AROUND THE WORLD

HAPPINESS AND TIME OFF

41.5%
OF MARRIED WOMEN ARE VERY HAPPY

35%
OF MARRIED MEN ARE VERY HAPPY

15.5%
OF DIVORCED WOMAN ARE VERY HAPPY

18.5%
OF DIVORCED MEN ARE VERY HAPPY

25.5%
OF SINGLE WOMAN ARE VERY HAPPY

18.5%
OF SINGLE MEN ARE VERY HAPPY

MARITAL SATISFACTION

THE HAPPY

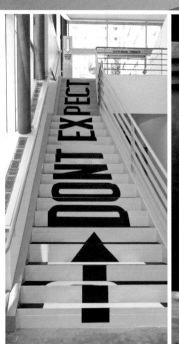

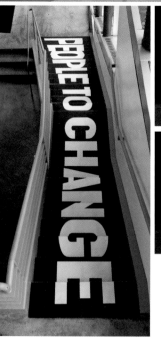

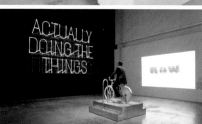

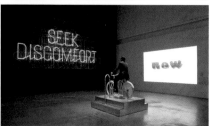

THIS PAGE: *The Happy Show* installation at Institute of Contemporary Art, Philadelphia, PA

OPPOSITE: *Trying to Look Good Limits My Life*, part of typographic project *20 Things I Have Learned in My Life So Far*, 2004

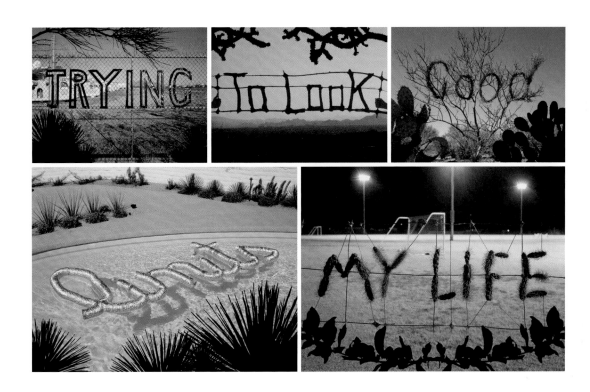

NOTES

1. Steven Heller, "Words to Design By," *Print*, August 15, 2012.

2. Herbert Spencer, *Pioneers of Modern Typography* (Cambridge, MA: The MIT Press, 1990), 67.

3. Art Directors Club, "Hall of Fame: W.A. Dwiggins," 1979, http://www.adcglobal.org/archive/hof/1979/?id=264

4. Jan Tschichold, *The New Typography: A Handbook for Modern Designers* (Berkeley: University of California Press, 2006), 68.

5. R. Roger Remington, "AIGA Medalist: Lester Beall," http://www.aiga.org/medalist-lesterbeall/, 1993.

6. Quentin Newark, *What is Graphic Design?* (Hove, UK: RotoVision, 2007), 134.

7. Steven Heller and David R. Brown, "AIGA Medalist: Herbert Matter," http://www.aiga.org/medalist-herbertmatter/, 1984.

8. Martha Scotford, "The Tenth Pioneer," *Eye*, no. 18, vol. 5, 1995.

9. Mike Joyce, email interview with author, 2013.

10. Jeremy Aynsley, *Pioneers of Modern Graphic Design*, (London: Mitchell Beazley, 2004), 106.

11. George Lois, email interview with author, 2013.

12. Jon Krasner, *Motion Graphic Design: Applied History and Aesthetics* (Boca Raton, FL: CRC Press), 20–21.

13. Julie Lasky, "AIGA Medalist: Georg Olden," http://www.aiga.org/medalist-georgolden/, 1988.

14. Tom Geismar, email interview with author, 2013.

15. David Airey, email interview with author, 2012.

16. Bill Baker, "Comics: Seymour Chwast — Driven to Draw," *The Morton Report*, http://www.themortonreport.com/, November 30, 2011.

17. Milton Glaser, "Ten Things I Have Learned," part of an AIGA talk in London, http://www.miltonglaser.com/milton/c:essays, 2001.

18. Rob Schwartz, "The Quest For 'Whoa!' A Conversation with the Legendary George Lois," *Forbes*, April 1, 2013

19. George Lois, email interview with author, 2013.

20. Jan Wilker, email interview with author, 2013.

21. April Greiman, email interview with author, 2013.

22. Michael Dooley and David Shields, "Words – and Images – on Ed Fella," *Print*, May 14, 2013.

23. Edward Fella, email interview with author, 2013.

24. John Maeda, email interview with author, 2013.

25. Steven Heller, email interview with author, 2013.

26. Stephen Doyle, email interview with author, 2013.

27. Michael Bierut, email interview with author, 2013.

28. Stefan Sagmeister, email interview with author, 2013.

29. Ibid.

SELECTED BIBLIOGRAPHY

AIGA. "AIGA Medal," Medalist biographies, 1920s–2010s, http://www.aiga.org/medalists/

Ambrose, Gavin, and Paul Harris. *The Visual Dictionary of Graphic Design*. New York: AVA Publishing, 2006.

Art Directors Club. "ADC Hall of Fame," http://www.adcglobal.org/archive/hof/

Aynsley, Jeremy. *Pioneers of Modern Graphic Design*. London: Mitchell Beazley, 2004.

Bauret, Gabriel. *Alexey Brodovitch*. New York: Assouline, 2005.

Brown, Robert K. and Susan Reinhold. *The Poster Art of A.M. Cassandre*. New York: E. P. Dutton, 1979

Chambers, Jason, "Meet One of the Pioneering Blacks in the Ad Industry," *Ad Age*, Feb. 16, 2009.

Craig, James and Bruce Barton. *Thirty Centuries of Graphic Design*. New York: Watson-Guptill Publication, 1987.

Cramsie, Patrick. *The Story of Graphic Design*. New York: Abrams, 2010.

Drew, Ned, and Paul Sternberger. *By Its Cover: Modern American Book Cover Design*. New York: Princeton Architectural Press, 2005.

Drucker, Johanna, and Emily McVarish. *Graphic Design History: A Critical Guide*. Upper Saddle River, NJ: Pearson Prentice Hall, 2009.

Eskilson, Stephen J. *Graphic Design: A New History*. New Haven, CT: Yale University Press, 2007.

Friedman, Mildred et. al. *Graphic Design in America: A Visual Language History*. Minneapolis/New York: Walker Art Center/Abrams, 1989.

Gerber, Anna, and Anja Lutz. *Influences: A Lexicon of Contemporary Graphic Design*. Berlin: Gestalten, 2006.

Gomez-Palacio, Bryony, and Armin Vit. *Graphic Design Referenced*. Beverly, MA: Rockport Publishers, 2009.

Heller, Steven, and Seymour Chwast. *Graphic Style: From Victorian to New Century*. New York: Harry N. Abrams, 1988.

Heller, Steven. *Design Literacy: Understanding Graphic Design*. New York: Allworth Press, 1997.

Heller, Steven and Marie Finamore (Eds.), *Design Culture: An Anthology of Writing from the AIGA Journal of Graphic Design*. New York: Allworth Press, 1997.

Heller, Steven. *Paul Rand*. London, Phaidon, 1999.

Heller, Steven, and Georgette Ballance, eds., *Graphic Design History*. New York: Allworth Press, 2001.

Heller, Steven. *The Graphic Design Reader*. New York: Allworth Press, 2002.

Heller, Steven, and Mirko Ilic. *The Anatomy of Design: Uncovering the Influences and Inspirations in Modern Graphic Design*. Beverly, MA: Rockport Publishers, 2007.

Heller, Steven; Ed. *I Heart Design: Remarkable Graphic Design Selected by Designers, Illustrators, and Critics*. Beverly, MA: Rockport Publishers, 2011.

Heller, Steven. "Erik Nitsche, Design Auteur," *Print*. November 22, 2011.

Heller, Steven, and Veronique Vienne, eds. *100 Ideas that Changed Graphic Design*. Laurence King Publishers. April 18, 2012.

Hollis, Richard. *Graphic Design: A Concise History*. London: Thames & Hudson, 1994.

Kohler, Eric. *In the Groove: Vintage Record Graphics 1940–1960*. San Francisco: Chronicle Books, 1999.

Kurlansky, Mervyn. *Masters of the 20th Century: The Icograda Design Hall of Fame*. New York: Graphic, 2001.

Livingston, Alan, and Isabella Livingston. *The Thames and Hudson Dictionary of Graphic Design and Designers*. London: Thames and Hudson, 2003.

Lupton, Ellen. *Thinking With Type: A Critical guide for Designers, Writers, Editors, & Students*. New York: Princeton Architectural Press, 2004.

Meggs, Philip B. *Six Chapters in Design: Bass, Chermayeff, Glaser, Rand, Tanaka, Tomaszewski*. San Francisco: Chronicle Books, 1997.

Meggs, Philip B. *A History of Graphic Design*. Hoboken, NJ: John Wiley and Sons, 1998.

Mount, Christopher. *Stenberg Brothers: Constructing a Revolution in Soviet Design*. New York: The Museum of Modern Art, 1997.

Poulin, Richard. *Graphic Design + Architecture: A 20th Century History*. Beverly, MA: Rockport Publishers, 2012.

Poulin, Richard. *The Language of Graphic Design: An Illustrated Handbook for Understanding Fundamental Design Principles.* Beverly, MA: Rockport Publishers, 2011.

Purvis, Alston W., and Cees W. de Jong. *Dutch Graphic Design: A Century of Innovation*. London: Thames and Hudson, 2006.

Purvis, Alston W., and Martijn F. Le Coultre. *Graphic Design 20th Century*. New York: Princeton Architectural Press, 2003.

Rathgeb, Markus. *Otl Aicher*. London: Phaidon Press, 2007.

Remington, R. Roger. *Nine Pioneers in American Graphic Design*. Cambridge MA: The MIT Press, 1989

Remington, Roger. *Lester Beall: Trailblazer of American Graphic Design*. New York: W. W. Norton & Company, 1996

Remington, R. Roger. *American Modernism: Graphic Design 1920 to 1960*. New Haven, CT: Yale University Press, 2003.

Remington. Roger R., and Robert S. P. Fripp. *Design and Science: The Life and Work of Will Burtin*. Aldershot, UK, and Burlington, VT: Lund Humphries, 2007.

Scher, Paula. *Make it Bigger*. New York: Princeton Architectural Press, 2005.

Scotford, Martha. *Cipe Pineles: A Life of Design*. New York: W. W. Norton & Company, 1999.

Shaughnessy, Adrian. *Graphic Design: A User's Manual*. London: Laurence King Publishing Ltd., 2009.

Spencer, Herbert. *Pioneers of Modern Typography*. Cambridge, MA: The MIT Press, 1990.

Studio 3. *A History of Graphic Design for Rainy Days*. Berlin: Gestalten, 2011.

Sutnar, Ladislav. *Prague New York—Design in Action*. Prague: Argo, 2003.

Weill, Alain. *Graphic Design: A History*. New York: Abrams, 2003.

Weston, Richard. *Modernism*. London: Phaidon Press, 1996.

Wheeler, Alina. *Designing Brand Identity: A Complete Guide to Creating, Building, and Maintaining Strong Brands*. Hoboken, NJ: John Wiley & Sons, 2003.

Wrede, Stuart. *The Modern Poster*. New York: The Museum of Modern Art, 1988.

ACKNOWLEDGMENTS

I'd like to express my sincere thanks to the many people who have made this book possible. I'm grateful that my editor Nikki Echler McDonald saw the potential of this project and helped make it a reality. Thanks to everyone at Peachpit Press, especially Tracey Croom, Charlene Charles Will, and Alison Serafini. Big thanks to my editorial team: Bryn Mooth, who smoothed my rough sentences while being a consistently calming voice of reason, and to Elaine Merrill, Liz Welch and Emily Glossbrenner. Also, I'd like to thank my friend Nancy Eklund Later for helping me shape the idea for this book, as did Kerry Colburn and Jennifer Worick. Thanks also to the experienced authors who kindly offered me advice: Steven Heller, Alston Purvis, Richard Poulin, Tim Samara, and Bryony Gomez-Palacio.

Without visual examples of great design work, this book would not exist (and it almost didn't). To the designers, estates, and organizations who contributed: Thank you for sharing such inspiring work. I am especially grateful to the people who were so generous with their images and source materials: Merrill Berman and Jim Frank of the Merrill C. Berman Collection, Emily Roz and Alexander Tochilovsky of the Herb Lubalin Study Center of Design and Typography, Aaron Cohen of ProjectObject, Scott Lindberg of New Documents, Rebecca Weiss of Swann Auction Galleries, Molly McCombs and Randy Ross of Modernism 101, Beth Kleber of The Milton Glaser Design Study Center and Archives, Jeffrey Head, Tim Shipe of the International Dada Archive at University of Iowa, Richard Kasvin of Chicago Center for the Print, Christian Annyas of The Movie Title Stills Collection, Sean Casey of the Rare Books & Manuscripts Department at Boston Public Library, Barbara Blumenthal of the Mortimer Rare Book Room at Smith College, and Kari Horowicz of the RIT Graphic Design Archive. Thanks also to J'Aimee Cronin, Adrienne Fields, and Lauren Graves from Artists Rights Society, and Kathryn Pawlick of VAGA.

I'm grateful to the late Steve Reoutt, who first opened my eyes to design history. Big thanks to my friend Herb Thornby for his hand-drawn illustrations of the designers in this book. I think it's important to put faces with these names, and Herb made that possible. Thanks also to Arturo Medrano for his assistance throughout.

And of course, my sincere gratitude goes to my family. I'm forever thankful for my late parents, John and Eileen Clifford, who always encouraged me and remain my biggest influences. Thanks to Tim for his support, patience, hard work, and understanding, and to Will for making my day, everyday.

INDEX

IMAGE CREDITS

t=top b=bottom r=right l=left c=center

Illustrations of all designers by Herb Thornby.

p. 8 courtesy Beinecke Rare Book And Manuscript Library, Yale University. p. 10 courtesy the Library of Congress. p. 11 courtesy Beinecke Rare Book and Manuscript Library, Yale University. pp. 12–15 courtesy the Library of Congress.

CHAPTER 1

pp. 19–23 © 2013 Artists Rights Society (ARS), New York / VG Bild-Kunst, Bonn; pp. 20–21 courtesy Swann Auction Galleries, p. 23 courtesy the Merrill C. Berman Collection, photo by Jim Frank. p. 24–25 Courtesy the Library of Congress. pp. 26–29 © 2013 Artists Rights Society (ARS), New York / VG Bild-Kunst, Bonn, courtesy the Library of Congress. pp. 30–31 © 2013 Artists Rights Society (ARS), New York / SIAE, Rome, courtesy Beinecke Rare Book and Manuscript Library, Yale University. pp. 33–36 © Simon Rendall; p. 33 courtesy the Library of Congress, p. 34–35 courtesy Swann Auction Galleries, p. 36 courtesy the Library of Congress. p. 37 © TIL from the London Transport Museum collection. p. 38 Courtesy Beinecke Rare Book and Manuscript Library, Yale University. p. 39 courtesy the Merrill C. Berman Collection, photo by Jim Frank. p. 40–41 courtesy Beinecke Rare Book and Manuscript Library, Yale University. p. 42 courtesy the Merrill C. Berman Collection, photo by Jim Frank. p. 43 courtesy Beinecke Rare Book and Manuscript Library, Yale University. p. 45 Art © Estate of Alexander Rodchenko/RAO Moscow/VAGA, New York, courtesy the Merrill C. Berman Collection, photo by Jim Frank. p. 46 Art © Estate of Georgii and Vladimir Stenberg/RAO, Moscow/VAGA, New York, Courtesy Swann Auction Galleries. p. 48–50t courtesy of The International Dada Archive, Special Collections, University of Iowa Libraries. p. 50b courtesy Beinecke Rare Book And Manuscript Library, Yale University. p. 51 courtesy of The International Dada Archive, Special Collections, University of Iowa Libraries. p. 52 © Can Stock Photo Inc. p. 53 © 2013 Artists Rights Society (ARS), New York / VG Bild-Kunst, Bonn, courtesy the Merrill C. Berman Collection,

photo by Jim Frank. P. 54–57 © 2013 Artists Rights Society (ARS), New York / VG Bild-Kunst, Bonn; p. 54 courtesy President and Fellows of Harvard College, p. 55 ©iStockphoto.com, p. 57 courtesy the Library of Congress. p 58 © MOURON. CASSANDRE. Lic 2013-16-07-01 www.cassandrefrance.com. P. 61 permission of S.D. Warren Company (d/b/a Sappi Fine Paper North America), courtesy Mortimer Rare Book Room, Smith College. p. 62 courtesy of the Trustees of the Boston Public Library/Rare Books. P. 64–67 © Tschichold family; p. 66 Courtesy Swann Auction Galleries, p 66l courtesy Modernism 101, p 66–67 courtesy the Merrill C. Berman Collection, photo by Jim Frank.

CHAPTER 2

pp. 71-72t Art © Lester Beall Jr. Trust/Licensed by VAGA, New York, NY; p. 71 courtesy the Library of Congress, p. 72t courtesy the Merrill C. Berman Collection, photo by Jim Frank. p. 73 courtesy International Paper Company. p. 75 © The Richard Avedon Foundation with permission of Hearst, and Michel Brodovitch, courtesy RIT Graphic Design Archives, Wallace Library, Rochester Institute of Technology. pp. 76–79 permission of Michel Brodovitch; p. 76–77 courtesy Modernism 101, p. 78–79 courtesy The Herb Lubalin Study Center of Design and Typography. p. 80–81 permission of Sony Music Entertainment, courtesy Scott Lindberg/New Documents. p. 82–87 permission of Alex Matter; p. 82 courtesy the Library of Congress, p. 83 courtesy Swann Auction Galleries, p. 84–85 courtesy Jeffrey Head, p. 86l and r courtesy Modernism 101, p. 87 courtesy Yale University Library. pp. 89–93 © Ladislav Sutnar, by permission of the Ladislav Sutnar Family; p. 89 courtesy RIT Graphic Design Archives, Wallace Library, Rochester Institute of Technology, pp. 90–91 courtesy The Herb Lubalin Study Center of Design and Typography, p. 92 courtesy the Merrill C. Berman Collection, photo by Jim Frank, p. 93t courtesy Swann Auction Galleries, p. 93b courtesy the Merrill C. Berman Collection, photo by Jim Frank. pp. 95–99 permission Elaine Lustig Cohen; p. 93 Courtesy Scott Lindberg/New Documents, p. 96tl Collection of Aaron Charles Cohen, p. 96tc courtesy The Herb Lubalin Study Center of Design and Typography,

p. 96tr courtesy John Clifford, p. 96bl courtesy The Herb Lubalin Study Center of Design and Typography, p. 96bc, 96br, , 97tl, 97tc, 97tr, 97bl collection of Aaron Charles Cohen, p. 97bc courtesy Scott Lindberg/New Documents, p. 97br courtesy The Herb Lubalin Study Center of Design and Typography, p. 98l courtesy Modernism 101, p.98r and 99 courtesy The Herb Lubalin Study Center of Design and Typography. pp. 100–103 permission of Carol Burtin Fripp; p. 100 with permission of Estate of Francesco Scavullo and Hearst, courtesy RIT Graphic Design Archives, Wallace Library, Rochester Institute of Technology, p. 101–103 courtesy RIT Graphic Design Archives, Wallace Library, Rochester Institute of Technology, p. 102 with permission from Hearst. p. 104tl permission of Alex Matter, courtesy Swann Auction Galleries. p. 104tr courtesy the Library of Congress. p. 104b permission Elaine Lustig Cohen, courtesy Scott Lindberg/New Documents. p. 106–109 © Westvaco Corporation, courtesy The Herb Lubalin Study Center of Design and Typography. p. 111–113 permission Renate Nitsche; p. 111 and 113 used with the permission of General Dynamics Corporation, p. 111 and 113tr and 113br collection Chicago Center for the Print, p. 112 John Clifford, p. 113tl and 113bl courtesy the Library of Congress. pp. 114–117 © 2013 Artists Rights Society (ARS), New York / ProLitteris, Zurich; p. 114 and 116 courtesy the Library of Congress, p. 115 courtesy Modernism 101, p. 117 courtesy Swann Auction Galleries. pp. 119–123 permission Paul Rand Revocable Trust; p. 119, 121t, 121b, 122 courtesy Modernism 101, p. 120 and 123 courtesy The Herb Lubalin Study Center Of Design and Typography. pp. 125–129 © The Estate Of Saul Bass; p. 127 courtesy Christian Annyas. pp. 130–133 permission Georg Olden Jr., courtesy of AIGA, www.aiga.org. pp. 134–137 permission Carol Burtin Fripp; p. 134 courtesy RIT Graphic Design Archives, Wallace Library, Rochester Institute of Technology, p. 135 courtesy The Herb Lubalin Study Center of Design and Typography, p. 136 courtesy Modernism 101, p. 137 Photography by Jerry Cooke, © The Jerry Cooke Archives, Inc. 2013, courtesy RIT Graphic Design Archives, Wallace Library, Rochester Institute of Technology.

CHAPTER 3

pp. 141–143 permission Chermayeff & Geismar, p. 142b permission Chermayeff & Geismar & Haviv. pp. 144–147 permission Yusaku Kamekura Award; p. 144 courtesy Modernism 101, p. 145 courtesy Swann Auction Galleries, pp. 146–147 courtesy the Merrill C. Berman Collection, photo by Jim Frank. p. 148–153 permission and courtesy The Herb Lubalin Study Center of Design and Typography. pp. 154–155 permission The Center for Design Study, courtesy The Herb Lubalin Study Center of Design and Typography. pp. 156–159 permission Seymour Chwast, Push Pin Group Inc.; p. 156 courtesy John Clifford, p. 157 courtesy The Milton Glaser Design Study Center and Archives, p. 158 courtesy The Library of Congress, p. 159 Courtesy Scott Lindberg/New Documents. p. 161–165 © Milton Glaser; p. 161, 163r, 164, 165 courtesy The Milton Glaser Design Study Center and Archives, p. 163l Courtesy The Library of Congress. pp. 166–167 created and designed by George Lois. p. 168 Wim Crouwel for Van Abbemuseum. pp. 169–171 permission Total Design (Wim Crouwel). pp. 172–173 permission Landor Associates. p. 175 © 1976 by ERCO GmbH. pp. 176–179 permission Vanderbyl Design. pp. 180–183 permission Peter Saville.

CHAPTER 4

pp. 187–191 permission April Greiman Made In Space. pp. 192–195 permission Emigre. pp. 196–197 permission Edward Fella. p. 200t and 200b permission MIT Media Lab. p. 201 permission The MIT Press. p. 203 permission Steven Heller. pp. 204–209 permission Doyle Partners. pp. 210–215 permission Paula Scher/Pentagram Design. pp. 216–221 permission Michael Bierut/ Pentagram Design. pp. 222–225 permission John Maeda. pp. 226–231 permission Sagmeister & Walsh.

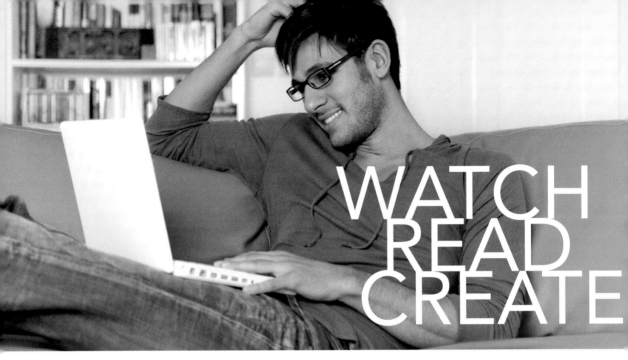

WATCH
READ
CREATE

Unlimited online access to all Peachpit, Adobe Press, Apple Training and New Riders videos and books, as well as content from other leading publishers including: O'Reilly Media, Focal Press, Sams, Que, Total Training, John Wiley & Sons, Course Technology PTR, Class on Demand, VTC and more.

No time commitment or contract required! Sign up for one month or a year. All for $19.99 a month

SIGN UP TODAY
peachpit.com/creativeedge

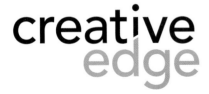